JANICE VANCLEAVE'S

Science Project Workbook

GRADES 3–6

WILEY

John Wiley & Sons, Inc.

Published by John Wiley & Sons, Inc., Hoboken, New Jersey
Published simultaneously in Canada

The contents of this book were previously published in *Janice VanCleave's Science Experiment Sourcebook,* copyright © 1997 Janice VanCleave, published by John Wiley & Sons, Inc.

The publisher and the author have made every reasonable effort to ensure that the experiments and activities in the book are safe when conducted as instructed but assume no responsibility for any damage caused or sustained while performing the experiments or activities in this book. Parents, guardians, and/or teachers should supervise young readers who undertake the experiments and activities in this book.

For general information about our other products and services, please contact our Customer Care Department within the United States at (800) 762-2974, outside the United States at (317) 572-3993 or fax (317) 572-4002.

Wiley also publishes its books in a variety of electronic formats. Some content that appears in print may not be available in electronic books. For more information about Wiley products, visit our web site at www.wiley.com.

ISBN 0-471-46647-6

Printed in the United States of America

10 9 8 7 6 5 4 3 2 1

Contents

Chemistry

Earth Science

Introduction for Teachers

Science is a way of solving problems and discovering why things happen the way they do. Why do stars twinkle? Why do you blink? What is stereophonic sound? Students can find the answers to these and many other questions by doing the experiments in this book.

This book presents 225 science experiments for students ages 8 to 12. The experiments cover five different fields of science:

- **Astronomy** The study of the planet we live on—earth—and all our neighbors in space.

- **Biology** The study of the way living organisms behave and interact.

- **Chemistry** The study of the way materials are put together and their behavior under different conditions.

- **Earth Science** The study of the unique habitat that all known living creatures share—the earth.

- **Physics** The study of energy and matter and the relationship between them.

THE EXPERIMENTS

Scientists identify a problem or an event and seek solutions or explanations through research and experimentation. A goal of each experiment in this book is to provide the step-by-step instructions necessary to complete the experiment successfully and accomplish the stated purpose of the experiment. The format of each experiment is as follows:

1. **Purpose:** The basic goals for the experiment.

2. **Materials:** A list of necessary supplies.

3. **Procedure:** Step-by-step instructions on how to perform the experiment.

At the back of the book you can find an Answer Key that presents the expected results of each experiment in this format:

1. **Results:** An explanation stating exactly what is expected to happen. This is an immediate learning tool. If the expected results are achieved, the experimenter has an immediate positive reinforcement. An error is also quickly recognized, and the need to start over or make corrections is readily apparent.

2. **Why?** An explanation of why the results were achieved is described in words that are understandable to the reader who may not be familiar with scientific terms. These new terms can also be found in the glossary.

How to Present Experiments

Select the topic that you wish to present. Then:

1. **Read the experiments in the topic section completely before starting.** When possible, practice doing the experiments yourself before you present them in class. This increases your understanding of the topic and makes you more familiar with the procedure and the materials. If you know the experiment well, it will be easier for you to give instructions and answer questions. The first experiment in each topic section will generally have the most information about the topic and can be used to introduce the topic to the class.

2. **Select a place to work.** The experiments in this book can be used with your entire class working in collaborative groups or at a science center with a small group or an individual. Choose work areas that provide space and access to the needed supplies.

3. **Choose a time.** Your class schedule may have a time for science. If not, select a time when you will have the fewest distractions so that the experiment can be completed. Once your instructions have been given, you may wish to allot a specific time for student experimentation and even set a

timer. At the end of the experimentation time, schedule 5 to 10 minutes to have everyone clean up.

4. **Collect and organize supplies well ahead of time.** You will experience less frustration and have more fun if all the necessary materials for the experiments are ready for instant use. You lose your train of thought and the attention of your class when you have to stop and search for supplies. (See "Tips on Materials" in the box below.)

Decide whether the students will be doing the experiment individually or in groups, and calculate from that how much of each material you will need for the class. You may prefer to designate a place in the classroom where the supplies will be placed each time a science experiment is performed. One idea is to separate the materials and put each type of material in its own box or area on the table. Boxes or trays are handy and safe ways for students to carry materials to their work area. Students are generally eager to help gather and organize supplies.

5. **Experiment.** Emphasize that safety is of the utmost importance and that the instructions should be followed exactly. With young children, you may wish to read the procedure for each step and discuss any applicable illustrations in the book. Then allow time for the children to follow the instructions. Instruct older children to follow along as you read the procedure and demonstrate each step. You might stop short of showing the final step so that the students see the results for the first time themselves. (See "Try This Technique" for a sample lesson plan.)

TIPS ON MATERIALS

- Many experiments call for water. If you don't have a sink in your classroom, you can supply water in a beverage dispenser with a push-button spout. This kind of container keeps water handy and helps minimize spills. Place the container on the edge of the supply table and put a small plastic wastebasket on the floor under the spigot to catch overflows.

- If an experiment involves cooling and you do not have access to a refrigerator, you can use an ice chest that holds a few sacks of ice or ice packs.

- To save time, you can precut some of the materials (except string, see the next item), either to the exact size needed or to a slightly larger size if measuring is going to be part of the activity.

- Do not cut string in advance because cut string generally gets twisted and is difficult to separate. Have the students measure and cut the needed lengths of string.

- For a class of younger students (or if you have only a short time to complete the experiment), prepare boxes containing all the needed materials to complete one experiment for each student or group of students. Most materials will fit in just a shoe box. If you have many classes that will be doing the same experiment, you may wish to check the boxes in and out.

- You may also want to keep labeled shoe boxes filled with basic supplies that are used in many experiments, such as scissors, tape, markers, and so forth.

6. Help students analyze the results.
When the results work out as expected, ask the students to provide a hypothesis (an idea about the solution to a problem, based on knowledge about the topic) as to why. Then refer to the "Why?" section in the back of the book to help you confirm the scientific explanation. When possible, let the scientific explanations be the answers to questions from curious students. Very young children are good observers, but usually they do not have enough science background to ask questions about scientific phenomena. You can guide these children with your own leading questions.

Remember that while the ultimate goal of a science activity is to teach a specific science concept, any and all observations made can be considered scientific data collecting. If the results are not the same as those described in the book, first go over the procedure, step by step, with the individual or group to make sure that no steps were left out. If all the steps were completed, try asking the students leading questions. The students can then provide their hypothesis as to why the results were not achieved. Start off by analyzing the materials. I like to ask questions such as "Do you think our tap water has too many chemicals in it?" and "Would a different brand affect the results?" Next, analyze other variables, such as lighting, temperature, and humidity. Introduce questions such as "Would it work better in sunlight?" or "Is there too much moisture in the air because it has been raining?" These brainstorming sessions can lead to further experimentation.

7. Keeping students on task. Young students, and many older ones, have difficulty in being attentive for long periods of time. Hands-on, individual instruction certainly helps, but this is not always possible. While there is no magic solution to the problem, two suggestions for making students more attentive are:

- Have all supplies ready so that the experiment starts quickly. Busy students are more attentive and less likely to be off task.

- Limit the science activity time. Even though there are several experiments per topic, do some of them at a later time. Students are more attentive during short, quick, fun activities.

Try This Technique
Information is more likely to be retained if the learner is an active, integral part of the learning process. A method that can lead to effective learning is to use a science experiment to introduce an idea, then follow with one or more experiments on the same scientific concept to reteach and evaluate student progress. In the following example, the scientific concept is "physical change" and the experiments provided are #120, "Super Chain," and #121, "Frosty," from pages 252 and 254 in this book.

Suggestions for Teaching "Super Chain"
Follow these steps to teach this experiment in the classroom:

1. Write the words "physical change" on the chalkboard.

2. Encourage the class to discover the definition of the term by asking questions such as the following:
   a. What does physical mean? (Physical pertains to properties of matter that are not chemical—such things as shape or size.)
   b. If "change" means "to make or become different," then what does "physical change" mean? (It is to change one or more of the properties of matter that are not chemical. A change in shape and size of a piece of paper could be done by tearing it in half. This change does not produce new substances.)

3. Read the procedure for the "Super Chain" experiment and demonstrate each step to the class.

4. Prepare the class to perform the experiment by passing out the materials needed.

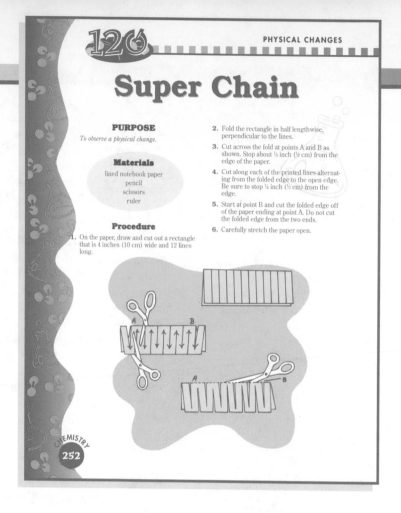

Super Chain

PURPOSE

To observe a physical change.

Materials

lined notebook paper
pencil
scissors
ruler

Procedure

1. On the paper, draw and cut out a rectangle that is 4 inches (10 cm) wide and 12 lines long.

2. Fold the rectangle in half lengthwise, perpendicular to the lines.

3. Cut across the fold at points A and B as shown. Stop about ¼ inch (½ cm) from the edge of the paper.

4. Cut along each of the printed lines alternating from the folded edge to the open edge. Be sure to stop ¼ inch (½ cm) from the edge.

5. Start at point B and cut the folded edge off of the paper ending at point A. Do not cut the folded edge from the two ends.

6. Carefully stretch the paper open.

CHEMISTRY
252

---

5. Two methods for student experimentation are:

   a. Read the procedure aloud again as the students perform the experiment themselves. After each step, observe the progress of each student to make sure that each one is ready for the next step. Proceed until all the steps have been read.

   b. Provide each student with a copy of the procedure steps. Observe the progress of each student and provide assistance if needed.

6. Allow the class to experiment with the chains they have made from the paper for several minutes. Then ask each student to answer these questions:

   a. What material was used to make the chain? (Paper)

   b. Did cutting the paper change it into another substance? (No)

   c. Does cutting a substance produce a physical change? (Yes)

7. Prepare for the next experiment using the following sample questions:

   a. A change in matter's size, shape, or state is what kind of change? (Physical)

   b. What are the basic states of matter? (Solid, liquid, and gas)

   c. What are the names of the processes that cause these physical changes of the states of matter?

   • A solid changes into a liquid (Melting)

   • A liquid changes into a solid (Freezing)

   • A liquid changes into a gas (Evaporation)

   • A gas changes into a liquid (Condensation)

   • A gas changes into a solid or a solid changes into a gas (Sublimation)

121

Frosty

PURPOSE

To determine how frost forms.

Materials

drinking glass

Procedure

1. Place a drinking glass in the freezer for 30 minutes.

2. Remove the glass and allow it to stand undisturbed for 30 seconds.

3. Scratch the cloudy formation on the outside of the glass with your fingernail.

4. Perform this experiment several times, selecting days with differing humidities.

CHEMISTRY
254

Suggestions for Teaching "Frosty"

The second experiment, "Frosty," provides new information about the topic of physical changes as a homework assignment. Follow these steps to help students complete the experiment on their own:

1. Provide copies of the experiment for each student.

2. Have the students complete a report on "Frosty." The report might consist of responses to the following requests:

   a. Draw a diagram of the glass before it was cooled. (Glass will look clear.)

   b. Draw a diagram of the glass after it was cooled. (Glass will look cloudy.)

   c. What forms on the outside of the glass? (Frost)

   d. Dew forms when water vapor in the air condenses on a cool surface. Explain why frost is not frozen dew. (Frost forms when water changes from a gas—water vapor—to a solid without first becoming a liquid. This change is called sublimation.)

Making Suggestions for New Approaches

Once any experiment has been performed, direct the class in thinking about how the results would be affected if one part of the experiment were changed. For example, in "Frosty" a glass container was specified. Guide the class in examining the possibility of trying the experiment with a different kind of container, such as plastic or metal. Start this type of thinking with a question such as "I wonder what would happen if you used a container that isn't made of glass?" Solicit ideas from each group and select those that are most practical. Ask each group to give a hypothesis as to what the results will be after they do the experiment with the change in materials.

Introduction for Students

The experiments in this book are grouped by topics, with two or more experiments per topic. You can learn more about any one of the topics by performing the experiments in that topic section. Any one of the sections can be used to design and develop a science project.

Using the Scientific Method

A science project is an investigation using the scientific method to discover the answer to some scientific problem. Before starting your project, you need to understand the scientific method. The scientific method is the "tool" that scientists use to find the answers to questions. It is the process of thinking through the possible solutions to a problem and testing each possibility for the best solution. The scientific method involves the following steps: doing research, identifying the problem, stating a hypothesis, conducting project experimentation, and reaching a conclusion.

Research

Research is the process of collecting information from your own experiences, knowledgeable sources, and data from exploratory experiments (as defined here, experiments in which the data are part of the research). Your first research will be used to select a project topic. This is called topic research. For example, you observe different seeds in the kitchen and wonder if they will grow. Because of this experience, you decide to learn how seeds grow. Your topic will be germination.

Once the topic is selected, you begin what is called project research. This is research to help you understand the topic, express a problem, propose a hypothesis, and design one or more project experiments—experiments designed to test the hypothesis. An example of project research would be to perform "Baby Bean," "Grow a Bean," and "Growing Season" on pages 98, 99, and 100 in this book. The results from these experiments and other research give you the needed information for the next step—identifying the problem.

Do use many references from printed sources—books, journals, magazines, and newspapers—as well as electronic sources—computer software and on-line services.

Do gather information from professionals—instructors, librarians, and scientists, such as physicians and veterinarians.

Do perform other exploratory experiments that you find about your topic of germination.

The Problem

The problem is the scientific question to be solved. It is best expressed as an open-ended question, which is a question that is answered with a statement, not just a yes or no. You have explored the physical makeup of pinto beans and how direction of planting and temperature affect growth, but is it possible that another factor—light—affected the results of these experiments? With this thought in mind, an example of a project problem might be "How does light affect the germination of bean seeds?"

Do limit your problem. Note that the previous question is about one period of seed development and one type of seed instead of all seeds. Finding the answer to a question such as "How does light affect seeds?" would require that you test different periods of seed development and an extensive variety of seed types.

Do choose a problem that can be solved experimentally. For example, the question "What is a flashlight?" can be answered by finding the definition of the word *flashlight* in the dictionary. "What makes a flashlight bulb glow?" can be answered by experimentation.

Hypothesis

A hypothesis is an idea about the solution to a problem, based on knowledge and research. While the hypothesis is a single statement, it is the key to a successful project. All of your project research is done with the goal of expressing a problem, proposing an answer to it—the hypothesis, and designing project experimentation. Then, all of your project experimenting will be performed to test the hypothesis. The hypothesis should make a claim about how two factors relate. For example, in the following sample hypothesis, the two relating factors are light and seed germination. One example of a hypothesis for the earlier problem question is:

"I believe that bean seeds do not need light during germination. I base my hypothesis on these facts:

• Seed packages instruct the user to plant seeds beneath the soil where it is dark.

• In my exploratory experiment, pinto beans germinated beneath the surface of soil in the absence of light."

Do state facts from past experiences or observations on which you based your hypothesis.

Do write down your hypothesis before beginning the project experimentation.

Don't change your hypothesis even if experimentation does not support it. If time permits, repeat or redesign the experiment.

Project Experimentation

Project experimentation is the process of testing a hypothesis. The things that have an effect on the experiment are called variables. There are three kinds of variables that you need to identify in your experiments: independent, dependent, and controlled. The independent variable is the variable you purposely manipulate (change). The dependent variable is the variable being observed that changes in response to the independent variable. The variables that are not changed are called controlled variables.

The problem in this chapter concerns the effect of light on seed germination. The independent variable for the experiment is light and the dependent variable is seed germination. Other factors could cause the dependent variable to change. To be sure that they don't affect the outcome, a control is set up. In a control, all variables are identical to the experimental setup—your original setup—except for the independent variable. Factors that are identical in both the experimental setup and the control setup are the controlled variables. For example, prepare the experiment by planting 3 or 4 different beans, one bean type per container. Place the containers in a dark closet so that they receive no light. If at the end of a set time period the seeds grow, you might decide that no light was needed for germination. But, before making this decision, you must determine experimentally if the seeds would grow with light. Thus, a control group of plants must be set up so that the container receives light throughout the testing period. The other variables for the experimental and control setup, such as type of container, soil, amount of water, temperature, and type of seeds used, must be kept the same. These are controlled variables.

Do have only one independent variable during an experiment.

Do repeat the experiment more than once to verify your results if time permits.

Do organize data.

Do have a control.

Project Conclusion

The project conclusion is a summary of the results of the project experimentation and a statement of how the results relate to the hypothesis. Reasons for experimental results that are contrary to the hypothesis are included. If applicable, the conclusion can end by giving ideas for further testing.

If your results do not support your hypothesis:

Don't change your hypothesis.

Don't leave out experimental results that do not support your hypothesis.

Do give possible reasons for the difference between your hypothesis and the experimental results.

Do give ways that you can experiment further to find a solution.

If your results support your hypothesis:

For example, you might say, "As stated in my hypothesis, I believe that light is not necessary during the germination of bean seeds. My experimentation supports the idea that bean seeds will germinate without light. After 7 days, the seeds tested were seen growing in full light and no light. It is possible that some light reached the "no light" containers that were placed in a dark closet. If I were to improve on this experiment, I would place the "no light" containers in a light-proof box and/or wrap them in a light-proof material, such as aluminum foil."

Ask your teacher for information about a project report and a project display. A research book about these topics and others dealing with science projects is *Janice VanCleave's Guide to the Best Science Fair Projects* (New York, Wiley, 1996).

ASTRONOMY

Where Is It?

PURPOSE

To determine the position of the sun in the sky.

Materials

yardstick (meter stick)
modeling clay
protractor
1-yard (1-m) piece of string
sharpened pencil
helper

Procedure

CAUTION: Never look directly at the sun.

1. Place the measuring stick on an outside table. Point one end toward the sun.

2. Use the clay to stand the protractor upright against the side of the measuring stick, with its center at the end of the stick.

3. Tie one end of the string around the pencil point. Stand the pencil on the measuring stick.

4. Move the pencil back and forth until the shadow of the pencil point strikes the end of the stick.

5. Ask your helper to pull the string to the end of the measuring stick and to read the angle where it crosses the protractor.

6. Repeat steps 4 and 5 at different times.

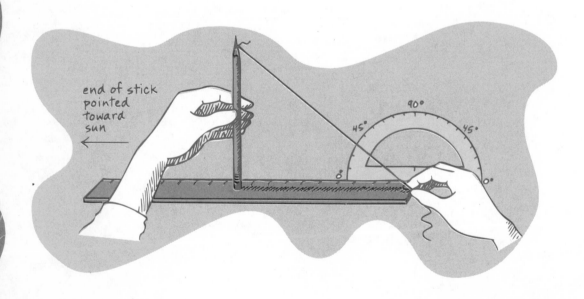

end of stick pointed toward sun

90°
45°
45°

Where Is It?

Observations and Data

What happens during the experiment? Write down what you observed as well as any measurements or calculations that you made. You may also want to draw sketches or take photos of your experiment.

_____

_____

_____

_____

_____

_____

_____

Results and Conclusions

What was the final result of your experiment? Was it what you expected? Why or why not?

_____

_____

_____

_____

_____

What's Next?

How could you improve on this experiment? Did the results make you think of any other questions that you could investigate with new experiments?

_____

_____

_____

_____

How High?

PURPOSE

To determine how distance can be compared using an astrolabe.

Materials

string
scissors
ruler
protractor
heavy bolt
drinking straw
masking tape
helper

Procedure

1. Measure and cut a 12-in. (30-cm) piece of string.

2. Tie one end of the string to the center of the protractor and attach the bolt to the other end of the string.

3. Tape the straw along the top edge of the protractor.

4. Look through the straw (keeping one eye closed) at the tops of distant objects and have your helper determine the angle of the hanging string.

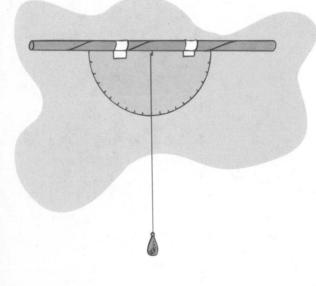

How High?

Observations and Data

What happens during the experiment? Write down what you observed as well as any measurements or calculations that you made. You may also want to draw sketches or take photos of your experiment.

_____

_____

_____

_____

_____

_____

Results and Conclusions

What was the final result of your experiment? Was it what you expected? Why or why not?

_____

_____

_____

_____

What's Next?

How could you improve on this experiment? Did the results make you think of any other questions that you could investigate with new experiments?

_____

_____

_____

_____

Mirage

PURPOSE

To determine why the sun's image is seen before sunrise and after sunset.

Materials

modeling clay
small bowl that you can see through
coin
helper
pitcher of water

Procedure

1. Press a walnut-size clay ball into the center of the small bowl.
2. Stick the coin in the center of the clay.
3. Place the bowl near the edge of a table.
4. Stand near the table so that you can see the entire coin.
5. Slowly move backwards until the coin is just barely out of sight.
6. Ask your helper to fill the bowl with water.

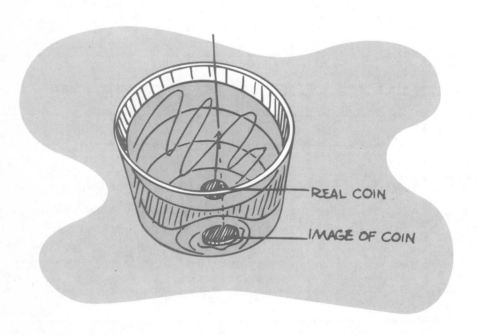

REAL COIN

IMAGE OF COIN

Mirage

Observations and Data

What happens during the experiment? Write down what you observed as well as any measurements or calculations that you made. You may also want to draw sketches or take photos of your experiment.

_____

_____

_____

_____

_____

_____

Results and Conclusions

What was the final result of your experiment? Was it what you expected? Why or why not?

_____

_____

_____

_____

_____

What's Next?

How could you improve on this experiment? Did the results make you think of any other questions that you could investigate with new experiments?

_____

_____

_____

_____

Blue Sky

PURPOSE

To determine why the earth is called the blue planet.

Materials

drinking glass
flashlight
eyedropper
milk
spoon

Procedure

1. Fill the glass with water.

2. In a darkened room, use the flashlight to direct a light beam through the center of the water.

3. Add 1 drop of milk to the water and stir.

4. Again, shine the light through the water.

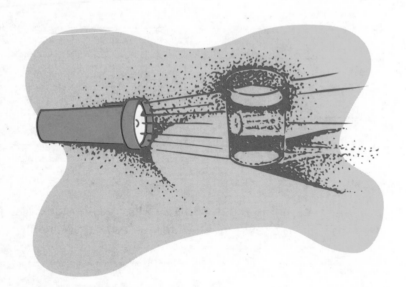

Blue Sky

Observations and Data

What happens during the experiment? Write down what you observed as well as any measurements or calculations that you made. You may also want to draw sketches or take photos of your experiment.

_____

_____

_____

_____

_____

_____

Results and Conclusions

What was the final result of your experiment? Was it what you expected? Why or why not?

_____

_____

_____

_____

What's Next?

How could you improve on this experiment? Did the results make you think of any other questions that you could investigate with new experiments?

_____

_____

_____

_____

Eclipse

PURPOSE

To demonstrate a solar eclipse.

Materials

pen
poster board
timer
helper

Procedure

CAUTION: Never look directly at the sun. It can damage your eyes.

1. Use the pen to draw the largest possible circle on the poster board.

2. Mark an X at one point on the outline of the circle.

3. Place the poster board on the ground in a sunny area outside.

4. Stand in the center of the paper, facing the X. Ask your helper to make a mark on the paper where the center of your shadow crosses the circle.

5. Repeat the previous step every 30 minutes, six or more times during the day.

5 Name

Eclipse

Observations and Data

What happens during the experiment? Write down what you observed as well as any measurements or calculations that you made. You may also want to draw sketches or take photos of your experiment.

_____

_____

_____

_____

_____

_____

Results and Conclusions

What was the final result of your experiment? Was it what you expected? Why or why not?

_____

_____

_____

_____

_____

What's Next?

How could you improve on this experiment? Did the results make you think of any other questions that you could investigate with new experiments?

_____

_____

_____

_____

Darker

PURPOSE

To determine why some areas of the earth are darker during a solar eclipse.

Materials

sheet of typing paper
flashlight
ruler

Procedure

1. Lay the paper on a table.

2. Hold the flashlight about 14 inches (35 cm) from the paper.

3. Place your hand between the light and the paper about 1 inch (2.5 cm) above the paper.

4. Spread your fingers apart.

5. Observe the color of the shadow made by your hand on the paper.

Darker

Observations and Data

What happens during the experiment? Write down what you observed as well as any measurements or calculations that you made. You may also want to draw sketches or take photos of your experiment.

_____

_____

_____

_____

_____

_____

Results and Conclusions

What was the final result of your experiment? Was it what you expected? Why or why not?

_____

_____

_____

_____

_____

What's Next?

How could you improve on this experiment? Did the results make you think of any other questions that you could investigate with new experiments?

_____

_____

_____

_____

Blocked

PURPOSE

To demonstrate a lunar eclipse.

Materials

baseball
several books
flashlight
golf ball

Procedure

1. Place the baseball on a table.

2. Stack some of the books about 12 inches (30 cm) from the baseball.

3. Lay the flashlight on the books and point it toward the baseball. If the light doesn't shine directly on the baseball, raise or lower the flashlight by increasing or decreasing the number and/or size of books used.

4. Hold the golf ball to the side of the baseball.

5. Slowly move the golf ball behind the baseball (the side opposite the flashlight).

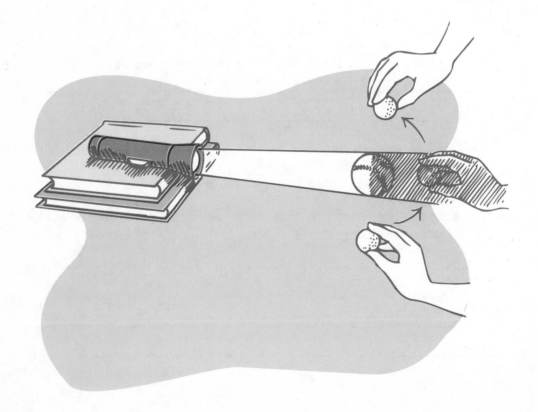

Blocked

Observations and Data

What happens during the experiment? Write down what you observed as well as any measurements or calculations that you made. You may also want to draw sketches or take photos of your experiment.

_____

_____

_____

_____

_____

_____

Results and Conclusions

What was the final result of your experiment? Was it what you expected? Why or why not?

_____

_____

_____

_____

_____

What's Next?

How could you improve on this experiment? Did the results make you think of any other questions that you could investigate with new experiments?

_____

_____

_____

_____

Direct

PURPOSE

To determine why Mars and the earth both have cold poles.

Materials

book
masking tape
2 sheets of black construction paper
2 thermometers

Procedure

1. Place the book on a flat surface in the sun.

2. Tape one piece of black paper on each side of the book.

3. Turn the book so that one sheet of paper receives direct sunlight.

4. Tape a thermometer on top of each sheet of black paper.

5. Read the temperature on both thermometers after 10 minutes.

Direct

Observations and Data

What happens during the experiment? Write down what you observed as well as any measurements or calculations that you made. You may also want to draw sketches or take photos of your experiment.

_____

_____

_____

_____

_____

_____

Results and Conclusions

What was the final result of your experiment? Was it what you expected? Why or why not?

_____

_____

_____

_____

_____

What's Next?

How could you improve on this experiment? Did the results make you think of any other questions that you could investigate with new experiments?

_____

_____

_____

_____

Slanted

PURPOSE

To determine why the poles of Mars and the earth are cold.

Materials

2 felt-tipped marking pens
1 sheet of white paper
compass
protractor

Procedure

1. Draw a half circle on the paper with a diameter of 8 inches (20 cm) using the compass.

2. Use the protractor to identify a 90-degree angle to the paper. Hold the two markers vertically so that they stand side by side.

3. Press the markers against the paper to make dots.

4. Lift both markers off the paper.

5. Hold the markers on top of one another at about a 10-degree angle to the paper. (Use a protractor to measure the angle.)

6. Lower the markers until the tip of the lower marker touches the paper within the top of the circle.

7. Slide the top marker down until its point touches the paper and press to make a second dot on the paper.

8. Compare the distance between the dots at the center to those at the top of the circle.

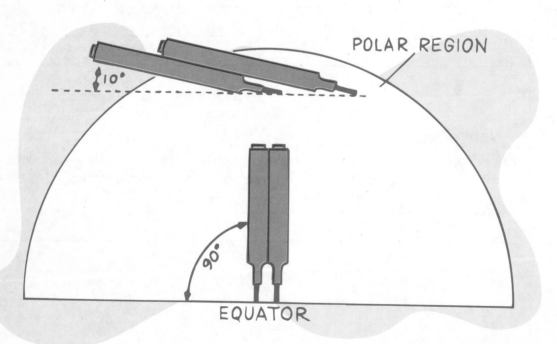

POLAR REGION

10°

90°

EQUATOR

Slanted

Observations and Data

What happens during the experiment? Write down what you observed as well as any measurements or calculations that you made. You may also want to draw sketches or take photos of your experiment.

_____

_____

_____

_____

_____

_____

Results and Conclusions

What was the final result of your experiment? Was it what you expected? Why or why not?

_____

_____

_____

_____

_____

What's Next?

How could you improve on this experiment? Did the results make you think of any other questions that you could investigate with new experiments?

_____

_____

_____

_____

Hidden

PURPOSE

To demonstrate how Mercury's position affects the observation of its surface.

Materials

desk lamp
pencil
ruler

Procedure

1. Turn the lamp on with the glowing bulb facing you. Caution: Do not look directly into the lamp.

2. Grasp the pencil in the center with the print on the pencil facing you.

3. Hold the pencil at arm's length from your face and about 6 in. (15 cm) from the glowing bulb.

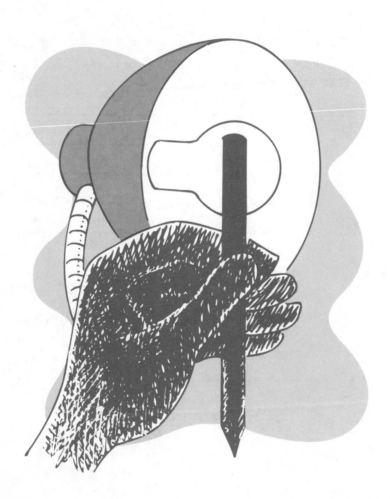

Hidden

Observations and Data

What happens during the experiment? Write down what you observed as well as any measurements or calculations that you made. You may also want to draw sketches or take photos of your experiment.

_____

_____

_____

_____

_____

_____

Results and Conclusions

What was the final result of your experiment? Was it what you expected? Why or why not?

_____

_____

_____

_____

_____

What's Next?

How could you improve on this experiment? Did the results make you think of any other questions that you could investigate with new experiments?

_____

_____

_____

_____

Peeper

PURPOSE

To determine when the planet Mercury is the most visible from earth.

Materials

cellophane tape
desk lamp
yardstick (meter stick)
black marking pen
basketball

Procedure

1. Center a piece of tape across the opening of a desk lamp. The tape should not touch the light bulb.

2. Use a marking pen to mark a small dot on the tape above the center of the light bulb.

3. Position the lamp so that the bulb faces you.

4. Turn the light on and stand 1 yd. (1 m) in front of the bulb.

5. Close your left eye and look at the dot on the tape with your open right eye.

6. Slowly move your body to the left until the dot appears just slightly to the right of the light bulb.

7. Stand in this position while holding the basketball in front of your face. Continue to keep your left eye closed.

8. Move the ball so that it blocks your view of the light bulb but allows you to see the dot on the tape.

Peeper

Observations and Data

What happens during the experiment? Write down what you observed as well as any measurements or calculations that you made. You may also want to draw sketches or take photos of your experiment.

_____

_____

_____

_____

_____

_____

Results and Conclusions

What was the final result of your experiment? Was it what you expected? Why or why not?

_____

_____

_____

_____

_____

What's Next?

How could you improve on this experiment? Did the results make you think of any other questions that you could investigate with new experiments?

_____

_____

_____

_____

Blasters

PURPOSE

To determine what might have produced the craters on the moon.

Materials

2-quart (2-liter) plastic bowl
flour
3 or 4 sheets of newspaper
baseball

Procedure

1. Fill the bowl ¾ full with flour.

2. Spread the newspaper on the floor.

3. Place the bowl of flour in the center of the newspaper.

4. Stand with the bowl at your feet and the ball level with your chest.

5. Drop the ball into the bowl.

Blasters

Observations and Data

What happens during the experiment? Write down what you observed as well as any measurements or calculations that you made. You may also want to draw sketches or take photos of your experiment.

_____

_____

_____

_____

_____

Results and Conclusions

What was the final result of your experiment? Was it what you expected? Why or why not?

_____

_____

_____

_____

_____

What's Next?

How could you improve on this experiment? Did the results make you think of any other questions that you could investigate with new experiments?

_____

_____

_____

_____

Plop!

PURPOSE

To determine the type of surface where craters are best formed.

Materials

8-inch (20-cm) square of aluminum foil
newspaper
1 golf ball-sized rock

Procedure

1. Lay the newspaper on the carpet.

2. Lay one foil square on top of the newspaper.

3. Stand at the edge of the foil.

4. Hold the rock waist high and drop it in the center of the foil.

5. Repeat steps 1 through 4 on a hard floor.

6. Examine both pieces of foil.

Plop!

Observations and Data

What happens during the experiment? Write down what you observed as well as any measurements or calculations that you made. You may also want to draw sketches or take photos of your experiment.

_____

_____

_____

_____

_____

_____

_____

Results and Conclusions

What was the final result of your experiment? Was it what you expected? Why or why not?

_____

_____

_____

_____

_____

What's Next?

How could you improve on this experiment? Did the results make you think of any other questions that you could investigate with new experiments?

_____

_____

_____

_____

Moving Target

PURPOSE

To simulate aiming a spacecraft for the moon.

Materials

scissors

ruler

string

masking tape

washer

book

paper towel

Procedure

1. Cut a 24-inch (60-cm) piece of string.

2. Tape one end of the string to one end of the ruler.

3. Tie the washer to the free end of the string.

4. Place the ruler on a table with about 4 inches (10 cm) of the ruler extending over the edge of the table.

5. Place a book on top of the ruler to secure it to the table.

6. Tear and wad up 10 grape-sized pieces of the paper towel.

7. Pull the hanging washer to the side and release it to start it swinging.

8. Sit about 1 yard (1 m) from the swinging washer.

9. Pitch one wad of paper at a time at the moving washer.

10. Record the number of paper wads that hit the swinging washer.

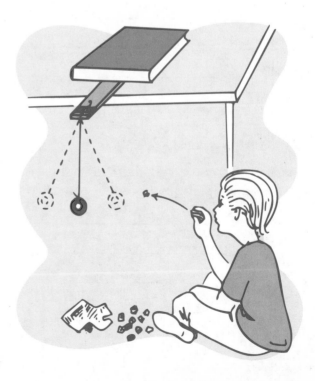

Moving Target

Observations and Data

What happens during the experiment? Write down what you observed as well as any measurements or calculations that you made. You may also want to draw sketches or take photos of your experiment.

_____

_____

_____

_____

_____

_____

Results and Conclusions

What was the final result of your experiment? Was it what you expected? Why or why not?

_____

_____

_____

_____

What's Next?

How could you improve on this experiment? Did the results make you think of any other questions that you could investigate with new experiments?

_____

_____

_____

_____

Face Forward

PURPOSE

To demonstrate that the moon rotates on its axis.

Materials

2 sheets of paper
masking tape
marker

Procedure

1. Draw a circle in the center of one sheet of paper.

2. Write the word EARTH in the center of the circle, and place the paper on the floor.

3. Mark a large X in the center of the second sheet of paper, and tape this paper to the wall.

4. Stand by the side of the paper on the floor and face the X on the wall.

5. Walk around the Earth, but continue to face the X.

6. Turn so that you face the paper labeled EARTH.

7. Walk around the Earth, but continue to face the Earth.

Face Forward

Observations and Data

What happens during the experiment? Write down what you observed as well as any measurements or calculations that you made. You may also want to draw sketches or take photos of your experiment.

_____

_____

_____

_____

_____

_____

Results and Conclusions

What was the final result of your experiment? Was it what you expected? Why or why not?

_____

_____

_____

_____

What's Next?

How could you improve on this experiment? Did the results make you think of any other questions that you could investigate with new experiments?

_____

_____

_____

_____

Changes

PURPOSE

To determine why the moon appears and disappears.

Materials

pencil
styrofoam ball the size of an apple
lamp

Procedure

1. Push the pencil into the styrofoam ball.

2. Position the lamp near a doorway.

3. Stand in a darkened room facing the lighted doorway.

4. Hold the ball in front of you and slightly higher than your head.

5. Slowly turn yourself around. Keep the ball in front of you as you turn.

6. Observe the ball as you turn.

Changes

Observations and Data

What happens during the experiment? Write down what you observed as well as any measurements or calculations that you made. You may also want to draw sketches or take photos of your experiment.

_____

_____

_____

_____

_____

_____

Results and Conclusions

What was the final result of your experiment? Was it what you expected? Why or why not?

_____

_____

_____

_____

What's Next?

How could you improve on this experiment? Did the results make you think of any other questions that you could investigate with new experiments?

_____

_____

_____

_____

Quicker

PURPOSE

To determine how distance affects a planet's period of revolution.

Materials

modeling clay
yardstick (meter stick)
ruler

Procedure

1. Place a walnut-sized ball of clay on one end of the ruler and on one end of the yardstick (meter stick).

2. Hold the yardstick and ruler vertically, side by side, with the edge without the clay ball on the ground.

3. Release both at the same time.

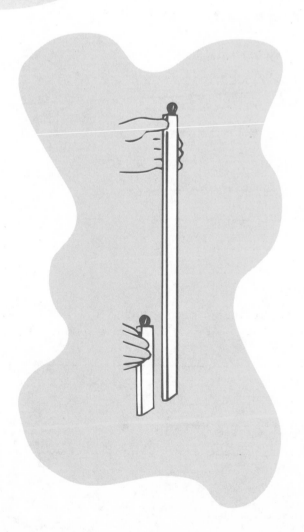

Quicker

Observations and Data

What happens during the experiment? Write down what you observed as well as any measurements or calculations that you made. You may also want to draw sketches or take photos of your experiment.

_____

_____

_____

_____

_____

_____

Results and Conclusions

What was the final result of your experiment? Was it what you expected? Why or why not?

_____

_____

_____

_____

_____

What's Next?

How could you improve on this experiment? Did the results make you think of any other questions that you could investigate with new experiments?

_____

_____

_____

_____

Speedy

PURPOSE

To determine the effect of distance on the orbiting speed of planets.

Materials

1 metal washer

1-yard (1-m) piece of string

Procedure

NOTE: This activity is to be performed in an open, outside area away from other people.

1. Tie the washer to the end of the 1-yard (1-m) length of string.

2. Hold the end of the string and extend your arm outward.

3. Swing your arm around so that the washer moves in a circular path beside your body.

4. Spin the washer at the slowest speed necessary to keep the string taut.

5. Hold the string in the center and spin the washer at the slowest speed necessary to keep the string taut.

6. Hold the string about 10 inches (25 cm) from the washer and spin as before.

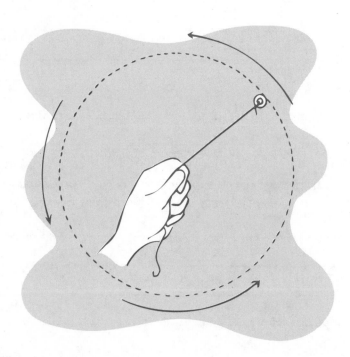

Speedy

Observations and Data

What happens during the experiment? Write down what you observed as well as any measurements or calculations that you made. You may also want to draw sketches or take photos of your experiment.

_____

_____

_____

_____

_____

_____

Results and Conclusions

What was the final result of your experiment? Was it what you expected? Why or why not?

_____

_____

_____

_____

_____

What's Next?

How could you improve on this experiment? Did the results make you think of any other questions that you could investigate with new experiments?

_____

_____

_____

_____

On the Move

PURPOSE

To determine why planets continue to move.

Materials

round cake pan
pencil
1 sheet construction paper
scissors
1 marble

Procedure

1. Use the cake pan to trace a circle on the paper.

2. Cut the circle out.

3. Place the pan on a flat surface.

4. Lay the paper inside the pan and place the marble on top of the paper.

5. Thump the marble so that it rolls around next to the wall of the pan.

6. Remove the paper from the pan.

7. Again, thump the marble so that it rolls around next to the wall of the pan.

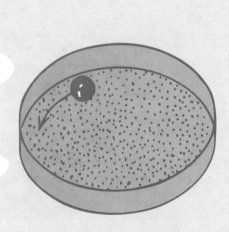

On the Move

Observations and Data

What happens during the experiment? Write down what you observed as well as any measurements or calculations that you made. You may also want to draw sketches or take photos of your experiment.

_____

_____

_____

_____

_____

_____

Results and Conclusions

What was the final result of your experiment? Was it what you expected? Why or why not?

_____

_____

_____

_____

What's Next?

How could you improve on this experiment? Did the results make you think of any other questions that you could investigate with new experiments?

_____

_____

_____

_____

Back Up

PURPOSE

To demonstrate the apparent backward motion of Mars.

Materials

Helper

Procedure

1. This is an outside activity.

2. Ask a helper to stand next to you and then start slowly walking forward.

3. Look past your helper's head and notice the background objects that he or she passes.

4. Start waking toward your helper at a faster speed than your helper.

5. Continue to observe the background past your helper's head.

6. Stop and ask your helper to stop when you are about 5 yd. (5 m) in front of him or her.

Back Up

Observations and Data

What happens during the experiment? Write down what you observed as well as any measurements or calculations that you made. You may also want to draw sketches or take photos of your experiment.

_____

_____

_____

_____

_____

_____

Results and Conclusions

What was the final result of your experiment? Was it what you expected? Why or why not?

_____

_____

_____

_____

_____

What's Next?

How could you improve on this experiment? Did the results make you think of any other questions that you could investigate with new experiments?

_____

_____

_____

_____

In and Out

PURPOSE

To demonstrate forces that keep satellites in orbit.

Materials

scissors
yardstick (meter stick)
string
masking tape
thread spool
metal spoon

Procedure

1. Cut 1 yard (1 m) of string.

2. Tie one end of the string to the roll of tape.

3. Thread the free end of the string through the hole in the spool.

4. Tie the spoon to the free end of the string.

5. Stand in an open area holding the tape in one hand and the spool with your other hand.

6. Give the spool a quick circular motion to start it spinning in a horizontal circle above your head.

7. Release the tape and allow it to hang freely.

8. Keep the spoon spinning by moving the thread spool in a circular motion.

9. Observe the movement of the tape roll.

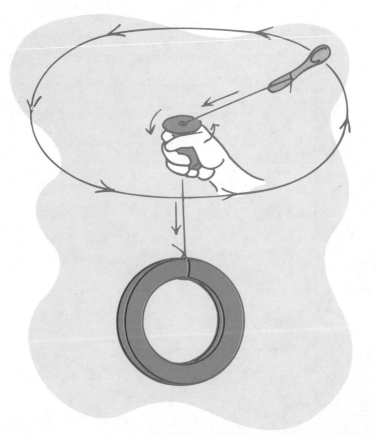

In and Out

Observations and Data

What happens during the experiment? Write down what you observed as well as any measurements or calculations that you made. You may also want to draw sketches or take photos of your experiment.

_____

_____

_____

_____

_____

_____

Results and Conclusions

What was the final result of your experiment? Was it what you expected? Why or why not?

_____

_____

_____

_____

_____

What's Next?

How could you improve on this experiment? Did the results make you think of any other questions that you could investigate with new experiments?

_____

_____

_____

_____

Orbiter

PURPOSE

To demonstrate the force that keeps satellites in orbit around the earth.

Materials

small-mouthed glass jar, 1 pint (500 ml)
marble

Procedure

1. Use your hand to hold the jar horizontally with its opening pointing to the side.

2. Place a marble inside the jar.

3. Gently place the mouth of the jar against the palm of your hand.

4. Move the jar around in a circular path until the marble quickly spins around on the inside of the jar.

5. Continue to move the jar around as you slowly turn the jar and your palm upside down. You may have to practice this movement to keep the marble moving at a constant speed.

6. Remove your palm from the mouth of the jar.

7. Stop moving the jar.

Orbiter

Observations and Data

What happens during the experiment? Write down what you observed as well as any measurements or calculations that you made. You may also want to draw sketches or take photos of your experiment.

_____

_____

_____

_____

_____

_____

Results and Conclusions

What was the final result of your experiment? Was it what you expected? Why or why not?

_____

_____

_____

_____

_____

What's Next?

How could you improve on this experiment? Did the results make you think of any other questions that you could investigate with new experiments?

_____

_____

_____

_____

Tumbler

PURPOSE

To demonstrate three kinds of satellite movements: roll, pitch, and yaw.

Materials

modeling clay
3 colored toothpicks—red, blue, and green
index card
marking pen
scissors

Procedure

1. Use modeling clay to form a spacecraft. The length, width, and height of your space vehicle must be less than the length of the toothpicks.

2. Insert the red toothpick through the center of the craft from front to back. This is toothpick A in the diagram.

3. Push the blue toothpick, toothpick B, through the approximate center of the craft from side to side.

4. Stick toothpick C, the green stick, through the spacecraft's approximate center from top to bottom.

5. Draw and cut out a small astronaut from an index card.

6. Stick the paper astronaut into the clay at the top of the spacecraft as indicated in the diagram.

7. With your hands, hold the ends of toothpick A.

8. Roll the stick back and forth between your fingers.

9. Observe the movement of the craft and the other toothpicks.

10. In turn, hold the other two toothpicks, rolling them back and forth between your fingers.

11. Again, observe the movement of the astronaut and spacecraft as the vehicle rotates.

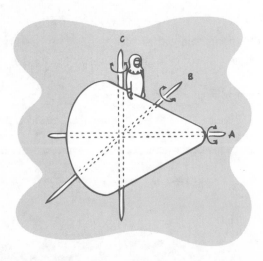

Tumbler

Observations and Data

What happens during the experiment? Write down what you observed as well as any measurements or calculations that you made. You may also want to draw sketches or take photos of your experiment.

_____

_____

_____

_____

_____

_____

Results and Conclusions

What was the final result of your experiment? Was it what you expected? Why or why not?

_____

_____

_____

_____

_____

What's Next?

How could you improve on this experiment? Did the results make you think of any other questions that you could investigate with new experiments?

_____

_____

_____

_____

Rings

PURPOSE

To determine what causes Saturn's rings.

Materials

3 sharpened pencils

masking tape

drawing compass

stiff cardboard, such as the
back of a writing tablet

scissors

cookie sheet

salt

adult helper

Procedure

1. Tape two of the pencils together so that
their points are even.

2. Use the compass to draw a circle with an 8-
inch (20-cm) diameter (length of a straight
line passing through the center of the circle with both endpoints on the circle) on
the cardboard.

3. Cut out the circle and have an adult use the
point of the compass to punch a hole in the
center.

4. Place the circle of cardboard, with the
rough side of the hole down, on the cookie
sheet.

5. Evenly cover the surface of the cardboard
with salt.

6. Ask your helper to stand the third pencil
point-down in the hole in the cardboard
circle.

7. Rest the points of the taped pencils against
the cardboard as your helper spins the
cardboard around one full turn.

Rings

Observations and Data

What happens during the experiment? Write down what you observed as well as any measurements or calculations that you made. You may also want to draw sketches or take photos of your experiment.

_____

_____

_____

_____

_____

_____

Results and Conclusions

What was the final result of your experiment? Was it what you expected? Why or why not?

_____

_____

_____

_____

_____

What's Next?

How could you improve on this experiment? Did the results make you think of any other questions that you could investigate with new experiments?

_____

_____

_____

_____

See Through

PURPOSE

To determine how Saturn can be seen through its rings.

Materials

scissors
ruler
white poster board
glue
black marking pen
straight pin
pencil
adult helper

Procedure

1. Cut 3 strips from the poster board that are each 1 × 6 inches (2.5 × 15 cm).

2. Evenly space the strips so that their centers cross.

3. Glue the centers of the strips together.

4. Use the marking pen to make two marks across the ends of each strip. Start the first mark ½ inch (1 cm) from the end of the strip and make the second mark 1 inch (2.5 cm) from the end.

5. Ask an adult to insert the pin through the center of the strips. Use the pin to enlarge the hole so that the paper blades easily spin. Then stick the end of the pin in a pencil eraser.

6. Spin the paper blades.

7. Observe the spinning blades.

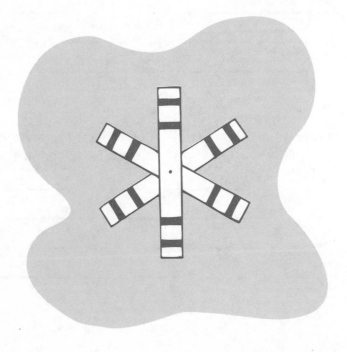

See Through

Observations and Data

What happens during the experiment? Write down what you observed as well as any measurements or calculations that you made. You may also want to draw sketches or take photos of your experiment.

_____

_____

_____

_____

_____

_____

Results and Conclusions

What was the final result of your experiment? Was it what you expected? Why or why not?

_____

_____

_____

_____

_____

What's Next?

How could you improve on this experiment? Did the results make you think of any other questions that you could investigate with new experiments?

_____

_____

_____

_____

Spreader

PURPOSE

To demonstrate how distance affects a star's apparent brightness.

Materials

flashlight

Procedure

NOTE: Perform this experiment in a darkened room.

1. Stand in the center of a darkened room and shine the flashlight at a wall.

2. Slowly walk toward the wall and observe how the light pattern produced on the wall changes.

Spreader

Observations and Data

What happens during the experiment? Write down what you observed as well as any measurements or calculations that you made. You may also want to draw sketches or take photos of your experiment.

_____

_____

_____

_____

_____

_____

Results and Conclusions

What was the final result of your experiment? Was it what you expected? Why or why not?

_____

_____

_____

_____

_____

What's Next?

How could you improve on this experiment? Did the results make you think of any other questions that you could investigate with new experiments?

_____

_____

_____

_____

Hazy

PURPOSE

To demonstrate why the Milky Way appears to be a hazy cloud.

Materials

paper hole punch
white paper
glue
black construction paper
masking tape

Procedure

1. Use the hole punch to cut about 20 circles from the white paper.

2. Glue the circles very close together, but not overlapping, in the center of the black paper.

3. Tape the paper to a tree or any outside object.

4. Stand close and look at the paper, then slowly back away until the separate circles can no longer be seen.

Hazy

Observations and Data

What happens during the experiment? Write down what you observed as well as any measurements or calculations that you made. You may also want to draw sketches or take photos of your experiment.

_____

_____

_____

_____

_____

_____

Results and Conclusions

What was the final result of your experiment? Was it what you expected? Why or why not?

_____

_____

_____

_____

_____

What's Next?

How could you improve on this experiment? Did the results make you think of any other questions that you could investigate with new experiments?

_____

_____

_____

_____

Twinkling Star

PURPOSE

To simulate twinkling stars.

Materials

12-by-12 inch (30-by-30-cm) square of
aluminum foil
2-quart (2-liter) glass bowl
tap water
flashlight
pencil

Procedure

1. Crumple the foil with your hands. Open up the crumpled foil and place it a table.

2. Fill the bowl with water and place it on top of the foil.

3. Darken the room and hold the flashlight about 12 inches (30 cm) above the bowl.

4. Gently tap the surface of the water with the pencil.

5. Observe the foil through the moving water.

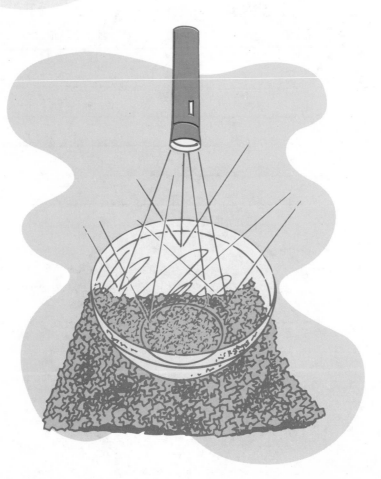

Twinkling Star

Observations and Data

What happens during the experiment? Write down what you observed as well as any measurements or calculations that you made. You may also want to draw sketches or take photos of your experiment.

_____

_____

_____

_____

_____

_____

Results and Conclusions

What was the final result of your experiment? Was it what you expected? Why or why not?

_____

_____

_____

_____

What's Next?

How could you improve on this experiment? Did the results make you think of any other questions that you could investigate with new experiments?

_____

_____

_____

_____

Brightest Star

PURPOSE

To locate the brightest star.

Materials

compass

Procedure

CAUTION: Never look directly at the sun.

1. Just before sunrise, go outside and find a good view of the sky above the horizon.

2. Use the compass to determine the directions of east and west.

3. Face the east and look for a very bright star in the sky above the horizon.

4. If you don't see the star at sunrise, look for it above the western horizon after sunset.

Brightest Star

Observations and Data

What happens during the experiment? Write down what you observed as well as any measurements or calculations that you made. You may also want to draw sketches or take photos of your experiment.

_____

_____

_____

_____

_____

_____

_____

Results and Conclusions

What was the final result of your experiment? Was it what you expected? Why or why not?

_____

_____

_____

_____

_____

What's Next?

How could you improve on this experiment? Did the results make you think of any other questions that you could investigate with new experiments?

_____

_____

_____

_____

Box Planetarium

PURPOSE

To demonstrate how planetariums produce images of the night sky.

Materials

shoe box
scissors
flashlight
black construction paper
cellophane tape
straight pin

Procedure

1. Cut a square from the end of the shoe box.

2. At the other end of the box, cut a circle just large enough to insert the end of the flashlight.

3. Cover the square opening with a piece of black paper. Secure the paper to the box with tape.

4. Use the pin to make 7 to 8 holes in the black paper.

5. Point the shoe box toward a blank wall.

6. In a darkened room, turn on the flashlight.

7. Move back and forth from the wall to form clear images of small light spots on the wall. Make the holes in the black paper larger if the spots on the wall are too small.

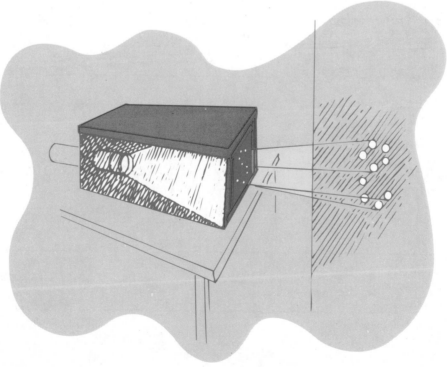

Box Planetarium

Observations and Data

What happens during the experiment? Write down what you observed as well as any measurements or calculations that you made. You may also want to draw sketches or take photos of your experiment.

_____

_____

_____

_____

_____

Results and Conclusions

What was the final result of your experiment? Was it what you expected? Why or why not?

_____

_____

_____

_____

_____

What's Next?

How could you improve on this experiment? Did the results make you think of any other questions that you could investigate with new experiments?

_____

_____

_____

_____

Star Projector

PURPOSE

To make a star projector.

Materials

round box, such as an empty oatmeal box
drawing compass
sheet of black construction paper
scissors
rubber band
chalk
flashlight
adult helper

Procedure

1. Ask an adult to remove both ends of the box.

2. Use the compass to draw a circle on the paper 2 inches (10 cm) wider than the end of the box.

3. Cut out the circle and place it over one end of the box. Secure the paper with the rubber band.

4. Use the chalk to draw the star pattern on the paper cover.

5. With the pointed end of the compass, make a hole through each star on the paper cover.

6. Place the flashlight inside the box. Darken the room and turn on the flashlight.

7. Turn the papered end of the box toward the ceiling. Move the flashlight back and forth in the box until a clear image of light spots appears on the ceiling.

star pattern on the box

OATS

31

Star Projector

Observations and Data

What happens during the experiment? Write down what you observed as well as any measurements or calculations that you made. You may also want to draw sketches or take photos of your experiment.

_____

_____

_____

_____

_____

_____

Results and Conclusions

What was the final result of your experiment? Was it what you expected? Why or why not?

_____

_____

_____

_____

What's Next?

How could you improve on this experiment? Did the results make you think of any other questions that you could investigate with new experiments?

_____

_____

_____

_____

Star Chart

PURPOSE

To record the position of the Big Dipper and Polaris.

Materials

scissors

ruler

string

large nail

white poster paper

marker

helper

Procedure

1. Cut a string 12 inches (30 cm) longer than your height.

2. Tie one end of the string to a nail.

3. On a clear, moonless night, lay a sheet of white poster paper on the ground.

4. Stand on the edge of the paper and point to a star in the Big Dipper while holding the free end of the string, allowing the nail to hang freely.

5. Ask a helper to mark a spot on the paper under the hanging nail.

6. Point to each of the stars in the Big Dipper as your helper marks their position on the paper.

7. Find and mark the position of the North Star by drawing a straight line from the two pointer stars in the bowl of the Big Dipper to the star in the handle of the Little Dipper.

Star Chart

Observations and Data

What happens during the experiment? Write down what you observed as well as any measurements or calculations that you made. You may also want to draw sketches or take photos of your experiment.

_____

_____

_____

_____

_____

_____

Results and Conclusions

What was the final result of your experiment? Was it what you expected? Why or why not?

_____

_____

_____

_____

_____

What's Next?

How could you improve on this experiment? Did the results make you think of any other questions that you could investigate with new experiments?

_____

_____

_____

_____

Spots

PURPOSE

To simulate the magnetic field around spots on the sun.

Materials

rubber gloves (the kind used for dishwashing)

scissors

soapless steel wool pad (purchase at a variety store in the paint section)

1-teaspoon (5-ml) measuring spoon

small round magnet

sheet of typing paper

Procedure

1. Put on the gloves and use the scissors to cut very tiny pieces from the steel wool pad. The smaller the pieces, the better. Cut enough pieces to fill the measuring spoon.

   CAUTION: Do not remove the gloves. They prevent the steel wool from damaging your skin.

2. Place the magnet on a wooden table and cover it with the paper.

3. Sprinkle the steel wool pieces on the paper above the magnet.

Spots

Observations and Data

What happens during the experiment? Write down what you observed as well as any measurements or calculations that you made. You may also want to draw sketches or take photos of your experiment.

_____

_____

_____

_____

_____

_____

Results and Conclusions

What was the final result of your experiment? Was it what you expected? Why or why not?

_____

_____

_____

_____

_____

What's Next?

How could you improve on this experiment? Did the results make you think of any other questions that you could investigate with new experiments?

_____

_____

_____

_____

Attractive

PURPOSE

To simulate the solar magnetic field.

Materials

bar magnet

8½ × 11 inch (22 × 28 cm) sheet of white paper

iron filings (found in magnetic drawing toys sold at toy stores)

small spray bottle

white vinegar

pencil

Procedure

1. Lay the magnet on a wooden table.

2. Cover the magnet with the sheet of paper.

3. Sprinkle iron filings over the surface of the paper.

4. Gently tap the paper with your finger until the filings settle into a pattern.

5. Fill the spray bottle ½ full with the vinegar.

6. Spray a fine mist of vinegar over the iron filings on the paper.

7. Allow the paper to remain undisturbed for an hour.

8. Lift the paper and shake the iron filings into the trash.

9. Draw a circle in the center of the pattern left by the rusty filings and label it "Sun."

Attractive

Observations and Data

What happens during the experiment? Write down what you observed as well as any measurements or calculations that you made. You may also want to draw sketches or take photos of your experiment.

_____

_____

_____

_____

_____

_____

Results and Conclusions

What was the final result of your experiment? Was it what you expected? Why or why not?

_____

_____

_____

_____

_____

What's Next?

How could you improve on this experiment? Did the results make you think of any other questions that you could investigate with new experiments?

_____

_____

_____

_____

Which Way?

PURPOSE

To make a shadow compass.

Materials

pen
paper plate
pencil

Procedure

CAUTION: Never look directly at the sun. It can damage your eyes.

1. Use the pen to mark the directions N, S, E, and W on the edge of the paper plate.

2. In the afternoon, lay the paper plate on the ground in a sunny area.

3. Push the point of the pencil through the center of the plate and into the ground about 1 inch (2.5 cm).

4. Move the pencil around until it no longer casts a shadow on the plate.

5. Wait until a shadow appears on the plate, then rotate the plate so that the shadow points toward the letter E.

Which Way?

Observations and Data

What happens during the experiment? Write down what you observed as well as any measurements or calculations that you made. You may also want to draw sketches or take photos of your experiment.

_____

_____

_____

_____

_____

_____

Results and Conclusions

What was the final result of your experiment? Was it what you expected? Why or why not?

_____

_____

_____

_____

_____

What's Next?

How could you improve on this experiment? Did the results make you think of any other questions that you could investigate with new experiments?

_____

_____

_____

_____

Clock Compass

PURPOSE

To demonstrate how a clock can be used as a compass.

Materials

scissors

ruler

1 sheet of white paper

pencil

12 × 12 inches (30 × 30 cm) cardboard

straight pin

clock

compass

Procedure

1. Cut a 6-inch (15-cm) diameter circle from the paper.

2. Write numbers on the paper circle as they appear on a clock.

3. Lay the paper circle in the center of the cardboard.

4. Stick a straight pin vertically through the center of the paper circle and into the cardboard.

5. Place the cardboard on an outside surface in direct sunlight.

6. Turn the paper circle until the shadow of the pin falls on the correct time. Do not use daylight savings time.

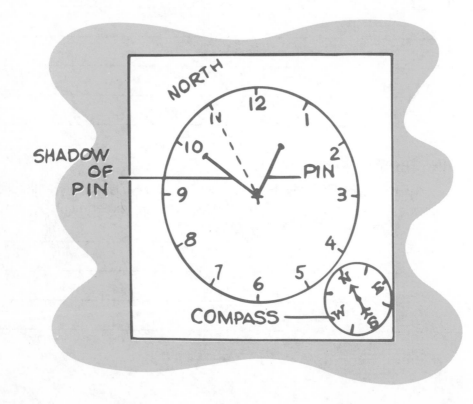

Clock Compass

Observations and Data

What happens during the experiment? Write down what you observed as well as any measurements or calculations that you made. You may also want to draw sketches or take photos of your experiment.

_____

_____

_____

_____

_____

_____

Results and Conclusions

What was the final result of your experiment? Was it what you expected? Why or why not?

_____

_____

_____

_____

_____

What's Next?

How could you improve on this experiment? Did the results make you think of any other questions that you could investigate with new experiments?

_____

_____

_____

_____

Flaming Colors

PURPOSE

To determine the colors that make up white light from the sun.

Materials

shallow baking pan
flat pocket mirror
1 sheet white typing paper

Procedure

CAUTION: This experiment must be done on a sunny day, and you must not look directly at the sun or use the mirror to reflect the sun's light toward another person's eyes.

1. Fill a shallow baking pan with water.
2. Place the pan on a table near a window so that it receives the morning sunlight.

3. Place a flat mirror inside the pan so that it rests at an angle against one side of the pan.
4. With one hand, hold a sheet of white paper in front of the mirror.
5. Use your other hand to move the mirror slightly. Adjust the position of the mirror and paper until a rainbow of colors appears on the white paper.
6. Slightly shake the mirror.

MIRROR

Flaming Colors

Observations and Data

What happens during the experiment? Write down what you observed as well as any measurements or calculations that you made. You may also want to draw sketches or take photos of your experiment.

_____

_____

_____

_____

_____

_____

Results and Conclusions

What was the final result of your experiment? Was it what you expected? Why or why not?

_____

_____

_____

_____

What's Next?

How could you improve on this experiment? Did the results make you think of any other questions that you could investigate with new experiments?

_____

_____

_____

_____

Rainbow

PURPOSE

To determine how the sun's position affects how a rainbow is made.

Materials

garden hose with sprayer

Procedure

NOTE: Since there is a possibility of getting wet, the best time to perform this experiment is on a warm day.

CAUTION: Never look directly at the sun.

1. Turn the water on and adjust the nozzle on the hose so that it sprays a fine mist of water.

2. Stand with the sun behind you and look for a rainbow in the water spray.

3. Turn around so that the sun is in front of you, and look for a rainbow in the water spray, again.

Rainbow

Observations and Data

What happens during the experiment? Write down what you observed as well as any measurements or calculations that you made. You may also want to draw sketches or take photos of your experiment.

_____

_____

_____

_____

_____

_____

Results and Conclusions

What was the final result of your experiment? Was it what you expected? Why or why not?

_____

_____

_____

_____

_____

What's Next?

How could you improve on this experiment? Did the results make you think of any other questions that you could investigate with new experiments?

_____

_____

_____

_____

Inverted

PURPOSE

To demonstrate how light travels through the lens of a refractive telescope.

Materials

dark construction paper, 1 sheet
scissors
gooseneck desk lamp
masking tape
ruler
magnifying lens

Procedure

1. Cut a paper circle from the dark paper to fit the opening of the lamp.

2. Cut an arrow design in the center of the paper circle.

3. Tape the circle over the lamp.

   CAUTION: Be sure that the paper does not rest on the lightbulb. The bulb will get hot.

4. Place the lamp about 6 ft. (2 m) from a wall.

5. Turn the lamp on, and darken the rest of the room.

6. Hold the magnifying lens about 12 in. (30 cm) from the lamp.

7. Move the magnifying lens back and forth from the lamp until a clear image is projected on the wall.

Inverted

Observations and Data

What happens during the experiment? Write down what you observed as well as any measurements or calculations that you made. You may also want to draw sketches or take photos of your experiment.

_____

_____

_____

_____

_____

_____

Results and Conclusions

What was the final result of your experiment? Was it what you expected? Why or why not?

_____

_____

_____

_____

_____

What's Next?

How could you improve on this experiment? Did the results make you think of any other questions that you could investigate with new experiments?

_____

_____

_____

_____

Sky Gazer

PURPOSE

To demonstrate how a refracting telescope works.

Materials

2 magnifying lenses
sheet of notebook paper

Procedure

1. In a darkened room, close one eye and look at an open window through one of the magnifying lenses.

2. Move the lens back and forth slowly until the objects outside the window are clearly in focus.

3. Without moving the lens, place the paper between you and the lens.

4. Move the paper back and forth until a clear image appears on the sheet.

5. Replace the paper with the second lens.

6. Move the second lens back and forth to find the position where the image looks clear when looking through both lenses.

Sky Gazer

Observations and Data

What happens during the experiment? Write down what you observed as well as any measurements or calculations that you made. You may also want to draw sketches or take photos of your experiment.

_____

_____

_____

_____

_____

_____

Results and Conclusions

What was the final result of your experiment? Was it what you expected? Why or why not?

_____

_____

_____

_____

_____

What's Next?

How could you improve on this experiment? Did the results make you think of any other questions that you could investigate with new experiments?

_____

_____

_____

_____

How Far?

PURPOSE

To demonstrate why it would be useful to place a large optical telescope on the moon.

Materials

clear plastic report folder
freezer

Procedure

1. Look through the plastic folder at a distant object.

2. Place the plastic folder in a freezer.

3. After 5 minutes, remove the folder from the freezer.

4. Again, look through the plastic folder at the same distant object.

How Far?

Observations and Data

What happens during the experiment? Write down what you observed as well as any measurements or calculations that you made. You may also want to draw sketches or take photos of your experiment.

_____

_____

_____

_____

_____

_____

Results and Conclusions

What was the final result of your experiment? Was it what you expected? Why or why not?

_____

_____

_____

_____

_____

What's Next?

How could you improve on this experiment? Did the results make you think of any other questions that you could investigate with new experiments?

_____

_____

_____

_____

Details

PURPOSE

To demonstrate the resolution of a lens.

Materials

scissors
black construction paper
flashlight
masking tape
straight pin

Procedure

1. Cut a circle of paper to fit over the end of the flashlight.

2. Secure the paper to the flashlight end with tape.

3. Use the pin to make two holes in the center of the paper circle about the width of the pencil lead apart.

4. Place the flashlight on a table.

5. Stand near the flashlight, facing the two spots of light emitted.

6. Slowly walk backwards until the spots look like one dot.

PINHOLES

Details

Observations and Data

What happens during the experiment? Write down what you observed as well as any measurements or calculations that you made. You may also want to draw sketches or take photos of your experiment.

_____

_____

_____

_____

_____

_____

Results and Conclusions

What was the final result of your experiment? Was it what you expected? Why or why not?

_____

_____

_____

_____

_____

What's Next?

How could you improve on this experiment? Did the results make you think of any other questions that you could investigate with new experiments?

_____

_____

_____

_____

Thick

PURPOSE

To determine why Venus' atmosphere is so hard to see through.

Materials

flashlight

wax paper

Procedure

1. Turn the flashlight on and place it on the edge of a chest of drawers.

2. Stand about 2 yards (2 m) from the chest of drawers.

3. Face the light and observe its brightness.

4. Hold the sheet of wax paper in front of your face.

5. Look through the wax paper at the light.

Thick

Observations and Data

What happens during the experiment? Write down what you observed as well as any measurements or calculations that you made. You may also want to draw sketches or take photos of your experiment.

_____

_____

_____

_____

_____

Results and Conclusions

What was the final result of your experiment? Was it what you expected? Why or why not?

_____

_____

_____

_____

_____

What's Next?

How could you improve on this experiment? Did the results make you think of any other questions that you could investigate with new experiments?

_____

_____

_____

_____

Bent

PURPOSE

To demonstrate how the thickness of an atmosphere affects how light is bent.

Materials

modeling clay
2 drinking cups
2 shiny pennies
tap water

Procedure

1. Stick a grape-sized piece of clay inside the bottom of each cup.

2. Press a penny in each piece of clay so that it is in the very center of the cup.

3. Fill one cup with water.

4. Place both cups on the edge of a table. The cups must be side by side and even with the edge of the table.

5. Stand close to the table. Then, take a few steps backward while observing the pennies in the cup.

6. Stop when you can no longer see either of the pennies.

Bent

Observations and Data

What happens during the experiment? Write down what you observed as well as any measurements or calculations that you made. You may also want to draw sketches or take photos of your experiment.

_____

_____

_____

_____

_____

_____

Results and Conclusions

What was the final result of your experiment? Was it what you expected? Why or why not?

_____

_____

_____

_____

What's Next?

How could you improve on this experiment? Did the results make you think of any other questions that you could investigate with new experiments?

_____

_____

_____

_____

Hot Box

PURPOSE

To determine why Venus is so hot.

Materials

2 thermometers
1 jar with lid (tall enough to hold the thermometers)

Procedure

1. Put one thermometer inside the jar and close the lid.

2. Place the second thermometer and the jar near a window in direct sunlight.

3. Record the temperature on both thermometers after 20 minutes.

Hot Box

Observations and Data

What happens during the experiment? Write down what you observed as well as any measurements or calculations that you made. You may also want to draw sketches or take photos of your experiment.

_____

_____

_____

_____

_____

_____

Results and Conclusions

What was the final result of your experiment? Was it what you expected? Why or why not?

_____

_____

_____

_____

_____

What's Next?

How could you improve on this experiment? Did the results make you think of any other questions that you could investigate with new experiments?

_____

_____

_____

_____

BIOLOGY

Zip

PURPOSE

To demonstrate how birds repair their feathers.

Materials

resealable plastic bag
feather

NOTE: Purchase the feather at a craft store. Do not use a feather found on the ground.

Procedure

1. Open the bag.

2. Put the open edges of the bag together and use your fingers to "zip" the bag closed.

3. Separate the vane on one side of the feather's shaft.

4. Use your fingers to push the separated section of the vane back together.

5. Move your fingers across the top and bottom of the feather in the same manner you "zipped" the plastic bag closed.

Zip

Observations and Data

What happens during the experiment? Write down what you observed as well as any measurements or calculations that you made. You may also want to draw sketches or take photos of your experiment.

_____

_____

_____

_____

_____

_____

_____

Results and Conclusions

What was the final result of your experiment? Was it what you expected? Why or why not?

_____

_____

_____

_____

What's Next?

How could you improve on this experiment? Did the results make you think of any other questions that you could investigate with new experiments?

_____

_____

_____

_____

Sipper

PURPOSE

To determine why hummingbirds have long, slender bills.

Materials

tall, slender vase
tap water
drinking straw

Procedure

1. Fill the vase half full with water. Lower the straw into the vase.

2. With your finger over the end of the straw, lift the straw so that its open end is above the water.

3. Lift your finger from the straw's opening.

Sipper

Observations and Data

What happens during the experiment? Write down what you observed as well as any measurements or calculations that you made. You may also want to draw sketches or take photos of your experiment.

_____

_____

_____

_____

_____

_____

Results and Conclusions

What was the final result of your experiment? Was it what you expected? Why or why not?

_____

_____

_____

_____

_____

What's Next?

How could you improve on this experiment? Did the results make you think of any other questions that you could investigate with new experiments?

_____

_____

_____

_____

Concentration

PURPOSE

To test your power of concentration.

Materials

chair

Procedure

1. Sit in the chair with your feet on the floor.

2. Use your right foot to trace a clockwise pattern on the floor.

3. Keep your foot going in a circle while you move your right hand around in a clockwise pattern in front of your body.

4. Continue tracing the circular pattern with your foot, but change the hand pattern to an up-and-down motion.

48

Concentration

Observations and Data

What happens during the experiment? Write down what you observed as well as any measurements or calculations that you made. You may also want to draw sketches or take photos of your experiment.

_____

_____

_____

_____

_____

_____

Results and Conclusions

What was the final result of your experiment? Was it what you expected? Why or why not?

_____

_____

_____

_____

_____

What's Next?

How could you improve on this experiment? Did the results make you think of any other questions that you could investigate with new experiments?

_____

_____

_____

_____

Change of Pattern

PURPOSE

To test your power of concentration.

Materials

a helper

Procedure

1. Ask your helper to pat the top of his or her head with one hand and to pat his or her stomach with the other hand.

2. Have him or her to continue patting the head, but to start rubbing the stomach in a circular motion.

3. Reverse the movements and have your helper rub his or her head while patting his stomach.

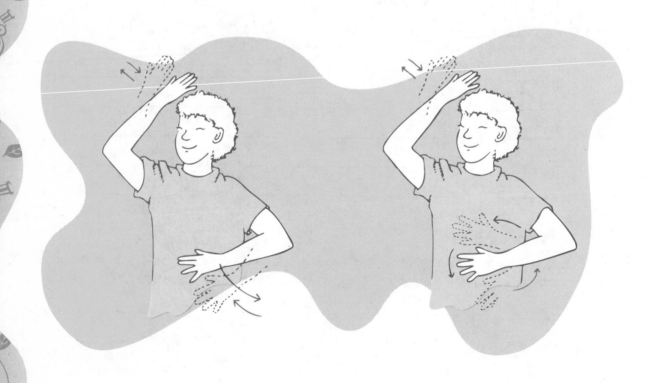

Change of Pattern

Observations and Data

What happens during the experiment? Write down what you observed as well as any measurements or calculations that you made. You may also want to draw sketches or take photos of your experiment.

_____

_____

_____

_____

_____

_____

Results and Conclusions

What was the final result of your experiment? Was it what you expected? Why or why not?

_____

_____

_____

_____

What's Next?

How could you improve on this experiment? Did the results make you think of any other questions that you could investigate with new experiments?

_____

_____

_____

_____

Hidden

PURPOSE

To demonstrate how color helps to protect an animal.

Materials

scissors

ruler

2 sheets of construction paper
(1 black and 1 orange)

2 sheets of newspaper (use sheets
with print only—no pictures)

pencil

helper

Procedure

1. Cut two 3-by-5-inch (7.5-by-12.5-cm) rectangles from each sheet of construction paper and from one sheet of newspaper.

2. Stack the rectangles together. Draw the largest fish possible on the top piece.

3. Cut out the fish, making sure to cut through all 6 layers of paper. Do not allow your helper to see the fish before the experiment starts.

4. Lay the uncut sheet of newspaper on the floor at the feet of your helper.

5. Ask your helper to close his or her eyes while you scatter the paper fish on the newspaper. Be sure to lay the newspaper fish with the print-only side facing up.

6. When you say "Go," have your helper open his or her eyes, quickly look at the newspaper, count the paper fish that are laying on the newspaper, and then immediately raise his or her eyes from the newspaper.

Hidden

Observations and Data

What happens during the experiment? Write down what you observed as well as any measurements or calculations that you made. You may also want to draw sketches or take photos of your experiment.

_____

_____

_____

_____

_____

_____

Results and Conclusions

What was the final result of your experiment? Was it what you expected? Why or why not?

_____

_____

_____

_____

_____

What's Next?

How could you improve on this experiment? Did the results make you think of any other questions that you could investigate with new experiments?

_____

_____

_____

_____

Blending

PURPOSE

To observe that the color of animals protects them from predators.

Materials

4 wooden stakes

string

ruler

scissors

colored pipe cleaners (multiple colors)

timer

helper

Procedure

1. Use the stakes and string to mark off a plot of grass about 20 feet (6 m) square.

2. Cut 20 one-half inch (13 mm) pieces of each color of pipe cleaner.

3. Ask a helper to scatter the pieces as evenly as possible in the marked-off plot of grass.

4. Pick up as many of the pieces as you can find in 5 minutes.

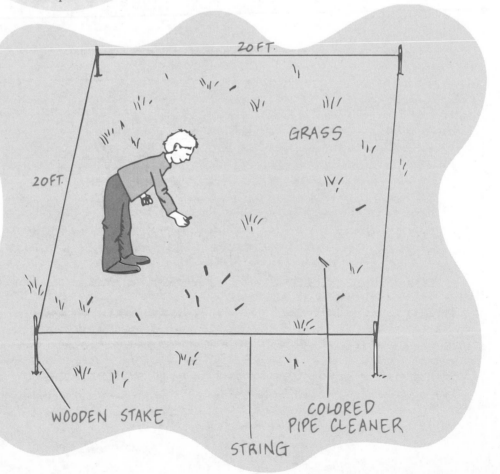

Blending

Observations and Data

What happens during the experiment? Write down what you observed as well as any measurements or calculations that you made. You may also want to draw sketches or take photos of your experiment.

_____

_____

_____

_____

_____

_____

Results and Conclusions

What was the final result of your experiment? Was it what you expected? Why or why not?

_____

_____

_____

_____

_____

What's Next?

How could you improve on this experiment? Did the results make you think of any other questions that you could investigate with new experiments?

_____

_____

_____

_____

Earthworm Farm

PURPOSE

To produce an environment suitable for earthworms.

Materials

2 cups (500 ml) soil

quart (liter) jar

tap water

1 cup (250 ml) peat moss

earthworms (purchase at a bait shop or dig your own)

apple peelings

dark construction paper

rubber band

Procedure

1. Pour the soil into the jar. Moisten the soil with water and keep it moist throughout the experiment.

2. Add the peat moss. Then put the worms into the jar.

3. Add the apple peelings.

4. Wrap the paper around the jar and secure with a rubber band. Place the jar in a shady, cool place.

5. Remove the paper and observe the jar every day for 7 days.

6. Return the worms to their natural surroundings—soil in a shady area outside.

Earthworm Farm

Observations and Data

What happens during the experiment? Write down what you observed as well as any measurements or calculations that you made. You may also want to draw sketches or take photos of your experiment.

_____

_____

_____

_____

_____

_____

Results and Conclusions

What was the final result of your experiment? Was it what you expected? Why or why not?

_____

_____

_____

_____

What's Next?

How could you improve on this experiment? Did the results make you think of any other questions that you could investigate with new experiments?

_____

_____

_____

_____

Night Crawlers

PURPOSE

To determine how earthworms respond to light.

Materials

scissors

shoe box with lid

flashlight

tape

notebook paper

tap water

paper towels

10 earthworms (purchase at a bait shop or dig your own)

timer

Procedure

1. Cut a hole slightly smaller than the flashlight's end in the end of the shoebox lid.

2. Tape a sheet of notebook paper to the lid so that it hangs about 1 inch (2.5 cm) from the floor of the shoe box, and about 4 inches (10 cm) from the end opposite the hole in the lid.

3. Place moistened paper towels in the bottom of the box.

4. Place the earthworms in the box under where the hole in the lid will be.

5. Position the flashlight over the hole and turn it on.

6. Leave the box undisturbed for 30 minutes, then open the lid and observe the position of the worms.

7. Return the worms to their natural surroundings—soil in a shady area outside.

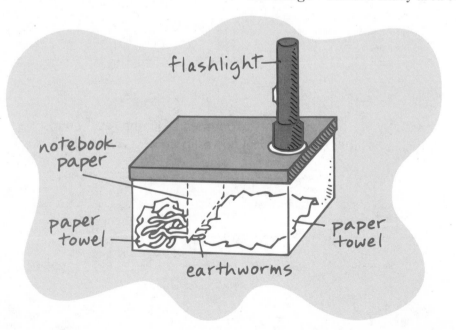

Night Crawlers

Observations and Data

What happens during the experiment? Write down what you observed as well as any measurements or calculations that you made. You may also want to draw sketches or take photos of your experiment.

_____

_____

_____

_____

_____

_____

Results and Conclusions

What was the final result of your experiment? Was it what you expected? Why or why not?

_____

_____

_____

_____

_____

What's Next?

How could you improve on this experiment? Did the results make you think of any other questions that you could investigate with new experiments?

_____

_____

_____

_____

Vanishing Ball

PURPOSE

To demonstrate the effect of the optic nerve on vision.

Materials

white paper
pencil
ruler

Procedure

1. In the center of the paper, draw two round ¼ inch (6 mm) colored dots, 4 inches (10 cm) apart.

2. Hold the paper at arm's length from your face.

3. Close your right eye and look at the dot on the right side with your open eye.

4. Slowly move the paper toward your face. Be sure to concentrate on the right dot and do not look at the one on the left.

5. Stop moving the paper when the left dot vanishes.

Vanishing Ball

Observations and Data

What happens during the experiment? Write down what you observed as well as any measurements or calculations that you made. You may also want to draw sketches or take photos of your experiment.

_____

_____

_____

_____

_____

_____

Results and Conclusions

What was the final result of your experiment? Was it what you expected? Why or why not?

_____

_____

_____

_____

_____

What's Next?

How could you improve on this experiment? Did the results make you think of any other questions that you could investigate with new experiments?

_____

_____

_____

_____

Blinking

PURPOSE

To determine if blinking is an involuntary action.

Materials

helper who wears glasses or
lightly tinted sunglasses

cotton ball

NOTE: If sunglasses are used, they must be lightly tinted so that you can easily see your helper's eyes through them.

Procedure

CAUTION: Do not substitute materials without adult approval. It could be dangerous to throw anything other than a cotton ball.

1. Have your helper wear his or her glasses.

2. Stand about 1 yard (1 m) away from your helper.

3. Without letting your helper know it's coming, throw a cotton ball directly at your helper's face. The glasses will keep the cotton ball from hitting your helper in the eyes.

Blinking

Observations and Data

What happens during the experiment? Write down what you observed as well as any measurements or calculations that you made. You may also want to draw sketches or take photos of your experiment.

_____

_____

_____

_____

_____

_____

Results and Conclusions

What was the final result of your experiment? Was it what you expected? Why or why not?

_____

_____

_____

_____

_____

What's Next?

How could you improve on this experiment? Did the results make you think of any other questions that you could investigate with new experiments?

_____

_____

_____

_____

Eye Lens

PURPOSE

To demonstrate how an eye lens works.

Materials

magnifying lens
ruler
sheet of typing paper

Procedure

1. Darken a room.

2. Hold the magnifying lens about 5 feet (1½ m) from an open window.

3. Position the paper on the opposite side of the lens from the window.

4. Slowly move the paper back and forth from the lens until a clear image of the window and objects outside appears.

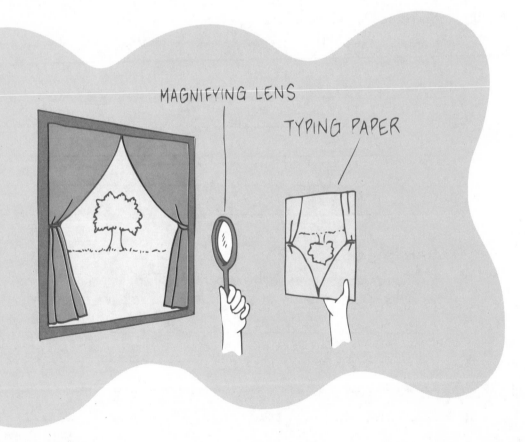

MAGNIFYING LENS

TYPING PAPER

Eye Lens

Observations and Data

What happens during the experiment? Write down what you observed as well as any measurements or calculations that you made. You may also want to draw sketches or take photos of your experiment.

_____

_____

_____

_____

_____

Results and Conclusions

What was the final result of your experiment? Was it what you expected? Why or why not?

_____

_____

_____

_____

_____

What's Next?

How could you improve on this experiment? Did the results make you think of any other questions that you could investigate with new experiments?

_____

_____

_____

_____

Fish Rings

PURPOSE

To determine the age of a fish.

Materials

fish scales (collect fish scales from a local fish market)

dark paper

hand lens

Procedure

1. Place a dried scale on the dark paper.

2. Using the hand lens, study the ring pattern on the scale.

3. Count the wide, lighter bands.

FISH SCALES

HAND LENS

DARK PAPER

Fish Rings

Observations and Data

What happens during the experiment? Write down what you observed as well as any measurements or calculations that you made. You may also want to draw sketches or take photos of your experiment.

_____

_____

_____

_____

_____

_____

Results and Conclusions

What was the final result of your experiment? Was it what you expected? Why or why not?

_____

_____

_____

_____

What's Next?

How could you improve on this experiment? Did the results make you think of any other questions that you could investigate with new experiments?

_____

_____

_____

_____

Cold Fish

PURPOSE

To determine if temperature affects how a fish breathes.

Materials

large-mouthed jar
aquarium with goldfish (or other small fish)
fish net
timer
large bowl
ice
tap water
thermometer
timer

Procedure

1. Fill the jar about three-fourths full with water from the aquarium. Use the net to transfer a fish to the jar.

2. Allow the fish 30 minutes to adjust to its new environment. Then, count the number of times the fish opens and closes its mouth in 1 minute.

3. Place the jar in the bowl. Fill the bowl half full with ice and then add enough water to fill the bowl. Do not add anything to the jar containing the fish.

4. Stand the thermometer inside the jar.

5. When the temperature in the jar reads 50 degrees Fahrenheit (10°C), count the number of times the fish opens and closes its mouth in 1 minute.

6. Pour the fish and the water in the jar back into the aquarium.

Cold Fish

Observations and Data

What happens during the experiment? Write down what you observed as well as any measurements or calculations that you made. You may also want to draw sketches or take photos of your experiment.

_____

_____

_____

_____

_____

_____

Results and Conclusions

What was the final result of your experiment? Was it what you expected? Why or why not?

_____

_____

_____

_____

What's Next?

How could you improve on this experiment? Did the results make you think of any other questions that you could investigate with new experiments?

_____

_____

_____

_____

Hearing

PURPOSE

To demonstrate how sound is heard.

Materials

metal spoon
2 ft. (61 cm) of kite string

Procedure

1. Tie the handle of the spoon in the center of the string.

2. Wrap the ends of the string around both index fingers. Be sure that both strings are the same length.

3. Place the tip of an index finger in each ear.

4. Lean over so that the spoon hangs freely and tap it against the side of a table.

KITE
STRING

— METAL SPOON

Hearing

Observations and Data

What happens during the experiment? Write down what you observed as well as any measurements or calculations that you made. You may also want to draw sketches or take photos of your experiment.

_____

_____

_____

_____

_____

Results and Conclusions

What was the final result of your experiment? Was it what you expected? Why or why not?

_____

_____

_____

_____

_____

What's Next?

How could you improve on this experiment? Did the results make you think of any other questions that you could investigate with new experiments?

_____

_____

_____

_____

Sound and Direction

PURPOSE

To test one's ability to determine the direction of a sound source.

Materials

a helper

Procedure

1. Have the helper sit in a chair.

2. Tell the helper to close his or her eyes.

3. Snap your fingers above his or her head and have the helper determine the area, front, top, or back of head, that you snap your fingers.

   NOTE: Be sure your fingers are held an equal distance between your helper's ears.

4. Do this several times, changing the snapping position each time.

Sound and Direction

Observations and Data

What happens during the experiment? Write down what you observed as well as any measurements or calculations that you made. You may also want to draw sketches or take photos of your experiment.

_____

_____

_____

_____

_____

_____

_____

Results and Conclusions

What was the final result of your experiment? Was it what you expected? Why or why not?

_____

_____

_____

_____

What's Next?

How could you improve on this experiment? Did the results make you think of any other questions that you could investigate with new experiments?

_____

_____

_____

_____

Fly Trap

PURPOSE

To observe the life cycle of a fly.

Materials

banana
1 quart jar (1 liter)
nylon stocking
rubber band

Procedure

1. Peel the banana and place the fruit inside the open jar.

2. Leave the jar open and undisturbed for 3 to 5 days.

3. Observe the jar daily. When 5 to 10 small fruit flies are seen inside the jar, cover the top with the stocking.

4. Secure the stocking over the mouth of the jar with a rubber band.

5. Leave the flies in the jar for 3 days, then release all of them.

6. Re-cover the jar with the stocking.

7. Observe the jar for 2 weeks.

Fly Trap

Observations and Data

What happens during the experiment? Write down what you observed as well as any measurements or calculations that you made. You may also want to draw sketches or take photos of your experiment.

_____

_____

_____

_____

_____

_____

Results and Conclusions

What was the final result of your experiment? Was it what you expected? Why or why not?

_____

_____

_____

_____

What's Next?

How could you improve on this experiment? Did the results make you think of any other questions that you could investigate with new experiments?

_____

_____

_____

_____

BZZZZZ

PURPOSE

To determine why insects make buzzing sounds.

Materials

rubber band (large enough to fit tightly
around the glass)
juice glass
index card

Procedure

1. Stretch the rubber band vertically around the glass, as shown in the diagram.

2. Pluck the rubber band with your finger.

3. Immediately touch the rubber band with a corner of the card.

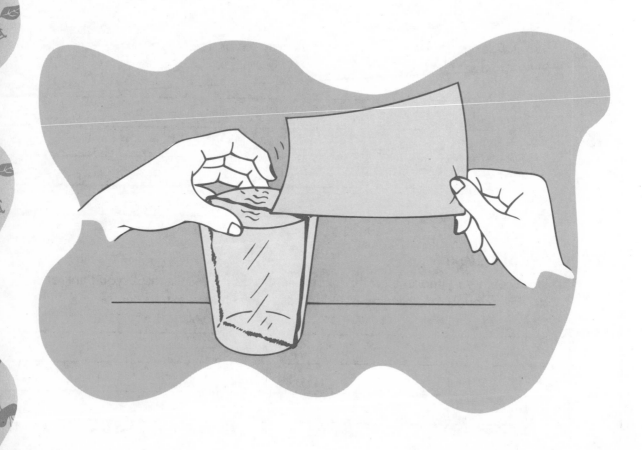

BZZZZZ

Observations and Data

What happens during the experiment? Write down what you observed as well as any measurements or calculations that you made. You may also want to draw sketches or take photos of your experiment.

_____

_____

_____

_____

_____

_____

Results and Conclusions

What was the final result of your experiment? Was it what you expected? Why or why not?

_____

_____

_____

_____

_____

What's Next?

How could you improve on this experiment? Did the results make you think of any other questions that you could investigate with new experiments?

_____

_____

_____

_____

Numb

PURPOSE

To demonstrate how the brain interprets messages from sensory receptors in the skin.

Materials

pencil

Procedure

1. Use your index finger and thumb of your right hand to rub the upper- and under-sides of the index finger of your left hand.

2. Hold the pencil in your left hand against the under-side of the index finger on that hand.

3. Rub the upper side of your left index finger and the pencil at the same time.

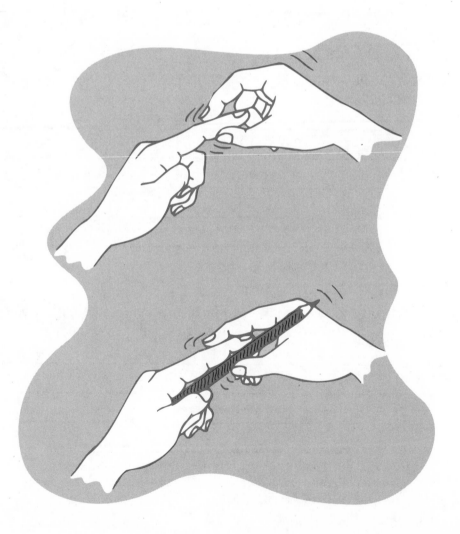

Numb

Observations and Data

What happens during the experiment? Write down what you observed as well as any measurements or calculations that you made. You may also want to draw sketches or take photos of your experiment.

_____

_____

_____

_____

_____

_____

Results and Conclusions

What was the final result of your experiment? Was it what you expected? Why or why not?

_____

_____

_____

_____

_____

What's Next?

How could you improve on this experiment? Did the results make you think of any other questions that you could investigate with new experiments?

_____

_____

_____

_____

How Do You Feel?

PURPOSE

To test the sensitivity of different parts of the skin.

Materials

two sharpened pencils
masking tape
helper

Procedure

1. Tape the pencils together so that the points are even.

TAPE

2. Ask a helper to look away as you GENTLY touch his or her forearm with both pencil points. Be sure the points touch the skin at the same time.

3. Ask how many points are felt.

4. Do the experiment again, but touch the pencil points to the tip of the helper's thumb or finger.

5. Again, ask how many points are felt.

How Do You Feel?

Observations and Data

What happens during the experiment? Write down what you observed as well as any measurements or calculations that you made. You may also want to draw sketches or take photos of your experiment.

_____

_____

_____

_____

_____

_____

Results and Conclusions

What was the final result of your experiment? Was it what you expected? Why or why not?

_____

_____

_____

_____

What's Next?

How could you improve on this experiment? Did the results make you think of any other questions that you could investigate with new experiments?

_____

_____

_____

_____

Food Producers

PURPOSE

To demonstrate that starch, a food substance, is produced in leaves.

Materials

leaf, pale green
pint (500 ml) jar with a lid
1 cup (250 ml) rubbing alcohol
paper towels
shallow dish
tincture of iodine
adult helper

Procedure

CAUTION: Keep alcohol away from your nose and mouth.

1. Place the pale green leaf in the jar. The paler the leaf, the easier it will be to extract the green pigment, chlorophyll.

2. Pour the alcohol into the jar. Put the lid on the jar.

3. Allow the jar to stand for 1 day.

4. Remove the leaf and dry it by blotting with a paper towel.

5. Lay the leaf in the shallow dish.

6. Ask your helper to add enough iodine to cover the leaf.

CAUTION: Keep iodine out of reach of small children. It is poisonous if swallowed. It stains clothes and skin.

Food Producers

Observations and Data

What happens during the experiment? Write down what you observed as well as any measurements or calculations that you made. You may also want to draw sketches or take photos of your experiment.

_____

_____

_____

_____

_____

_____

Results and Conclusions

What was the final result of your experiment? Was it what you expected? Why or why not?

_____

_____

_____

_____

_____

What's Next?

How could you improve on this experiment? Did the results make you think of any other questions that you could investigate with new experiments?

_____

_____

_____

_____

Independence

PURPOSE

To demonstrate the independence of plants.

Materials

1-gallon (4-liter) jar with a large mouth
and lid
small potted plant

Procedure

1. Moisten the soil of the plant.

2. Place the entire plant, pot and all, inside the gallon jar.

3. Close the jar with its lid.

4. Place the jar somewhere that receives sunlight for part of the day.

5. Leave the jar closed for 30 days.

Independence

Observations and Data

What happens during the experiment? Write down what you observed as well as any measurements or calculations that you made. You may also want to draw sketches or take photos of your experiment.

_____

_____

_____

_____

_____

_____

Results and Conclusions

What was the final result of your experiment? Was it what you expected? Why or why not?

_____

_____

_____

_____

What's Next?

How could you improve on this experiment? Did the results make you think of any other questions that you could investigate with new experiments?

_____

_____

_____

_____

Light Seekers

PURPOSE

To determine if plants do seek the light.

Materials

houseplant

Procedure

1. Place the plant next to a window for 3 days.

2. Rotate the plant 180° and allow it to stand for another 3 days.

Light Seekers

Observations and Data

What happens during the experiment? Write down what you observed as well as any measurements or calculations that you made. You may also want to draw sketches or take photos of your experiment.

_____

_____

_____

_____

_____

_____

Results and Conclusions

What was the final result of your experiment? Was it what you expected? Why or why not?

_____

_____

_____

_____

_____

What's Next?

How could you improve on this experiment? Did the results make you think of any other questions that you could investigate with new experiments?

_____

_____

_____

_____

Flower Maze

PURPOSE

To demonstrate that plants grow toward light.

Materials

paper cup
potting soil
3 pinto beans
tap water
scissors
cardboard
shoe box with a lid
masking tape

Procedure

1. Fill the cup with soil and plant the beans in the soil.

2. Moisten the soil and allow the beans to sprout (about 5 to 7 days).

3. Cut two cardboard pieces to fit inside the shoe box.

4. Secure the cardboard with tape to form a maze, as shown in the diagram.

5. Cut a hole at one end of the lid.

6. Place the bean plant inside the shoe box at one end.

7. Secure the box lid with the hole on the opposite end from the plant.

8. Open the lid daily to observe the plant's growth. Water the soil when needed.

9. Continue to observe until the plant grows out the hole in the lid.

Flower Maze

Observations and Data

What happens during the experiment? Write down what you observed as well as any measurements or calculations that you made. You may also want to draw sketches or take photos of your experiment.

_____

_____

_____

_____

_____

_____

Results and Conclusions

What was the final result of your experiment? Was it what you expected? Why or why not?

_____

_____

_____

_____

_____

What's Next?

How could you improve on this experiment? Did the results make you think of any other questions that you could investigate with new experiments?

_____

_____

_____

_____

Eyes Up

PURPOSE

To show that potatoes can propagate.

Materials

4 potatoes
quart (liter) jar
potting soil
tap water
adult helper

Procedure

1. Place the potatoes inside a dark cabinet. Check the skin of each potato daily for small white growths called "eyes."

2. Ask an adult helper to cut a square out of the potato around the eye.

3. Fill the jar with potting soil.

4. Bury the eye about 2 inches (5 cm) below the soil's surface with the eye sticking up.

5. Keep the soil moist with tap water, but not wet.

6. Observe the jar for 2 weeks.

POTATO

POTATO EYES

Eyes Up

Observations and Data

What happens during the experiment? Write down what you observed as well as any measurements or calculations that you made. You may also want to draw sketches or take photos of your experiment.

_____

_____

_____

_____

_____

_____

Results and Conclusions

What was the final result of your experiment? Was it what you expected? Why or why not?

_____

_____

_____

_____

_____

What's Next?

How could you improve on this experiment? Did the results make you think of any other questions that you could investigate with new experiments?

_____

_____

_____

_____

Cuttings

PURPOSE

To grow a new plant from a cutting.

Materials

house plant, such as ivy
scissors
small jar
tap water

Procedure

1. Cut off a stem with leaves from the plant.

2. Place the cut end of the stem in the jar filled with water.

3. Observe the bottom of the stem for several days.

IVY

WATER

Cuttings

Observations and Data

What happens during the experiment? Write down what you observed as well as any measurements or calculations that you made. You may also want to draw sketches or take photos of your experiment.

_____

_____

_____

_____

_____

_____

Results and Conclusions

What was the final result of your experiment? Was it what you expected? Why or why not?

_____

_____

_____

_____

_____

What's Next?

How could you improve on this experiment? Did the results make you think of any other questions that you could investigate with new experiments?

_____

_____

_____

_____

Grow a Bean

PURPOSE

To determine if the way seeds are planted affects the direction of root growth.

Materials

paper towels

clear drinking glass

masking tape

marking pen

4 pole snap beans, such as Kentucky Wonder

tap water

Procedure

1. Fold one paper towel and line the inside of the glass with it. Wad several paper towels and stuff them into the glass to hold the paper lining tightly against the glass.

2. Place a strip of tape around the outside of the glass.

3. On four sides of the glass, mark the tape with an arrow to indicate up, down, left, and right.

4. Place one bean between the glass and the paper towel lining under each arrow. Point the bean's concave side in the direction indicated by the arrow.

5. Moisten the paper towels in the glass with water. The paper should be moist, not dripping wet.

6. Keep the paper moist and observe for 5 to 7 days.

Grow a Bean

Observations and Data

What happens during the experiment? Write down what you observed as well as any measurements or calculations that you made. You may also want to draw sketches or take photos of your experiment.

_____

_____

_____

_____

_____

_____

Results and Conclusions

What was the final result of your experiment? Was it what you expected? Why or why not?

_____

_____

_____

_____

_____

What's Next?

How could you improve on this experiment? Did the results make you think of any other questions that you could investigate with new experiments?

_____

_____

_____

_____

Growing Season

PURPOSE

To demonstrate the effect of temperature on seed growth.

Materials

2 drinking glasses
paper towels
8 pinto beans
tap water

Procedure

1. Prepare both glasses as follows:

   a. Fold one paper towel and line the inside of the glass with it.

   b. Wad several paper towels and stuff them into the glass to hold the paper lining against the glass.

   c. Place four beans between the glass and the paper towel lining. Evenly space the beans around the center of the glass.

2. Moisten the paper towels in the glasses with water. The paper should be moist but not dripping wet.

3. Place one glass in the refrigerator and keep the other at normal room temperature.

4. Keep the paper in both glasses moist and observe for 7 or more days.

Growing Season

Observations and Data

What happens during the experiment? Write down what you observed as well as any measurements or calculations that you made. You may also want to draw sketches or take photos of your experiment.

_____

_____

_____

_____

_____

_____

Results and Conclusions

What was the final result of your experiment? Was it what you expected? Why or why not?

_____

_____

_____

_____

_____

What's Next?

How could you improve on this experiment? Did the results make you think of any other questions that you could investigate with new experiments?

_____

_____

_____

_____

Fingerprints

PURPOSE

To collect and observe the patterns of fingerprints.

Materials

pencil
white paper
transparent tape
magnifying lens

Procedure

1. Rub the sharpened end of a pencil across a sheet of paper 15 to 20 times to collect a layer of graphite on the paper.

2. Rub your left index finger across the graphite on the paper.

3. Tear off about one inch (2½ cm) of tape and stick it across the darkened tip of your finger.

4. Remove the tape and stick it on a sheet of typing paper.

5. Repeat the process using the tips of other fingers.

6. Observe the patterns produced by each finger with a magnifying lens.

TAPE

Fingerprints

Observations and Data

What happens during the experiment? Write down what you observed as well as any measurements or calculations that you made. You may also want to draw sketches or take photos of your experiment.

_____

_____

_____

_____

_____

_____

Results and Conclusions

What was the final result of your experiment? Was it what you expected? Why or why not?

_____

_____

_____

_____

_____

What's Next?

How could you improve on this experiment? Did the results make you think of any other questions that you could investigate with new experiments?

_____

_____

_____

_____

Gripper

PURPOSE

To determine how the ridges on fingertips affect the ability to pick up objects.

Materials

dishwashing gloves
assortment of small coins

Procedure

1. Put one glove on the hand you write with.

2. Spread the coins out on a table.

3. Pick up each coin one at a time with the hand covered with the rubber glove. Place each coin back on the table before lifting the next coin.

4. Make note of the ease or difficulty in lifting each coin from the table's surface.

5. Note the texture of the fingers of the gloves.

6. Remove the glove from your hand.

7. Turn the glove that does not fit your writing hand inside out.

8. Put the inside-out glove on your writing hand.

9. Again, pick each coin up one at a time with the hand covered with the rubber glove. Place each coin back on the table before lifting the next coin.

10. Make note of the ease or difficulty in lifting each coin from the table's surface.

11. Again, note the texture of the fingers of the glove.

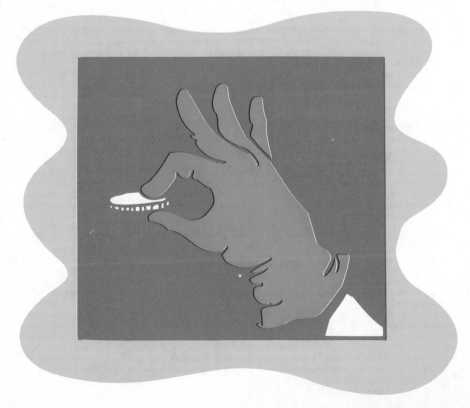

Gripper

Observations and Data

What happens during the experiment? Write down what you observed as well as any measurements or calculations that you made. You may also want to draw sketches or take photos of your experiment.

_____

_____

_____

_____

_____

_____

Results and Conclusions

What was the final result of your experiment? Was it what you expected? Why or why not?

_____

_____

_____

_____

What's Next?

How could you improve on this experiment? Did the results make you think of any other questions that you could investigate with new experiments?

_____

_____

_____

_____

 75

Skin Color

PURPOSE

To observe the effect of light on skin color.

Materials

Band-Aid™

Procedure

1. Place a Band-Aid around the end of one finger.

2. Leave the bandage on for 2 days.

3. Remove the bandage and observe the color of the skin over the entire finger.

BAND-AID

BEULAH'S BAND-AIDS

Skin Color

Observations and Data

What happens during the experiment? Write down what you observed as well as any measurements or calculations that you made. You may also want to draw sketches or take photos of your experiment.

_____

_____

_____

_____

_____

_____

Results and Conclusions

What was the final result of your experiment? Was it what you expected? Why or why not?

_____

_____

_____

_____

What's Next?

How could you improve on this experiment? Did the results make you think of any other questions that you could investigate with new experiments?

_____

_____

_____

_____

76

Stronger

PURPOSE

To determine how sniffing affects the intensity of smells.

Materials

vanilla extract
2 cotton balls
baby food jar
timer

Procedure

1. Place a few drops of the vanilla on one of the cotton balls.

2. Drop the moistened cotton ball into the jar.

3. Hold the opening of the jar under, but not touching, your nose.

4. Breathe normally for one or two breaths and note the strength of the smell of the vanilla.

5. Discard the cotton ball in the jar.

6. Wait 5 minutes, then repeat steps 1 and 2 with the other cotton ball, again holding the opening of the jar under, but not touching, your nose.

7. Take a good sniff by inhaling deeply.

Stronger

Observations and Data

What happens during the experiment? Write down what you observed as well as any measurements or calculations that you made. You may also want to draw sketches or take photos of your experiment.

_____

_____

_____

_____

_____

_____

Results and Conclusions

What was the final result of your experiment? Was it what you expected? Why or why not?

_____

_____

_____

_____

_____

What's Next?

How could you improve on this experiment? Did the results make you think of any other questions that you could investigate with new experiments?

_____

_____

_____

_____

Fooling Your Tongue

PURPOSE

To demonstrate how smell affects taste.

Materials

apple
eyedropper
vanilla extract
cotton ball

Procedure

1. Take a bite of apple.

2. Chew it thoroughly and swallow.

3. Observe how the apple tastes.

4. Add several drops of vanilla extract to the cotton ball.

5. Hold the cotton ball near, but not touching, your nose as you take a second bite out of the apple.

6. Continue to smell the cotton ball as you chew the bite of apple.

Fooling Your Tongue

Observations and Data

What happens during the experiment? Write down what you observed as well as any measurements or calculations that you made. You may also want to draw sketches or take photos of your experiment.

_____

_____

_____

_____

_____

_____

Results and Conclusions

What was the final result of your experiment? Was it what you expected? Why or why not?

_____

_____

_____

_____

What's Next?

How could you improve on this experiment? Did the results make you think of any other questions that you could investigate with new experiments?

_____

_____

_____

_____

Geometric Designs

PURPOSE

To determine if all spider webs have the same geometric design.

Materials

spider webs
hairspray
baby powder
glue stick
dark construction paper
scissors
adult helper

Procedure

NOTE: The best time to find spider webs is in the early morning of a spring or summer day.

1. Pick out a suitable web for collecting and wait a few hours for any dew to dry.

   CAUTION: Be sure the spider is gone before continuing.

2. Spray the web with hairspray and immediately cover the web with powder.

3. Spray the paper with hairspray and push the sticky side against the web. Ask an adult to cut the web's support strands.

4. Allow the paper and web to dry.

5. Repeat steps 1 through 4 to collect as many different kinds of webs as possible. Compare the webs.

Geometric Designs

Observations and Data

What happens during the experiment? Write down what you observed as well as any measurements or calculations that you made. You may also want to draw sketches or take photos of your experiment.

_____

_____

_____

_____

_____

_____

Results and Conclusions

What was the final result of your experiment? Was it what you expected? Why or why not?

_____

_____

_____

_____

_____

What's Next?

How could you improve on this experiment? Did the results make you think of any other questions that you could investigate with new experiments?

_____

_____

_____

_____

Telegraph Lines

PURPOSE

To determine how a spider evaluates the size of an intruder.

Materials

string

helper

Procedure

1. Stretch the string between two stationary objects. A door knob and a table leg are good choices.

2. Gently place the tips of your fingers on top of one end of the string.

3. Have your helper pluck the opposite end of the string while you look away.

4. Your helper should pluck the strings with varying degrees of firmness: gently to very firmly. You do not want to see how firmly the string is being plucked.

Telegraph Lines

Observations and Data

What happens during the experiment? Write down what you observed as well as any measurements or calculations that you made. You may also want to draw sketches or take photos of your experiment.

_____

_____

_____

_____

_____

_____

_____

Results and Conclusions

What was the final result of your experiment? Was it what you expected? Why or why not?

_____

_____

_____

_____

_____

What's Next?

How could you improve on this experiment? Did the results make you think of any other questions that you could investigate with new experiments?

_____

_____

_____

_____

Hummer

PURPOSE

To determine how you make sounds.

Procedure

1. Hum a tune with your mouth open.

2. Continue to hum, but close your mouth.

3. Pinch your nose closed with your fingers and hum with your mouth open.

4. Close your mouth, hum a tune, and pinch your nose closed again.

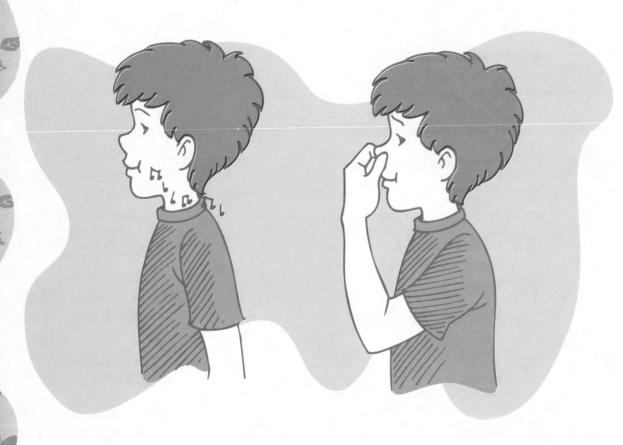

Hummer

Observations and Data

What happens during the experiment? Write down what you observed as well as any measurements or calculations that you made. You may also want to draw sketches or take photos of your experiment.

_____

_____

_____

_____

_____

_____

Results and Conclusions

What was the final result of your experiment? Was it what you expected? Why or why not?

_____

_____

_____

_____

_____

What's Next?

How could you improve on this experiment? Did the results make you think of any other questions that you could investigate with new experiments?

_____

_____

_____

_____

ZZZZs

PURPOSE

To determine what makes a person snore.

Materials

wax paper
scissors
ruler

Procedure

1. Measure and cut a 6-in. (15-cm) square of wax paper.

2. Place your hands on the sides of the paper square.

3. Hold the paper against your lips.

4. Hum your favorite song.

5. Hum the same song without the paper.

ZZZZs

Observations and Data

What happens during the experiment? Write down what you observed as well as any measurements or calculations that you made. You may also want to draw sketches or take photos of your experiment.

_____

_____

_____

_____

_____

_____

Results and Conclusions

What was the final result of your experiment? Was it what you expected? Why or why not?

_____

_____

_____

_____

_____

What's Next?

How could you improve on this experiment? Did the results make you think of any other questions that you could investigate with new experiments?

_____

_____

_____

_____

Climbers

PURPOSE

To see how water moves through a leaf.

Materials

juice glass
tap water
red food coloring
scissors
large tree leaf, such as an oak leaf
crayons or colored markers
3 sheets of typing paper

Procedure

1. Fill the glass about one-fourth full with water.

2. Add enough food coloring to make the water a deep red color.

3. Use the scissors to cut across the end of the leaf's stem.

4. Stand the leaf in the glass of colored water.

5. Observe the leaf and make a colored drawing of it. Label the drawing Day 1.

6. Repeat step 5 at about the same time each day for the next 2 days. Label the drawings Day 2 and Day 3.

Climbers

Observations and Data

What happens during the experiment? Write down what you observed as well as any measurements or calculations that you made. You may also want to draw sketches or take photos of your experiment.

_____

_____

_____

_____

_____

_____

Results and Conclusions

What was the final result of your experiment? Was it what you expected? Why or why not?

_____

_____

_____

_____

_____

What's Next?

How could you improve on this experiment? Did the results make you think of any other questions that you could investigate with new experiments?

_____

_____

_____

_____

Water Loss

PURPOSE

To demonstrate transpiration, the loss of water from leaves.

Materials

growing plant
plastic sandwich bag
tape (cellophane)

Procedure

1. Place the sandwich bag over one leaf.
2. Secure the bag to the stem with the tape.
3. Place the plant in sunlight for 2 to 3 hours.
4. Observe the inside of the bag.

PLASTIC BAG

TAPE

POTTED PLANT

Water Loss

Observations and Data

What happens during the experiment? Write down what you observed as well as any measurements or calculations that you made. You may also want to draw sketches or take photos of your experiment.

_____

_____

_____

_____

_____

_____

Results and Conclusions

What was the final result of your experiment? Was it what you expected? Why or why not?

_____

_____

_____

_____

_____

What's Next?

How could you improve on this experiment? Did the results make you think of any other questions that you could investigate with new experiments?

_____

_____

_____

_____

Water Flow

PURPOSE

To demonstrate how water is transported through plant stems.

Materials

scissors

measuring cup (250 ml)

tap water

2 glasses

red and blue food coloring

1 white carnation with a long stem (purchase at a floral shop)

adult helper

Procedure

1. Have an adult helper cut the stem in half lengthwise from the end to about half way up toward the flower.

2. Pour ½ cup of water into each glass.

3. Add enough food coloring to make the water in each glass a deep color. One will be blue and the other red.

4. Place one end of the flower stem in the blue water and the other end in the red water.

5. Leave the flower standing in the water for 48 hours.

RED WATER BLUE WATER

Water Flow

Observations and Data

What happens during the experiment? Write down what you observed as well as any measurements or calculations that you made. You may also want to draw sketches or take photos of your experiment.

_____

_____

_____

_____

_____

_____

Results and Conclusions

What was the final result of your experiment? Was it what you expected? Why or why not?

_____

_____

_____

_____

_____

What's Next?

How could you improve on this experiment? Did the results make you think of any other questions that you could investigate with new experiments?

_____

_____

_____

_____

Desert Plants

PURPOSE

To demonstrate the rate of evaporation from different leaf structures.

Materials

3 paper towels
tap water
baking sheet
waxed paper
2 paper clips

Procedure

1. Dampen the paper towels with water. They should be wet, but not dripping.

2. Lay one paper towel flat on the baking sheet.

3. Roll up a second paper towel and place it next to the flat one on the pan.

4. Roll the last paper towel as you did the second one, but cover the outside of the roll with waxed paper.

5. Secure the ends, top and bottom, of the waxed paper roll with paper clips.

6. Place the waxed paper roll on the pan.

7. Position the pan with its paper rolls where it will receive direct sunlight.

8. Unroll the paper rolls after 24 hours and feel the paper.

Desert Plants

Observations and Data

What happens during the experiment? Write down what you observed as well as any measurements or calculations that you made. You may also want to draw sketches or take photos of your experiment.

_____

_____

_____

_____

_____

_____

Results and Conclusions

What was the final result of your experiment? Was it what you expected? Why or why not?

_____

_____

_____

_____

What's Next?

How could you improve on this experiment? Did the results make you think of any other questions that you could investigate with new experiments?

_____

_____

_____

_____

Stand Up

PURPOSE

To demonstrate how the change in turgor pressure causes plant stems to wilt.

Materials

wilted stalk of celery
1 drinking glass
blue food coloring

Procedure

1. Ask an adult to cut a slice from the bottom of a wilted celery stalk.

2. Put enough food coloring into a glass half full of water to turn it dark blue.

3. Allow the celery to stand overnight in the blue water.

WILTED CELERY

BLUE WATER

Stand Up

Observations and Data

What happens during the experiment? Write down what you observed as well as any measurements or calculations that you made. You may also want to draw sketches or take photos of your experiment.

_____

_____

_____

_____

_____

_____

Results and Conclusions

What was the final result of your experiment? Was it what you expected? Why or why not?

_____

_____

_____

_____

_____

What's Next?

How could you improve on this experiment? Did the results make you think of any other questions that you could investigate with new experiments?

_____

_____

_____

_____

Morning Glory

PURPOSE

To demonstrate how some flowers open quickly.

Materials

newspaper
marking pen
ruler
scissors
large bowl

Procedure

1. Draw a flower on a sheet of newspaper by following these instructions:

a. Draw a 6-in. (15-cm) diameter circle on the paper.

b. Draw four lines to divide the circle into eight equal parts.

c. Use the lines as a guide to draw flower petals as in the diagram.

2. Cut out the paper flower.

3. Fold each petal toward the center of the flower and crease it so that it lays flat. The petals will overlap.

4. Fill the bowl with water.

5. Place the folded paper flower, petal side up, on top of the water in the bowl.

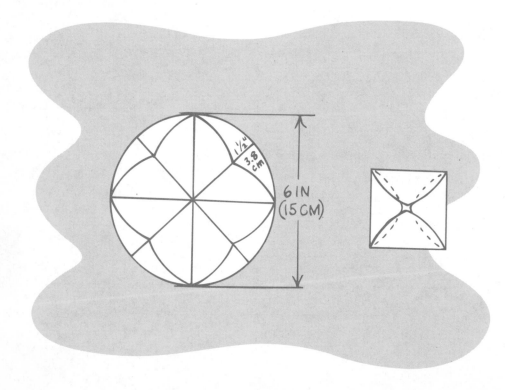

Morning Glory

Observations and Data

What happens during the experiment? Write down what you observed as well as any measurements or calculations that you made. You may also want to draw sketches or take photos of your experiment.

_____

_____

_____

_____

_____

Results and Conclusions

What was the final result of your experiment? Was it what you expected? Why or why not?

_____

_____

_____

_____

_____

What's Next?

How could you improve on this experiment? Did the results make you think of any other questions that you could investigate with new experiments?

_____

_____

_____

_____

Retainer

PURPOSE

To demonstrate the overlapping of images in your mind.

Materials

white poster board
marking pen
scissors
paper hole punch
ruler
string

Procedure

1. Draw and cut a circle with a 4-in. (10-cm) diameter from the poster board.

2. Use the hole punch to make two holes on each side of the paper circle.

3. Measure and cut two 24-in (60-cm) pieces of string.

4. Thread the string through the holes as shown in the diagram.

5. Use the marker to draw a large empty fishbowl on one side of the paper circle, and a small fish on the opposite side.

6. Hold the strings and twirl the paper disk around in a circle about 25 times to twist the strings.

7. Pull the strings straight out with your fingers.

8. Observe the spinning paper disk.

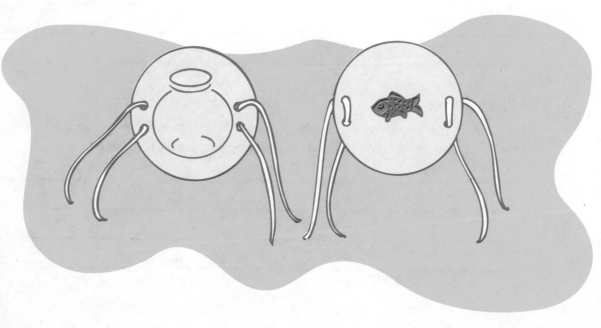

Retainer

Observations and Data

What happens during the experiment? Write down what you observed as well as any measurements or calculations that you made. You may also want to draw sketches or take photos of your experiment.

_____

_____

_____

_____

_____

_____

Results and Conclusions

What was the final result of your experiment? Was it what you expected? Why or why not?

_____

_____

_____

_____

_____

What's Next?

How could you improve on this experiment? Did the results make you think of any other questions that you could investigate with new experiments?

_____

_____

_____

_____

Winker

PURPOSE

To demonstrate the persistence of vision by making a phenakistoscope (a viewing device).

Materials

marking pen

scissors

ruler

poster board—10 in. (25 cm) square

push pin

pencil

mirror

Procedure

1. Draw and cut a 10-in. (25-cm) diameter circle from a piece of poster board.

2. On one side of the paper disk, use the pencil to divide the circle into 12 equal parts.

3. At each of the 12 divisions, cut a slot about ¼ in. (.63 cm) wide and 1 in. (2.5 cm) deep.

4. Draw faces on the unmarked side of the disk. On each of the 12 faces, change the position of the eyelid on one eye as in the diagram.

5. Insert a push pin through the center of the disk and into the eraser of a pencil. Spin the disk to hollow out the hole made by the pin so that it turns easily.

6. While standing in front of a mirror, hold the end of the pencil so that the side with the faces points toward the mirror.

7. Spin the paper as you look through the slots in the disk at the mirror.

Winker

Observations and Data

What happens during the experiment? Write down what you observed as well as any measurements or calculations that you made. You may also want to draw sketches or take photos of your experiment.

_____

_____

_____

_____

_____

_____

Results and Conclusions

What was the final result of your experiment? Was it what you expected? Why or why not?

_____

_____

_____

_____

_____

What's Next?

How could you improve on this experiment? Did the results make you think of any other questions that you could investigate with new experiments?

_____

_____

_____

_____

Night Vision

PURPOSE

To demonstrate your ability to view contrasting colors at night.

Materials

scissors

ruler

construction paper: black, dark brown, and white

cellophane tape

cardboard box about $1 \times 1 \times 2$ feet $(30 \times 30 \times 60$ cm)

stool about 2½ feet (75 cm) tall

Procedure

1. Cut two 4-inch (10-cm) wide letter V's from the brown paper and one from the white paper.

2. Tape the brown letter at the top of the black paper and the white letter at the bottom of the paper.

3. Tape the black sheet of paper in the bottom of the box.

4. Place a stool in a dimly lit hallway or room.

5. Place the box on the stool so that the black paper is upright and shaded by the shadow of the box.

6. Stand so that you are as close to the box as possible, and are able to see the letters on the black paper.

7. Observe how clearly each letter can be read as you slowly walk backwards about 15 feet (5 m).

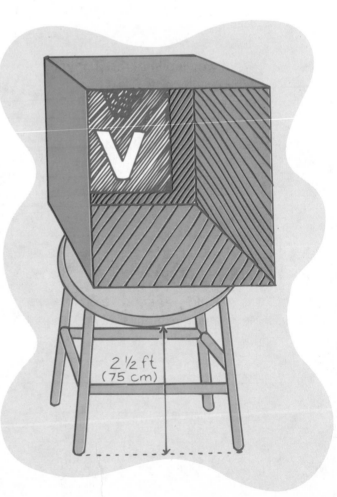

2 ½ ft (75 cm)

Night Vision

Observations and Data

What happens during the experiment? Write down what you observed as well as any measurements or calculations that you made. You may also want to draw sketches or take photos of your experiment.

_____

_____

_____

_____

_____

_____

Results and Conclusions

What was the final result of your experiment? Was it what you expected? Why or why not?

_____

_____

_____

_____

What's Next?

How could you improve on this experiment? Did the results make you think of any other questions that you could investigate with new experiments?

_____

_____

_____

_____

CHEMISTRY

Soakers

PURPOSE

To compare the water-absorbing ability of paper diapers and cloth diapers.

Materials

two 2-quart (2-liter) bowls
tap water
paper diaper
baking pan
cloth diaper
timer
ruler

Procedure

NOTE: Dispose of the paper diaper material in the trash. Do not put any of the material down the drain.

1. Fill both bowls with water. Be sure the water levels are the same in both bowls.

2. Place the paper diaper in one of the bowls.

3. Hold the diaper under the water for 10 seconds. Lift the diaper and place it on the baking pan.

4. Place the cloth diaper in the second bowl.

5. Hold the diaper under the water for 10 seconds, lift and place it on the baking pan.

6. Compare the level of the water left in each of the bowls by holding a ruler upright inside first one bowl, then the other.

Soakers

Observations and Data

What happens during the experiment? Write down what you observed as well as any measurements or calculations that you made. You may also want to draw sketches or take photos of your experiment.

_____

_____

_____

_____

_____

_____

Results and Conclusions

What was the final result of your experiment? Was it what you expected? Why or why not?

_____

_____

_____

_____

What's Next?

How could you improve on this experiment? Did the results make you think of any other questions that you could investigate with new experiments?

_____

_____

_____

_____

92

Stick On

PURPOSE

To demonstrate how air is cleaned by adsorbent chemicals.

Materials

1 cup (250 ml) baking soda

shoe box with a lid

measuring tablespoon (15 ml)

2 pint-size Ziploc® bags

marking pen

adult helper

1 onion

saucer

Procedure

1. Pour 1 cup (250 ml) of baking soda into a shoe box.

2. Remove one tablespoon (15 ml) of baking soda from the box and place it in a Ziploc® bag. With the marking pen, label the bag "UNUSED."

3. Evenly spread the rest of the baking soda over the bottom of the box.

4. Ask an adult helper to peel an onion and cut it in four parts.

5. Place the pieces of onion in a saucer.

6. Set the saucer of onions inside the shoe box.

7. Place the lid on the box.

8. After 24 hours, remove a tablespoon (15 ml) of the baking soda and place it in a Ziploc® bag. Label the bag "USED."

9. Open the bags one at a time and smell the contents.

USED

UNUSED

ZIP LOCK BAG WITH 1 TABLESPOON OF BAKING SODA

CLOSED SHOE BOX

ONION WEDGES
BAKING SODA

Stick On

Observations and Data

What happens during the experiment? Write down what you observed as well as any measurements or calculations that you made. You may also want to draw sketches or take photos of your experiment.

_____

_____

_____

_____

_____

_____

Results and Conclusions

What was the final result of your experiment? Was it what you expected? Why or why not?

_____

_____

_____

_____

What's Next?

How could you improve on this experiment? Did the results make you think of any other questions that you could investigate with new experiments?

_____

_____

_____

_____

Cabbage Indicator

PURPOSE

To prepare a cabbage indicator that can be used to test for acids and bases.

Materials

red cabbage
food blender
distilled water
tea strainer
large bowl
quart (liter) jar with lid
masking tape
marking pen
adult helper

Procedure

1. Fill the blender half way with cabbage leaves, then cover them with distilled water.

2. Ask an adult to blend the water and cabbage.

3. Ask your helper to strain the contents of the blender into the bowl.

4. Pour the cabbage juice from the bowl into the jar. Label the jar Cabbage Indicator.

5. Close the lid on the jar and store it in the refrigerator until needed for Experiments 94 and 95.

93

Cabbage Indicator

Observations and Data

What happens during the experiment? Write down what you observed as well as any measurements or calculations that you made. You may also want to draw sketches or take photos of your experiment.

_____

_____

_____

_____

_____

_____

Results and Conclusions

What was the final result of your experiment? Was it what you expected? Why or why not?

_____

_____

_____

_____

_____

What's Next?

How could you improve on this experiment? Did the results make you think of any other questions that you could investigate with new experiments?

_____

_____

_____

_____

Acid Testing

PURPOSE

To use cabbage indicator to identify an acid.

Materials

2 tablespoons (30 ml) cabbage indicator
(from Experiment 93)
white saucer
1 teaspoon (5 ml) pickle juice
spoon

Procedure

1. Place the cabbage indicator in the saucer.
2. Observe the color of the cabbage indicator.
3. Add the pickle juice to the indicator. Stir.
4. Observe the color of the liquid in the saucer.

Acid Testing

Observations and Data

What happens during the experiment? Write down what you observed as well as any measurements or calculations that you made. You may also want to draw sketches or take photos of your experiment.

_____

_____

_____

_____

_____

_____

_____

Results and Conclusions

What was the final result of your experiment? Was it what you expected? Why or why not?

_____

_____

_____

_____

_____

What's Next?

How could you improve on this experiment? Did the results make you think of any other questions that you could investigate with new experiments?

_____

_____

_____

_____

Base Testing

PURPOSE

To use cabbage indicator to identify a base.

Materials

2 tablespoons (30 ml) cabbage indicator
(from Experiment 93)

white saucer

antacid tablet

spoon

timer

Procedure

1. Place the cabbage indicator in the saucer.

2. Observe the color of the cabbage indicator.

3. Add the antacid tablet to the indicator and allow it to sit for 2 to 3 minutes. Stir.

4. Observe the color of the liquid in the saucer.

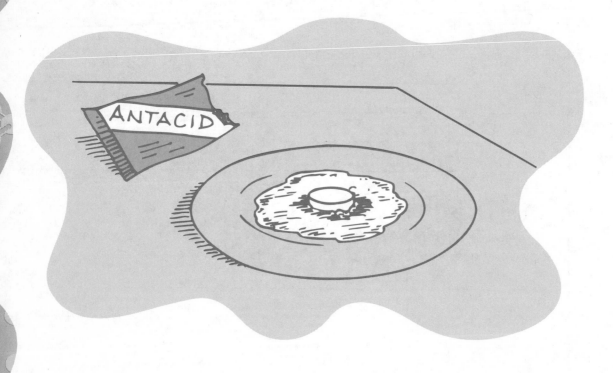

Base Testing

Observations and Data

What happens during the experiment? Write down what you observed as well as any measurements or calculations that you made. You may also want to draw sketches or take photos of your experiment.

_____

_____

_____

_____

_____

_____

Results and Conclusions

What was the final result of your experiment? Was it what you expected? Why or why not?

_____

_____

_____

_____

_____

What's Next?

How could you improve on this experiment? Did the results make you think of any other questions that you could investigate with new experiments?

_____

_____

_____

_____

Holes

PURPOSE

To determine why there are holes in bread slices.

Materials

1 bowl, 1 qt. (1 liter)

measuring cup (250 ml)

1 cup (250 ml) flour

measuring tablespoon (15 ml)

3 tablespoons (45 ml) sugar

1 package yeast, ¼ oz. (7 g)

stirring spoon

1 bowl, 2 qt. (2 liter)

1 paper towel

Procedure

1. In a 1-quart (1-liter) bowl mix together 1 cup (250 ml) of flour, 3 tablespoons (45 ml) of sugar, 1 package of yeast, and 1 cup (250 ml) of warm water from the faucet. Stir.

2. Into the empty 2-quart (2-liter) bowl pour 3 cups (750 ml) of warm water from the faucet.

3. Set the small bowl with the flour mixture into the larger bowl of warm water.

4. Cover the top of the bowls with the paper towel.

5. Lift the paper towel every 30 minutes for 4 hours and observe the surface of the mixture in the bowl.

Holes

Observations and Data

What happens during the experiment? Write down what you observed as well as any measurements or calculations that you made. You may also want to draw sketches or take photos of your experiment.

_____

_____

_____

_____

_____

_____

Results and Conclusions

What was the final result of your experiment? Was it what you expected? Why or why not?

_____

_____

_____

_____

_____

What's Next?

How could you improve on this experiment? Did the results make you think of any other questions that you could investigate with new experiments?

_____

_____

_____

_____

Hard Water

PURPOSE

To determine what makes water hard.

Materials

2 baby-food jars with lids
distilled water
½ teaspoon (2.5 ml) Epsom salts
spoon
eyedropper
dishwashing liquid

Procedure

1. Fill both jars ½ full with distilled water.

2. To one jar of water, add the Epsom salts. Stir well.

3. Add 3 drops of dishwashing liquid to each jar.

4. Secure the lids on the jars.

5. Shake the jars vigorously back and forth 15 times.

6. Allow the jar to stand for 10 seconds.

7. Observe and describe the appearance of the suds.

Hard
Water

Observations and Data

What happens during the experiment? Write down what you observed as well as any measurements or calculations that you made. You may also want to draw sketches or take photos of your experiment.

_____

_____

_____

_____

_____

_____

Results and Conclusions

What was the final result of your experiment? Was it what you expected? Why or why not?

_____

_____

_____

_____

_____

What's Next?

How could you improve on this experiment? Did the results make you think of any other questions that you could investigate with new experiments?

_____

_____

_____

_____

Lumpy

PURPOSE

To demonstrate why milk curdles.

Materials

¼ cup (63 ml) whole milk
small bowl
2 tablespoons (30 ml) white vinegar
spoon
timer

Procedure

1. Pour the milk into the bowl.

2. Add the vinegar and stir.

3. Allow the contents of the bowl to stand for about 5 minutes.

Lumpy

Observations and Data

What happens during the experiment? Write down what you observed as well as any measurements or calculations that you made. You may also want to draw sketches or take photos of your experiment.

_____

_____

_____

_____

_____

_____

Results and Conclusions

What was the final result of your experiment? Was it what you expected? Why or why not?

_____

_____

_____

_____

_____

What's Next?

How could you improve on this experiment? Did the results make you think of any other questions that you could investigate with new experiments?

_____

_____

_____

_____

Drinkable Iron

PURPOSE

To test for the presence of iron in fruit juices.

Materials

1-pint (500-ml) glass jar
3 tea bags
warm tap water
4 tablespoons (60 ml) pineapple juice
4 tablespoons (60 ml) apple juice
4 tablespoons (60 ml) white grape juice
4 tablespoons (60 ml) cranberry juice
5 clear plastic glasses
measuring spoons

Procedure

1. Make a strong tea solution by placing the tea bags in the pint jar, then fill it with warm water.

2. Allow the jar to stand for 1 hour.

3. Pour each juice sample into a different glass, as shown in the illustration.

4. Add 4 tablespoons (60 ml) of tea to each glass and stir. Wash the spoon with water after each use.

5. Allow the glasses to sit undisturbed for 20 minutes.

6. Carefully lift each glass and look up through the bottom of the glass. Make note of the juice that has dark particles settling on the bottom of the glass.

7. Allow the glasses to sit for 2 hours more.

8. Again, look for dark particles on the bottom of the glasses.

Drinkable Iron

Observations and Data

What happens during the experiment? Write down what you observed as well as any measurements or calculations that you made. You may also want to draw sketches or take photos of your experiment.

_____
_____
_____
_____
_____
_____

Results and Conclusions

What was the final result of your experiment? Was it what you expected? Why or why not?

_____
_____
_____
_____
_____

What's Next?

How could you improve on this experiment? Did the results make you think of any other questions that you could investigate with new experiments?

_____
_____
_____
_____

Needles

PURPOSE

To grow needle-shaped crystals of Epsom salts.

Materials

1 small baby-food jar
tap water
2 tablespoons (30 ml) Epsom salts
spoon
scissors
1 sheet of dark construction paper
saucer

Procedure

1. Fill the jar ½ full with water.

2. Add the Epsom salts to the water. Stir.

3. Cut a circle from the construction paper to fit the inside of the saucer.

4. Pour a thin layer of the salt solution over the paper. Try not to pour out the undissolved salt.

5. Place the saucer in a warm place and wait several days.

Needles

Observations and Data

What happens during the experiment? Write down what you observed as well as any measurements or calculations that you made. You may also want to draw sketches or take photos of your experiment.

_____

_____

_____

_____

_____

_____

Results and Conclusions

What was the final result of your experiment? Was it what you expected? Why or why not?

_____

_____

_____

_____

_____

What's Next?

How could you improve on this experiment? Did the results make you think of any other questions that you could investigate with new experiments?

_____

_____

_____

_____

Lace

PURPOSE

To grow a layer of lacy salt crystals.

Materials

measuring cup

tap water

tall, slender, clear jar

3 tablespoons (45 ml) table salt

spoon

scissors

ruler

black construction paper

Procedure

1. Pour ½ cup (250 ml) water into the jar.

2. Add the salt and stir.

3. Cut a ½-inch strip from the construction paper. The height of the paper should be about one-half the height of the jar.

4. Stand the paper strip against the inside of the jar.

5. Place the jar in a visible place where it will be undisturbed.

6. Allow the jar to sit for 3 to 4 weeks. Observe it daily.

Lace

Observations and Data

What happens during the experiment? Write down what you observed as well as any measurements or calculations that you made. You may also want to draw sketches or take photos of your experiment.

_____

_____

_____

_____

_____

_____

Results and Conclusions

What was the final result of your experiment? Was it what you expected? Why or why not?

_____

_____

_____

_____

_____

What's Next?

How could you improve on this experiment? Did the results make you think of any other questions that you could investigate with new experiments?

_____

_____

_____

_____

102

Dripper

PURPOSE

To demonstrate the formation of stalagmites and stalactites.

Materials

2 baby food jars
Epsom salts
tap water
spoon
2 washers
18-inch (45-cm) piece of cotton string
sheet of dark construction paper

Procedure

NOTE: This activity works best in humid weather.

1. Fill each jar with Epsom salts. Add just enough water to cover the Epsom salts and stir.

2. Tie a washer to each end of the string.

3. Place one washer in each of the jars and place the sheet of paper between the jars.

4. Position the jars to that the string hangs between them with the lowest part of the loop about 1 inch (2.5 cm) above the paper.

5. Allow the jars to stand undisturbed and out of any draft for 1 week or longer.

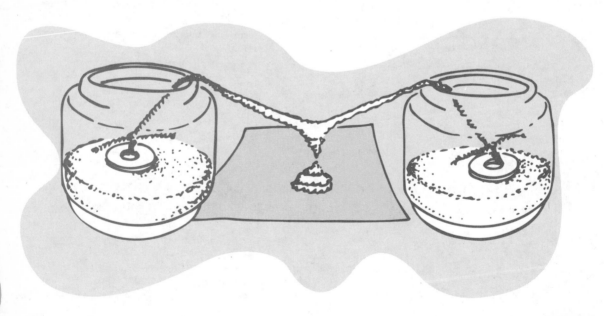

Dripper

Observations and Data

What happens during the experiment? Write down what you observed as well as any measurements or calculations that you made. You may also want to draw sketches or take photos of your experiment.

_____

_____

_____

_____

_____

_____

Results and Conclusions

What was the final result of your experiment? Was it what you expected? Why or why not?

_____

_____

_____

_____

_____

What's Next?

How could you improve on this experiment? Did the results make you think of any other questions that you could investigate with new experiments?

_____

_____

_____

_____

Wash Out!

PURPOSE

To determine how stains are cleaned by enzymes found in detergents.

Materials

1 quart (liter) glass jar

tap water

measuring spoon

powdered laundry detergent with enzymes

large spoon

marking pen

masking tape

1 fresh, peeled hard-boiled egg

magnifying lens

Procedure

1. Fill the jar three-fourths full with tap water.

2. Add 1 tablespoon (15 ml) of the laundry detergent to the jar of water and stir.

3. Place the egg in the jar and put it in a warm area, such as near a window with direct sunlight.

4. Each day, for 7 or more days, lift the egg out of the jar with the spoon and use the magnifying lens for close-up inspection.

5. Each day, replace the egg in a fresh solution of the mixture of laundry detergent and water.

Wash Out!

Observations and Data

What happens during the experiment? Write down what you observed as well as any measurements or calculations that you made. You may also want to draw sketches or take photos of your experiment.

_____

_____

_____

_____

_____

_____

Results and Conclusions

What was the final result of your experiment? Was it what you expected? Why or why not?

_____

_____

_____

_____

What's Next?

How could you improve on this experiment? Did the results make you think of any other questions that you could investigate with new experiments?

_____

_____

_____

_____

Browning Apple

PURPOSE

An investigation of the effect that oxygen has on the darkening of fruit.

Materials

apple
vitamin C tablet

Procedure

1. Cut the unpeeled apple in half.

2. Crush the vitamin C tablet and sprinkle the powder over the cut surface of one of the apple halves.

3. Allow both apple sections to sit uncovered for one hour.

4. Observe the color of each section.

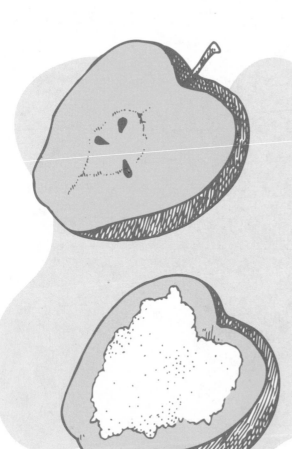

Name

Browning Apple

Observations and Data

What happens during the experiment? Write down what you observed as well as any measurements or calculations that you made. You may also want to draw sketches or take photos of your experiment.

_____

_____

_____

_____

_____

_____

Results and Conclusions

What was the final result of your experiment? Was it what you expected? Why or why not?

_____

_____

_____

_____

What's Next?

How could you improve on this experiment? Did the results make you think of any other questions that you could investigate with new experiments?

_____

_____

_____

_____

Tug-of-War

PURPOSE

To determine why some materials get wetter than others.

Materials

drinking glass
liquid cooking oil
eyedropper
tap water

Procedure

1. Turn the glass upside down on a table and rub a drop of oil on one half of its bottom surface.

2. Fill the eyedropper with water and squeeze a drop of water on both the oiled and the unoiled areas of the glass.

3. Observe the shape of the water drops.

WATER DROPS

OIL

Tug-of-War

Observations and Data

What happens during the experiment? Write down what you observed as well as any measurements or calculations that you made. You may also want to draw sketches or take photos of your experiment.

_____

_____

_____

_____

_____

_____

Results and Conclusions

What was the final result of your experiment? Was it what you expected? Why or why not?

_____

_____

_____

_____

_____

What's Next?

How could you improve on this experiment? Did the results make you think of any other questions that you could investigate with new experiments?

_____

_____

_____

_____

Magic Paper

PURPOSE

To observe the attraction between molecules.

Materials

sheet of typing paper
2-by-6-inch (5-by-15-cm) piece of newspaper
rubber cement
talcum powder
scissors (Do not use school scissors.)

Procedure

1. Lay the typing paper on a table and place the newspaper in its center.

2. Evenly spread a thin, solid covering of rubber cement over the top surface of the newspaper.

3. Allow the rubber cement to dry for 5 minutes.

4. Sprinkle talcum powder evenly over the cement.

5. Cut the newspaper into two 1-by-6-inch (2.5-by-15-cm) strips.

6. Place the strips together with the powdered surfaces touching.

7. Cut across one end of the strips by inserting the paper as far into the scissors as possible and cutting with the largest part of the blade.

8. Gently raise the other end of one of the strips.

9. Hold up only the raised edge, allowing the strip to hang.

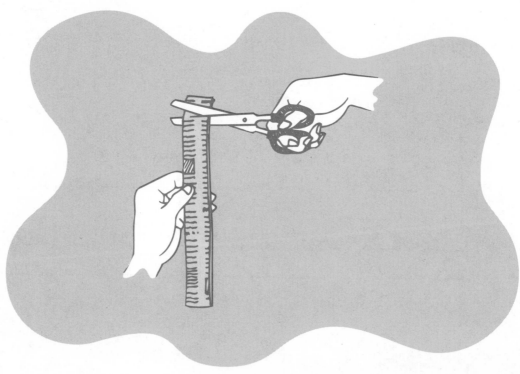

Magic Paper

Observations and Data

What happens during the experiment? Write down what you observed as well as any measurements or calculations that you made. You may also want to draw sketches or take photos of your experiment.

_____

_____

_____

_____

_____

_____

Results and Conclusions

What was the final result of your experiment? Was it what you expected? Why or why not?

_____

_____

_____

_____

_____

What's Next?

How could you improve on this experiment? Did the results make you think of any other questions that you could investigate with new experiments?

_____

_____

_____

_____

Clicking Coin

PURPOSE

To observe the effects of expanding gas.

Materials

2-liter soda bottle
quarter
cup of water

Procedure

1. Place the empty, uncapped soda bottle in the freezer for 5 minutes.

2. Wet the quarter by dipping it in the cup of water. Remove the bottle from the freezer and immediately cover the mouth with the wet coin.

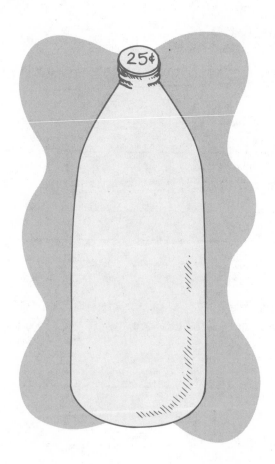

Clicking Coin

Observations and Data

What happens during the experiment? Write down what you observed as
well as any measurements or calculations that you made. You may also want
to draw sketches or take photos of your experiment.

_____

_____

_____

_____

_____

_____

Results and Conclusions

What was the final result of your experiment? Was it what you expected?
Why or why not?

_____

_____

_____

_____

What's Next?

How could you improve on this experiment? Did the results make you think of
any other questions that you could investigate with new experiments?

_____

_____

_____

_____

Bubbler

PURPOSE

To demonstrate the effect of gas pressure in a closed container.

Materials

scissors

ruler

drinking straw

modeling clay

½ cup (125 ml) tap water

dishwashing liquid

eyedropper

saucer

½ cup (125 ml) white vinegar

1 teaspoon (5 ml) baking soda

bathroom tissue

soda bottle

Procedure

1. Cut a 4-inch (10-cm) piece from the straw and wrap a walnut-size piece of clay around its center. Save the remaining piece of the straw to use as a stirrer.

2. Place 2 drops of dishwashing liquid and 2 drops of water into the saucer. Stir.

3. Pour the water and the vinegar into the bottle.

4. Spread the baking soda across the center of the tissue section.

5. Roll the tissue up and twist the ends of the paper.

6. Drop the packet into the bottle. Immediately place one end of the straw in the bottle and seal the mouth of the bottle with the clay.

7. Dip your finger into the soap and water mixture and rub the mixture across the open end of the straw.

Bubbler

Observations and Data

What happens during the experiment? Write down what you observed as well as any measurements or calculations that you made. You may also want to draw sketches or take photos of your experiment.

_____

_____

_____

_____

_____

_____

Results and Conclusions

What was the final result of your experiment? Was it what you expected? Why or why not?

_____

_____

_____

_____

What's Next?

How could you improve on this experiment? Did the results make you think of any other questions that you could investigate with new experiments?

_____

_____

_____

_____

Hotter

PURPOSE

To demonstrate an exothermic reaction.

Materials

5-ounce (150-ml) paper cup
small plastic spoon
plaster of paris
tap water

Procedure

1. In the paper cup, mix together 4 spoonfuls of plaster of paris with 2 spoonfuls of water.

   NOTE: Do not wash any plaster down the sink, as it can clog the drain.

2. Determine if a temperature change occurs by touching the surface of the plaster with your fingers periodically for 1 hour.

Hotter

Observations and Data

What happens during the experiment? Write down what you observed as well as any measurements or calculations that you made. You may also want to draw sketches or take photos of your experiment.

_____

_____

_____

_____

_____

_____

Results and Conclusions

What was the final result of your experiment? Was it what you expected? Why or why not?

_____

_____

_____

_____

What's Next?

How could you improve on this experiment? Did the results make you think of any other questions that you could investigate with new experiments?

_____

_____

_____

_____

Colder

PURPOSE

To demonstrate an endothermic reaction.

Materials

thermometer
¼ cup (63 ml) cold tap water
timer
2 effervescent antacid tablets

Procedure

1. Stand the thermometer in the cup of water.

2. After 5 minutes, note the temperature of the water.

3. Place the antacid tablets in the water near the bulb of the thermometer.

4. When the tablets stop fizzing, observe the temperature of the water and note any change.

Colder

Observations and Data

What happens during the experiment? Write down what you observed as well as any measurements or calculations that you made. You may also want to draw sketches or take photos of your experiment.

_____

_____

_____

_____

_____

_____

Results and Conclusions

What was the final result of your experiment? Was it what you expected? Why or why not?

_____

_____

_____

_____

What's Next?

How could you improve on this experiment? Did the results make you think of any other questions that you could investigate with new experiments?

_____

_____

_____

_____

No Room

PURPOSE

To try to inflate a balloon inside a bottle.

Materials

cola bottle or any small-mouth bottle
balloon

NOTE: The balloon must be large enough to fit over the mouth of the bottle.

Procedure

1. Hold on to the top of the balloon and push the bottom inside the bottle.

2. Stretch the top of the balloon over the mouth of the bottle.

3. Try to inflate the balloon by blowing into it.

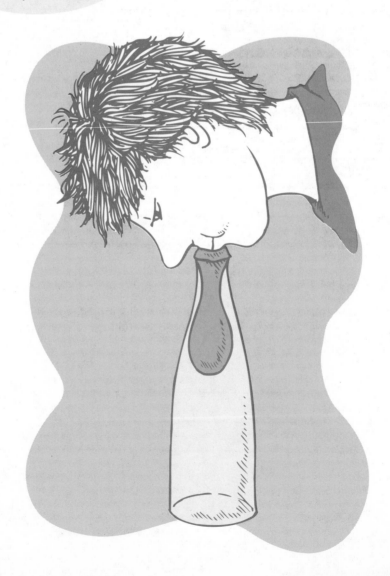

No Room

Observations and Data

What happens during the experiment? Write down what you observed as well as any measurements or calculations that you made. You may also want to draw sketches or take photos of your experiment.

_____

_____

_____

_____

_____

_____

_____

Results and Conclusions

What was the final result of your experiment? Was it what you expected? Why or why not?

_____

_____

_____

_____

_____

What's Next?

How could you improve on this experiment? Did the results make you think of any other questions that you could investigate with new experiments?

_____

_____

_____

_____

Blow Up

PURPOSE
To determine if a gas fills an open container.

Materials
drinking straw
empty glass soda bottle
9-inch (22.5-cm) round balloon

Procedure
1. Hold the top of the balloon and push the bottom of the balloon inside the bottle.
2. Insert the straw into the bottle beside the balloon.
3. Blow into the mouth of the balloon.

Blow Up

Observations and Data

What happens during the experiment? Write down what you observed as well as any measurements or calculations that you made. You may also want to draw sketches or take photos of your experiment.

_____

_____

_____

_____

_____

_____

Results and Conclusions

What was the final result of your experiment? Was it what you expected? Why or why not?

_____

_____

_____

_____

_____

What's Next?

How could you improve on this experiment? Did the results make you think of any other questions that you could investigate with new experiments?

_____

_____

_____

_____

Dry Paper

PURPOSE

To demonstrate that even though gases cannot always be seen, they do take up space.

Materials

bucket (taller than the glass)
tap water
1 paper towel
9-ounce (270-cm) clear, plastic glass

Procedure

1. Fill the bucket ½ full with water.

2. Wad the paper towel into a ball and push it to the bottom of the glass.

3. Turn the glass upside down. The paper wad must remain against the bottom of the glass. Make the paper ball a little bigger if it falls.

4. *IMPORTANT:* Hold the glass vertically with its mouth pointing down. Push the glass straight down into the bucket filled ½ full of water.

5. *IMPORTANT:* DO NOT TILT the glass as you lift it out of the water.

6. Remove the paper and examine it.

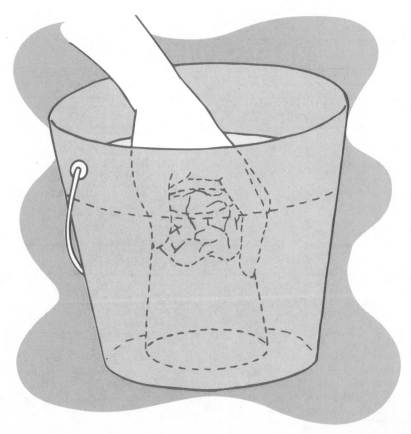

Dry Paper

Observations and Data

What happens during the experiment? Write down what you observed as well as any measurements or calculations that you made. You may also want to draw sketches or take photos of your experiment.

_____

_____

_____

_____

_____

_____

Results and Conclusions

What was the final result of your experiment? Was it what you expected? Why or why not?

_____

_____

_____

_____

_____

What's Next?

How could you improve on this experiment? Did the results make you think of any other questions that you could investigate with new experiments?

_____

_____

_____

_____

Stretchy

PURPOSE

To determine how heat affects the movement of molecules in a rubber band.

Materials

pencil

one 5-ounce (150-ml) paper cup

scissors

ruler

string

rubber band, about 3 inches (7.5 cm) long

salt

masking tape

hair dryer *(Use only with adult supervision)*

adult helper

Procedure

1. Use the pencil to punch two holes under the rim of the paper cup on opposite sides.

2. Cut an 8-inch (20-cm) piece of string. Tie the ends through each hole in the cup to form a loop.

3. Cut the rubber band once to make one 6-inch (15-cm) -long strip and tie one end of the rubber band to the string loop on the cup.

4. Cut an 18-inch (45-cm) length of string and attach it to the free end of the rubber band.

5. Fill the cup about half full with salt.

6. Set the cup on the floor under the edge of a table and tape the string to the top of the table so the cup is just resting on the floor.

7. Ask an adult to hold the hair dryer turned to high heat about 2 inches (5 cm) from the rubber band and move it up and down the band.

8. Observe the position of the cup as the rubber band is heated for about 10 seconds.

Stretchy

Observations and Data

What happens during the experiment? Write down what you observed as well as any measurements or calculations that you made. You may also want to draw sketches or take photos of your experiment.

_____

_____

_____

_____

_____

_____

Results and Conclusions

What was the final result of your experiment? Was it what you expected? Why or why not?

_____

_____

_____

_____

_____

What's Next?

How could you improve on this experiment? Did the results make you think of any other questions that you could investigate with new experiments?

_____

_____

_____

_____

In Motion

PURPOSE

To determine how temperature affects dissolving substances in water.

Materials

2 ice cubes
2 small clear drinking glasses
cold and warm tap water
flat toothpick
box of flavored gelatin (flavors such as grape, cherry, or strawberry work best)

Procedure

1. Place the ice cubes in one glass and fill it with cold water.

2. Fill the other glass with warm water.

3. Use the large end of the toothpick to scoop up the flavored gelatin.

4. Observe from the side of the glass as you gently shake the gelatin over the glass of warm water.

5. Remove the ice from the first glass. Repeat steps 3 and 4 with the glass of cold water.

In Motion

Observations and Data

What happens during the experiment? Write down what you observed as well as any measurements or calculations that you made. You may also want to draw sketches or take photos of your experiment.

_____

_____

_____

_____

_____

_____

Results and Conclusions

What was the final result of your experiment? Was it what you expected? Why or why not?

_____

_____

_____

_____

_____

What's Next?

How could you improve on this experiment? Did the results make you think of any other questions that you could investigate with new experiments?

_____

_____

_____

_____

Glob

PURPOSE

To discover how a non-Newtonian fluid behaves.

Materials

4-oz (120-ml) bottle of white school glue

1 pint (500-ml) jar

food coloring, any color

1 bowl, 2 qt. (liter)

measuring cup (250 ml)

1 pint (500 ml) distilled water

1 teaspoon (5 ml) borax powder (found in the supermarket with laundry detergents)

measuring teaspoon (5 ml)

stirring spoon

Procedure

1. Pour the glue into a pint (500-ml) jar.

2. Fill the empty glue bottle with distilled water and pour the water into the jar containing the glue. Add 10 drops of food coloring and stir well.

3. Put 1 cup (250 ml) distilled water and 1 teaspoon (5 ml) borax powder into the bowl. Stir until the powder dissolves.

4. Slowly pour the colored glue into the bowl containing the borax. Stir as you pour.

5. Take the thick glob that forms out of the bowl. Knead the glob with your hands until it is smooth and dry.

6. Try these experiments with the glob:

   a. Roll it into a ball and bounce it on a smooth surface.

   b. Hold it in your hands and quickly pull the ends in opposite directions.

   c. Hold it in your hands and slowly pull the ends in opposite directions.

Glob

Observations and Data

What happens during the experiment? Write down what you observed as well as any measurements or calculations that you made. You may also want to draw sketches or take photos of your experiment.

_____

_____

_____

_____

_____

_____

Results and Conclusions

What was the final result of your experiment? Was it what you expected? Why or why not?

_____

_____

_____

_____

_____

What's Next?

How could you improve on this experiment? Did the results make you think of any other questions that you could investigate with new experiments?

_____

_____

_____

_____

Sticky Sand

PURPOSE

To discover how a non-Newtonian fluid behaves.

Materials

measuring spoons
tap water
2-quart (liter) bowl
1 cup (250 ml) cornstarch
spoon

Procedure

1. Pour 8 tablespoons (120 ml) of water into the bowl.

2. Slowly add the cornstarch to the water. Stir well after each addition.

   NOTE: The mixture should be so thick that it is very hard to stir.

   Add a few drops of water if all of the starch will not dissolve or a little starch if the mixture looks thin.

3. Place your hand on the surface of the mixture in the bowl and very gently push downward.

4. When your hand has sunk into the mixture, try to lift your hand out of the bowl.

Sticky Sand

Observations and Data

What happens during the experiment? Write down what you observed as well as any measurements or calculations that you made. You may also want to draw sketches or take photos of your experiment.

_____

_____

_____

_____

_____

_____

_____

Results and Conclusions

What was the final result of your experiment? Was it what you expected? Why or why not?

_____

_____

_____

_____

_____

What's Next?

How could you improve on this experiment? Did the results make you think of any other questions that you could investigate with new experiments?

_____

_____

_____

_____

Faded

PURPOSE

To determine how sunlight affects color.

Materials

scissors

ruler

sheet of red construction paper

stiff paper, such as a file folder

Procedure

1. Cut a 6-by-6-inch (15-by-15-cm) square from both the construction paper and the stiff paper.

2. Cut a large star from the center of the square of stiff paper.

3. Lay the square of stiff paper, with the star section removed, over the square of red paper.

4. Place the pieces of paper near a window that receives direct sunlight.

5. After 2 days, remove the stiff paper.

Faded

Observations and Data

What happens during the experiment? Write down what you observed as well as any measurements or calculations that you made. You may also want to draw sketches or take photos of your experiment.

_____

_____

_____

_____

_____

_____

Results and Conclusions

What was the final result of your experiment? Was it what you expected? Why or why not?

_____

_____

_____

_____

_____

What's Next?

How could you improve on this experiment? Did the results make you think of any other questions that you could investigate with new experiments?

_____

_____

_____

_____

Chemical Heating

PURPOSE

To show that a chemical reaction can produce heat.

Materials

cooking or outdoor thermometer

1 jar with lid (The thermometer must fit inside the closed jar.)

1 steel wool pad without soap

¼ cup (60 ml) vinegar

measuring cup (250 ml)

Procedure

1. Place the thermometer inside the jar and close the lid. Record the temperature after 5 minutes.

2. Soak one-half of the steel wool pad in vinegar for 1 or 2 minutes.

3. Squeeze out any excess liquid from the steel wool and wrap it around the bulb of the thermometer.

4. Place the thermometer and the steel wool inside the jar. Close the lid.

5. Record the temperature after 5 minutes.

Chemical Heating

Observations and Data

What happens during the experiment? Write down what you observed as well as any measurements or calculations that you made. You may also want to draw sketches or take photos of your experiment.

_____

_____

_____

_____

_____

_____

Results and Conclusions

What was the final result of your experiment? Was it what you expected? Why or why not?

_____

_____

_____

_____

_____

What's Next?

How could you improve on this experiment? Did the results make you think of any other questions that you could investigate with new experiments?

_____

_____

_____

_____

Super Chain

PURPOSE

To observe a physical change.

Materials

lined notebook paper
pencil
scissors
ruler

Procedure

1. On the paper, draw and cut out a rectangle that is 4 inches (10 cm) wide and 12 lines long.

2. Fold the rectangle in half lengthwise, perpendicular to the lines.

3. Cut across the fold at points A and B as shown. Stop about ¼ inch (½ cm) from the edge of the paper.

4. Cut along each of the printed lines alternating from the folded edge to the open edge. Be sure to stop ¼ inch (½ cm) from the edge.

5. Start at point B and cut the folded edge off of the paper ending at point A. Do not cut the folded edge from the two ends.

6. Carefully stretch the paper open.

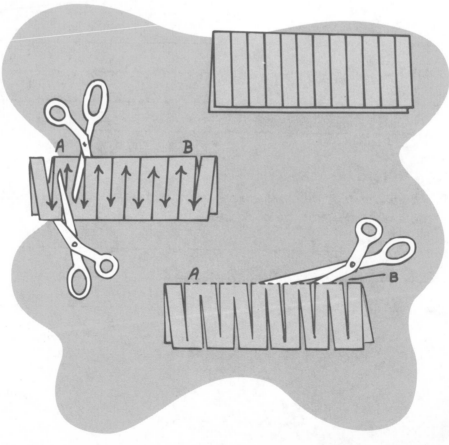

Super Chain

Observations and Data

What happens during the experiment? Write down what you observed as well as any measurements or calculations that you made. You may also want to draw sketches or take photos of your experiment.

_____

_____

_____

_____

_____

_____

Results and Conclusions

What was the final result of your experiment? Was it what you expected? Why or why not?

_____

_____

_____

_____

What's Next?

How could you improve on this experiment? Did the results make you think of any other questions that you could investigate with new experiments?

_____

_____

_____

_____

Frosty

PURPOSE

To determine how frost forms.

Materials

drinking glass

Procedure

1. Place a drinking glass in the freezer for 30 minutes.

2. Remove the glass and allow it to stand undisturbed for 30 seconds.

3. Scratch the cloudy formation on the outside of the glass with your fingernail.

4. Perform this experiment several times, selecting days with differing humidities.

Frosty

Observations and Data

What happens during the experiment? Write down what you observed as well as any measurements or calculations that you made. You may also want to draw sketches or take photos of your experiment.

_____

_____

_____

_____

_____

_____

_____

Results and Conclusions

What was the final result of your experiment? Was it what you expected? Why or why not?

_____

_____

_____

_____

_____

What's Next?

How could you improve on this experiment? Did the results make you think of any other questions that you could investigate with new experiments?

_____

_____

_____

_____

Tasty Solution

PURPOSE

To determine the fastest way to dissolve candy.

Materials

3 bite-sized pieces of soft candy

Procedure

1. Place one of the candy pieces in your mouth. *DO NOT* chew, and *DO NOT* move your tongue around.

2. Record the time it takes for this candy piece to dissolve.

3. Place a second candy piece in your mouth. *DO* move the candy back and forth with your tongue, but *DO NOT* chew.

4. Record the time it takes to dissolve this candy piece.

5. Place the third piece of candy in your mouth. *DO* move the candy back and forth with your tongue as you chew.

6. Record the time it takes to dissolve this third piece of candy.

Tasty Solution

Observations and Data

What happens during the experiment? Write down what you observed as well as any measurements or calculations that you made. You may also want to draw sketches or take photos of your experiment.

_____

_____

_____

_____

_____

_____

_____

Results and Conclusions

What was the final result of your experiment? Was it what you expected? Why or why not?

_____

_____

_____

_____

_____

What's Next?

How could you improve on this experiment? Did the results make you think of any other questions that you could investigate with new experiments?

_____

_____

_____

_____

Speedy Soup

PURPOSE

To show how temperature affects how long it takes for a material to dissolve.

Materials

2 cups
warm and cold tap water
2 bouillon cubes
spoon

Procedure

1. Fill one cup with cold tap water.

2. Add one bouillon cube.

3. Allow this cup to sit undisturbed while the second cup is prepared.

4. Fill the second cup with warm tap water.

5. Add one bouillon cube to the water and stir.

123

Speedy Soup

Observations and Data

What happens during the experiment? Write down what you observed as well as any measurements or calculations that you made. You may also want to draw sketches or take photos of your experiment.

_____

_____

_____

_____

_____

_____

Results and Conclusions

What was the final result of your experiment? Was it what you expected? Why or why not?

_____

_____

_____

_____

_____

What's Next?

How could you improve on this experiment? Did the results make you think of any other questions that you could investigate with new experiments?

_____

_____

_____

_____

Cooler

PURPOSE

To demonstrate that evaporation takes away heat.

Materials

clay flowerpot

bucket, large enough to hold the clay flowerpot

bowl, large enough to set the clay flowerpot in

table

2 thermometers

2 drinking glasses, large enough to hold a thermometer

electric fan

Procedure

1. Place the clay flowerpot in a bucket of water and let it soak for one day.

2. Fill a bowl with water to a depth of about 1 in. (2.5 cm) and set the bowl on a table.

3. Stand a thermometer in a glass and set the glass in the center of the bowl.

4. Turn the wet flowerpot upside down and stand it in the bowl so that it covers the glass and the thermometer. Put a clay plug in the hole in the flowerpot.

5. Stand a thermometer in a second glass, and set the glass on the table next to the bowl.

6. Record the reading on both thermometers.

7. Position a fan so that it blows equally on the flowerpot and on the glass standing on the table.

8. Record the reading on both thermometers every 10 minutes for 1 hour.

NOTE: Quickly replace the pot after each reading.

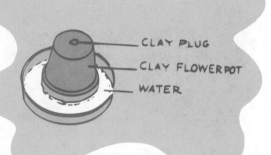

Cooler

Observations and Data

What happens during the experiment? Write down what you observed as well as any measurements or calculations that you made. You may also want to draw sketches or take photos of your experiment.

_____

_____

_____

_____

_____

_____

Results and Conclusions

What was the final result of your experiment? Was it what you expected? Why or why not?

_____

_____

_____

_____

_____

What's Next?

How could you improve on this experiment? Did the results make you think of any other questions that you could investigate with new experiments?

_____

_____

_____

_____

Frozen Orange Cubes

PURPOSE

To determine whether orange juice will freeze like water.

Materials

orange juice
ice tray
tap water
small bowl

Procedure

1. Fill half of the ice tray with orange juice.

2. Fill the remaining half of the tray with water.

3. Set the tray in the freezer overnight.

4. Remove the frozen cubes and place in the bowl.

5. Carefully try to bite into a cube of orange juice and a cube of water.

125

Frozen Orange Cubes

Observations and Data

What happens during the experiment? Write down what you observed as well as any measurements or calculations that you made. You may also want to draw sketches or take photos of your experiment.

_____

_____

_____

_____

_____

_____

Results and Conclusions

What was the final result of your experiment? Was it what you expected? Why or why not?

_____

_____

_____

_____

_____

What's Next?

How could you improve on this experiment? Did the results make you think of any other questions that you could investigate with new experiments?

_____

_____

_____

_____

Crystal Ink

PURPOSE

To produce a message written with shiny crystals.

Materials

table salt

measuring teaspoon (5 ml)

measuring cup (250 ml)

stove with an oven

art brush

1 sheet black construction paper

WARNING: Adult supervision is needed for use of the oven.

Procedure

1. Add 3 teaspoons (15 ml) of salt to ¼ cup (60 ml) water.

2. Ask an adult helper to warm the oven to 150°F. (66°C).

3. Use an art brush to write a message on the black paper. Stir the salt solution with the brush before making each letter. It is important to do this in order to produce a clear message.

4. Have the adult helper turn the oven off and place the paper in the oven on top of the wire racks.

5. Allow the paper to heat for 5 minutes or until it dries.

126

Crystal Ink

Observations and Data

What happens during the experiment? Write down what you observed as well as any measurements or calculations that you made. You may also want to draw sketches or take photos of your experiment.

_____

_____

_____

_____

_____

_____

Results and Conclusions

What was the final result of your experiment? Was it what you expected? Why or why not?

_____

_____

_____

_____

_____

What's Next?

How could you improve on this experiment? Did the results make you think of any other questions that you could investigate with new experiments?

_____

_____

_____

_____

A Different Form

PURPOSE

To produce a different form of matter.

Materials

1 teaspoon (5 ml) baking soda
1-quart (1-liter) plastic soda bottle
3 tablespoons (45 ml) vinegar
one 18-in (2.3-cm) balloon
cellophane tape

Procedure

1. Pour the baking soda into the bottle.

2. Pour the vinegar into the balloon.

3. Attach the open end of the balloon to the mouth of the bottle. Use the tape to secure the balloon to the bottle.

4. Raise the balloon to allow the vinegar to pour into the bottle.

A Different Form

Observations and Data

What happens during the experiment? Write down what you observed as well as any measurements or calculations that you made. You may also want to draw sketches or take photos of your experiment.

_____

_____

_____

_____

_____

Results and Conclusions

What was the final result of your experiment? Was it what you expected? Why or why not?

_____

_____

_____

_____

What's Next?

How could you improve on this experiment? Did the results make you think of any other questions that you could investigate with new experiments?

_____

_____

_____

_____

Suspended

PURPOSE

To observe the Tyndall effect.

Materials

small cardboard box, large enough to cover a quart (liter) jar

scissors

2 quart (liter) jars

tap water

1 teaspoon (5 ml) flour

spoon

flashlight

adult helper

Procedure

1. Ask an adult to do the following to prepare the box:

   a. Use the point of the scissors to make a small hole in the end of the box. The height of the hole should be half the height of the jars being used.

   b. Cut a 1-inch (2.5-cm) square viewing hole in front of the box. The hole must be near the corner of the box and as high as the small round hole on the side.

2. Fill the jars three-fourths full with water.

3. Add flour to one of the jars and stir.

4. Place each jar, in turn, in front of the viewing hole.

5. Ask your helper to hold the flashlight near the small hole. Observe the contents of each jar through the viewing hole.

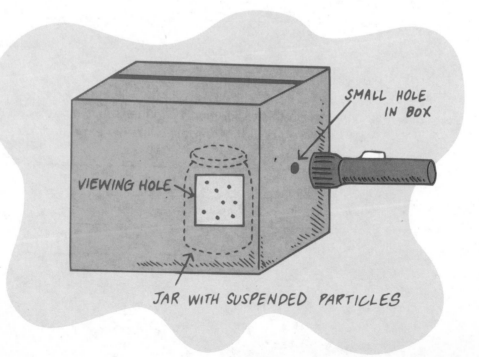

SMALL HOLE IN BOX

VIEWING HOLE

JAR WITH SUSPENDED PARTICLES

Suspended

Observations and Data

What happens during the experiment? Write down what you observed as well as any measurements or calculations that you made. You may also want to draw sketches or take photos of your experiment.

_____

_____

_____

_____

_____

_____

Results and Conclusions

What was the final result of your experiment? Was it what you expected? Why or why not?

_____

_____

_____

_____

_____

What's Next?

How could you improve on this experiment? Did the results make you think of any other questions that you could investigate with new experiments?

_____

_____

_____

_____

Immiscible

PURPOSE

To observe the separation of an emulsion.

Materials

½ cup (125 ml) tap water
1-quart (1-liter) glass jar with a lid
blue food coloring
spoon
¼ cup (60 ml) liquid oil

Procedure

1. Pour the water into the jar.

2. Add 5 drops of the food coloring and stir.

3. Slowly add the liquid oil.

4. Secure the lid and shake the jar vigorously 10 times.

5. Put the jar on a table and observe what happens.

Immiscible

Observations and Data

What happens during the experiment? Write down what you observed as well as any measurements or calculations that you made. You may also want to draw sketches or take photos of your experiment.

_____

_____

_____

_____

_____

_____

_____

Results and Conclusions

What was the final result of your experiment? Was it what you expected? Why or why not?

_____

_____

_____

_____

_____

What's Next?

How could you improve on this experiment? Did the results make you think of any other questions that you could investigate with new experiments?

_____

_____

_____

_____

Erupting Colors

PURPOSE

To produce erupting color bubbles.

Materials

clear glass bowl, 2 qt. (liter)
measuring tablespoon (15 ml)
liquid cooking oil
food coloring—red, blue, green
cup (250 ml)
fork

Procedure

1. Fill the bowl with water.

2. Pour 1 tablespoon of cooking oil into the cup.

3. Add 4 drops of each of the food coloring colors.

4. Use the fork to beat the oil and colors until thoroughly mixed.

5. Pour the mixture of oil and food colors onto the water in the bowl.

6. Observe the surface and side of the bowl for 5 to 10 minutes.

Erupting Colors

Observations and Data

What happens during the experiment? Write down what you observed as well as any measurements or calculations that you made. You may also want to draw sketches or take photos of your experiment.

_____

_____

_____

_____

_____

_____

Results and Conclusions

What was the final result of your experiment? Was it what you expected? Why or why not?

_____

_____

_____

_____

_____

What's Next?

How could you improve on this experiment? Did the results make you think of any other questions that you could investigate with new experiments?

_____

_____

_____

_____

Separator

PURPOSE

To separate a suspension by spinning.

Materials

24-inch (60-cm) piece of strong cord
small bucket
tap water
spoon
¼ cup (63 ml) flour
clear drinking glass

Procedure

1. Tie the ends of the cord to the handle of the bucket.

2. Fill the bucket one-fourth full with water.

3. Stir the flour into the water.

4. Carry the pail and glass outside. In an area clear of objects and people, hold the cord and swing the bucket around 15 times.

5. Pour a small amount of the liquid from the bucket into the empty glass.

6. If the liquid looks cloudy, swing the bucket 15 times again and pour another small amount of liquid into the glass.

7. Continue to swing and pour until the liquid looks clear.

Separator

Observations and Data

What happens during the experiment? Write down what you observed as well as any measurements or calculations that you made. You may also want to draw sketches or take photos of your experiment.

_____

_____

_____

_____

_____

_____

Results and Conclusions

What was the final result of your experiment? Was it what you expected? Why or why not?

_____

_____

_____

_____

_____

What's Next?

How could you improve on this experiment? Did the results make you think of any other questions that you could investigate with new experiments?

_____

_____

_____

_____

132

Drinkable Iron

PURPOSE

To determine why water forms beads on certain surfaces.

Materials

saucer

baby powder

red, blue, or green food coloring in a dropper bottle

Procedure

1. Cover the saucer with a thin layer of powder.

2. Place several drops of food coloring on the powder layer.

NOTE: Keep the results of this activity for Experiment 133.

BABY POWDER

Drinkable Iron

Observations and Data

What happens during the experiment? Write down what you observed as well as any measurements or calculations that you made. You may also want to draw sketches or take photos of your experiment.

_____

_____

_____

_____

_____

_____

Results and Conclusions

What was the final result of your experiment? Was it what you expected? Why or why not?

_____

_____

_____

_____

_____

What's Next?

How could you improve on this experiment? Did the results make you think of any other questions that you could investigate with new experiments?

_____

_____

_____

_____

Spreader

PURPOSE

To demonstrate the decrease of water's surface tension.

Materials

dishwashing liquid

saucer

toothpick

saucer with beads of colored water
from Experiment 132

Procedure

1. Pour a drop of dishwashing liquid on the saucer.

2. Dip the end of the toothpick into the drop of dishwashing liquid.

3. Touch the wet end of the toothpick to several colored beads on the powder.

Spreader

Observations and Data

What happens during the experiment? Write down what you observed as well as any measurements or calculations that you made. You may also want to draw sketches or take photos of your experiment.

_____

_____

_____

_____

_____

_____

Results and Conclusions

What was the final result of your experiment? Was it what you expected? Why or why not?

_____

_____

_____

_____

_____

What's Next?

How could you improve on this experiment? Did the results make you think of any other questions that you could investigate with new experiments?

_____

_____

_____

_____

Floating Sticks

PURPOSE

To observe the pulling power of water molecules.

Materials

3 toothpicks
quart (liter) glass bowl
liquid dish soap

Procedure

1. Fill the bowl three-quarters full with water.

2. Place two toothpicks side by side on the surface in the center of the water.

3. Treat the third toothpick by dipping its point in liquid detergent.

   NOTE: Only a very small amount of detergent is needed.

4. Touch the treated toothpick tip between the floating sticks.

Floating Sticks

Observations and Data

What happens during the experiment? Write down what you observed as well as any measurements or calculations that you made. You may also want to draw sketches or take photos of your experiment.

_____

_____

_____

_____

_____

_____

Results and Conclusions

What was the final result of your experiment? Was it what you expected? Why or why not?

_____

_____

_____

_____

What's Next?

How could you improve on this experiment? Did the results make you think of any other questions that you could investigate with new experiments?

_____

_____

_____

_____

Moving Drop

PURPOSE

To demonstrate the attractive force between water molecules.

Materials

1-foot (30-cm) sheet of wax paper
toothpick
eyedropper
water

Procedure

1. Spread the wax paper on a table.

2. Use the eyedropper to position three or four separate small drops of water on the paper.

3. Wet the toothpick with water.

4. Bring the tip of the wet pick near, but not touching, one of the water drops. Repeat with the other drops.

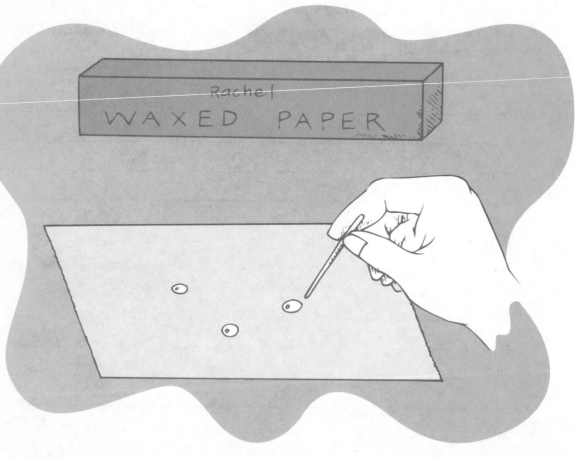

Moving Drop

Observations and Data

What happens during the experiment? Write down what you observed as well as any measurements or calculations that you made. You may also want to draw sketches or take photos of your experiment.

_____

_____

_____

_____

_____

_____

_____

Results and Conclusions

What was the final result of your experiment? Was it what you expected? Why or why not?

_____

_____

_____

_____

_____

What's Next?

How could you improve on this experiment? Did the results make you think of any other questions that you could investigate with new experiments?

_____

_____

_____

_____

EARTH SCIENCE

Push Up

PURPOSE

To demonstrate the strength of atmospheric pressure.

Materials

bowl large enough to hold a glass on its side

tap water

drinking glass

Procedure

1. Fill the bowl ¾ full with water.

2. Turn the glass on its side and push it beneath the surface of the water. The glass should fill with water.

3. Keep the glass under the water and turn it so that its mouth points down.

4. Slowly lift the glass leaving about 1 inch (1.25 cm) of the mouth under the water's surface.

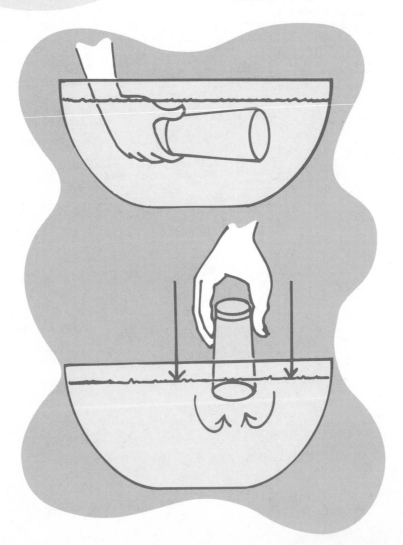

Push Up

Observations and Data

What happens during the experiment? Write down what you observed as well as any measurements or calculations that you made. You may also want to draw sketches or take photos of your experiment.

_____

_____

_____

_____

_____

_____

Results and Conclusions

What was the final result of your experiment? Was it what you expected? Why or why not?

_____

_____

_____

_____

What's Next?

How could you improve on this experiment? Did the results make you think of any other questions that you could investigate with new experiments?

_____

_____

_____

_____

Spacer

PURPOSE

To determine the size of a single hole needed to pour liquid out of a can.

Materials

3 empty soda cans
paper towels
scissors
duct tape

Procedure

1. Remove the opening tab from the tops of three soda cans.

2. Fill the three cans with water from a faucet.

3. Use paper towels to dry the tops of each can.

4. Use the scissors to cut two strips of tape 1 in. (2.5 cm) square.

5. Leave the opening in one of the cans uncovered (A).

6. Cover three-fourths of the opening in one of the cans with one strip of tape (B).

7. Use the second piece of tape to cover one-half of the opening in another can (C).

8. Hold one can at a time over a sink. Tilt each can at the same angle.

9. Observe any flow of liquid out of the cans.

Spacer

Observations and Data

What happens during the experiment? Write down what you observed as well as any measurements or calculations that you made. You may also want to draw sketches or take photos of your experiment.

_____

_____

_____

_____

_____

_____

Results and Conclusions

What was the final result of your experiment? Was it what you expected? Why or why not?

_____

_____

_____

_____

_____

What's Next?

How could you improve on this experiment? Did the results make you think of any other questions that you could investigate with new experiments?

_____

_____

_____

_____

Folds

PURPOSE

To demonstrate how compressional forces affect crustal movement.

Materials

4 paper towels

glass of water

Procedure

1. Stack the paper towels on a table.
2. Fold the stack of paper in half.
3. Wet the paper with water.
4. Place your hands on the edges of the wet paper.
5. Slowly push the sides of paper toward the center.

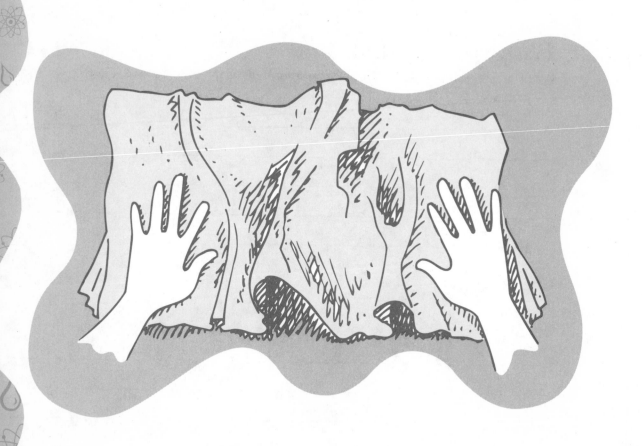

Folds

Observations and Data

What happens during the experiment? Write down what you observed as well as any measurements or calculations that you made. You may also want to draw sketches or take photos of your experiment.

_____

_____

_____

_____

_____

_____

_____

Results and Conclusions

What was the final result of your experiment? Was it what you expected? Why or why not?

_____

_____

_____

_____

_____

What's Next?

How could you improve on this experiment? Did the results make you think of any other questions that you could investigate with new experiments?

_____

_____

_____

_____

Easy Over?

PURPOSE

To demonstrate the pressure required to fold the earth's crust.

Materials

1 sheet of newspaper

Procedure

1. Fold the paper in half.
2. Continue to fold the paper as many times as you can.

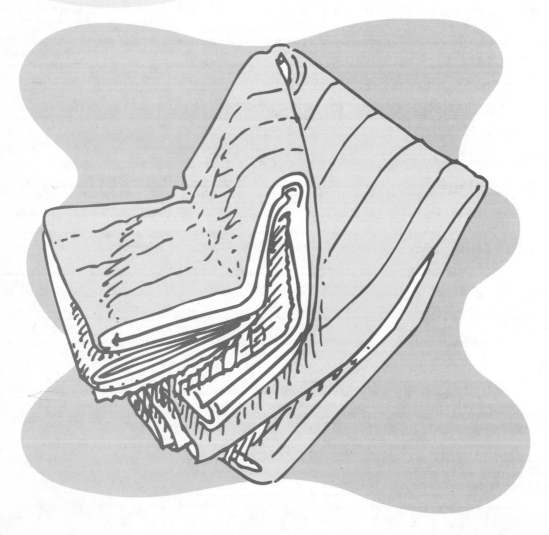

Easy Over?

Observations and Data

What happens during the experiment? Write down what you observed as well as any measurements or calculations that you made. You may also want to draw sketches or take photos of your experiment.

_____

_____

_____

_____

_____

_____

_____

Results and Conclusions

What was the final result of your experiment? Was it what you expected? Why or why not?

_____

_____

_____

_____

_____

What's Next?

How could you improve on this experiment? Did the results make you think of any other questions that you could investigate with new experiments?

_____

_____

_____

_____

Widening

PURPOSE

To demonstrate the expansion of the Atlantic Ocean.

Materials

scissors
ruler
sheet of typing paper
shoe box
modeling clay

Procedure

1. Cut two 3-by-11-inch (7-by-28-cm) strips from the paper.

2. Cut out a ½-by-3½-inch (1-by-9-cm) slit from the center of the bottom of the shoe box, as shown in the diagram.

3. Cut out a 3-by-6-inch (7.5-by-15-cm) section in the center of one of the box's largest sides.

4. Put the paper strips together, and run them up through the slit in the box. Pull the strips out about 3 inches (7.5 cm), fold them back on opposite sides, and place a piece of clay on the end of each strip.

5. Hold the papers under the box and slowly push the strips up through the slit.

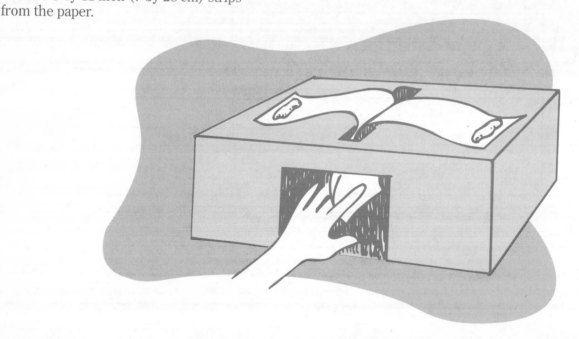

Widening

Observations and Data

What happens during the experiment? Write down what you observed as well as any measurements or calculations that you made. You may also want to draw sketches or take photos of your experiment.

_____

_____

_____

_____

_____

_____

Results and Conclusions

What was the final result of your experiment? Was it what you expected? Why or why not?

_____

_____

_____

_____

What's Next?

How could you improve on this experiment? Did the results make you think of any other questions that you could investigate with new experiments?

_____

_____

_____

_____

Squeezed

PURPOSE

To determine how compression forces can bend layers of rock.

Materials

2 large thin sponges
tap water

Procedure

1. Moisten the sponges with water to make them flexible.

2. Lay the moist sponges on top of each other.

3. Place your hands on opposite ends of the sponge "sandwich."

4. While holding the "sandwich" in front of you, slowly push the ends about 2 inches (5 cm) toward the center. The sponge "sandwich" will fold up or down.

5. Repeat step 4, but tilt your hands a little to make the "sandwich" fold in the opposite direction.

Squeezed

Observations and Data

What happens during the experiment? Write down what you observed as well as any measurements or calculations that you made. You may also want to draw sketches or take photos of your experiment.

_____

_____

_____

_____

_____

_____

Results and Conclusions

What was the final result of your experiment? Was it what you expected? Why or why not?

_____

_____

_____

_____

What's Next?

How could you improve on this experiment? Did the results make you think of any other questions that you could investigate with new experiments?

_____

_____

_____

_____

Bulging Ball

PURPOSE

To determine why the earth bulges at the equator.

Materials

construction paper—16 in. (40 cm) long
paper hole punch
scissors
ruler
paper glue
pencil

Procedure

1. Measure and cut 2 separate strips, 1¼ in. × 16 in. (3 cm × 40 cm), from construction paper.

2. Cross the strips at their centers and glue.

3. Bring the four ends together, overlap, and glue, forming a sphere.

4. Allow the glue to dry.

5. Cut a hole through the center of the overlapped ends with the hole punch.

6. Push about 2 in. (5 cm) of the pencil through the hole.

7. Hold the pencil between your palms.

8. Move your hands back and forth to make the paper sphere spin.

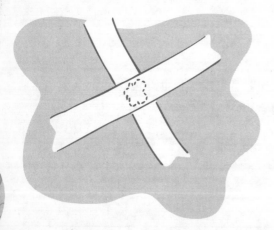

Bulging Ball

Observations and Data

What happens during the experiment? Write down what you observed as well as any measurements or calculations that you made. You may also want to draw sketches or take photos of your experiment.

_____

_____

_____

_____

_____

_____

_____

Results and Conclusions

What was the final result of your experiment? Was it what you expected? Why or why not?

_____

_____

_____

_____

_____

What's Next?

How could you improve on this experiment? Did the results make you think of any other questions that you could investigate with new experiments?

_____

_____

_____

_____

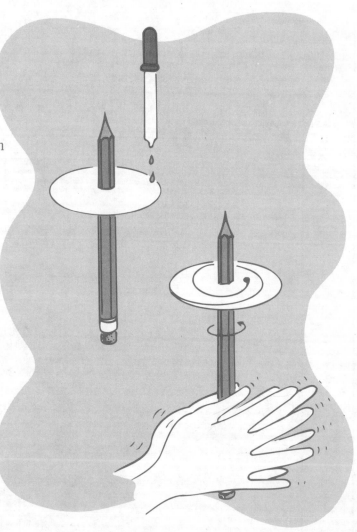

Twirler

PURPOSE

To demonstrate the effect of the earth's rotation on wind and water currents.

Materials

construction paper
pencil
scissors
ruler
eyedropper

Procedure

1. Cut an 8-in. (20-cm) diameter circle from the construction paper.

2. Push the point of the pencil through the center of the circle.

3. Place a drop of water on top of the paper near the pencil.

4. Hold the pencil between the palms of your hands and twirl the pencil in a counterclockwise direction.

Twirler

Observations and Data

What happens during the experiment? Write down what you observed as well as any measurements or calculations that you made. You may also want to draw sketches or take photos of your experiment.

_____

_____

_____

_____

_____

_____

Results and Conclusions

What was the final result of your experiment? Was it what you expected? Why or why not?

_____

_____

_____

_____

_____

What's Next?

How could you improve on this experiment? Did the results make you think of any other questions that you could investigate with new experiments?

_____

_____

_____

_____

Jolted

PURPOSE

To determine how faults produce earth-quakes.

Materials

2 wooden blocks, each about
2 by 4 by 6 inches (5 by 10 by 15 cm)
2 sheets of medium-grade sandpaper
masking tape

Procedure

1. Wrap each wooden block with a sheet of sandpaper, and secure with tape.

2. Hold one block in each hand. The blocks should be held straight up and down.

3. Push the blocks together tightly.

4. While continuing to push the blocks together, try to slide the blocks in different directions.

Jolted

Observations and Data

What happens during the experiment? Write down what you observed as well as any measurements or calculations that you made. You may also want to draw sketches or take photos of your experiment.

_____

_____

_____

_____

_____

_____

Results and Conclusions

What was the final result of your experiment? Was it what you expected? Why or why not?

_____

_____

_____

_____

_____

What's Next?

How could you improve on this experiment? Did the results make you think of any other questions that you could investigate with new experiments?

_____

_____

_____

_____

Side-to-Side

PURPOSE

To determine how buildings respond to lateral (side-to-side) movements produced by earthquakes.

Materials

sheet of coarse (rough) sandpaper
Slinky

Procedure

1. Place the sandpaper on a table.

2. Stand the Slinky on the end on the sandpaper.

3. Grab the edge of the sandpaper with your fingers, and quickly pull the paper about 6 inches (15 cm) toward the side of the table.

4. Observe the movement of the Slinky.

Side-to-Side

Observations and Data

What happens during the experiment? Write down what you observed as well as any measurements or calculations that you made. You may also want to draw sketches or take photos of your experiment.

_____

_____

_____

_____

_____

Results and Conclusions

What was the final result of your experiment? Was it what you expected? Why or why not?

_____

_____

_____

_____

_____

What's Next?

How could you improve on this experiment? Did the results make you think of any other questions that you could investigate with new experiments?

_____

_____

_____

_____

Covered

PURPOSE

To demonstrate the effect of rain on hills with and without ground cover.

Materials

3 large shallow baking pans

table

modeling clay

ruler

2 cups of soil

quart (liter) bowl filled with a mixture of leaves, grass, and small twigs

1 drinking glass

Procedure

1. Place a shallow baking pan on a table.

2. Use clay to position two pans so that they are raised about 2 in. (5 cm) at one end, with their other ends resting inside the pan on the table as in the diagram.

3. Spread one cup of soil across the top section of the pans.

4. Cover the soil on one of the pans with the mixture of grass, leaves, and small twigs.

5. Hold a tilted glass full of water about 6 in. (15 cm) above the uncovered soil and allow the water to slowly pour onto the soil.

6. Repeat the procedure on the covered soil.

7. Compare the amount of soil collected at the bottom of each elevated pan.

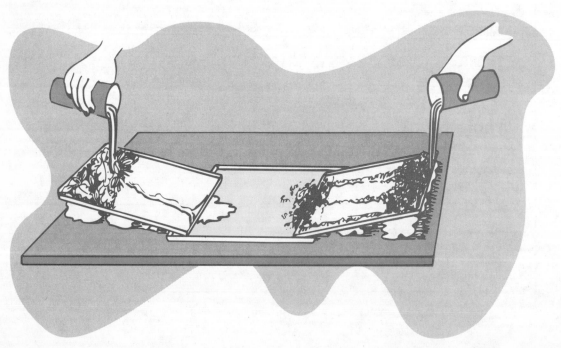

Covered

Observations and Data

What happens during the experiment? Write down what you observed as well as any measurements or calculations that you made. You may also want to draw sketches or take photos of your experiment.

_____

_____

_____

_____

_____

_____

_____

Results and Conclusions

What was the final result of your experiment? Was it what you expected? Why or why not?

_____

_____

_____

_____

What's Next?

How could you improve on this experiment? Did the results make you think of any other questions that you could investigate with new experiments?

_____

_____

_____

_____

Speedy

PURPOSE

To demonstrate how the speed of running water affects the wearing away of soil.

Materials

pencil

paper cup

scissors

drinking straw

modeling clay

cookie sheet

ruler

soil

1-gallon (4-liter) plastic jug, filled with tap water

Procedure

1. Use the pencil to make a hole in the side of the paper cup near the bottom.

2. Cut the straw in half and insert one of the pieces into the hole in the cup. Seal around the hole with clay.

3. Lay the cookie sheet on the ground and raise one end about 2 inches (5 cm) by putting soil under it.

4. Cover the sheet with a thin layer of soil. Set the cup on the sheet as shown.

5. Hold your finger over the end of the straw as you fill the cup with water.

6. Release the end of the straw and observe the movement of the water.

7. Repeat steps 4 through 6, raising the end of the sheet about 6 inches (15 cm). Keep the materials for Experiment 148.

Speedy

Observations and Data

What happens during the experiment? Write down what you observed as well as any measurements or calculations that you made. You may also want to draw sketches or take photos of your experiment.

_____

_____

_____

_____

_____

_____

Results and Conclusions

What was the final result of your experiment? Was it what you expected? Why or why not?

_____

_____

_____

_____

_____

What's Next?

How could you improve on this experiment? Did the results make you think of any other questions that you could investigate with new experiments?

_____

_____

_____

_____

Wander

PURPOSE

To determine why streams are not always straight.

Materials

materials from Experiment 147
several small rocks

Procedure

1. On the cookie sheet from Experiment 147, push one rock into the soil directly in front of the straw.

2. Continue to fill the cup with water until the running water cuts a definite path in the soil.

3. Change the direction of the stream by placing rocks in the path of the water.

Wander

Observations and Data

What happens during the experiment? Write down what you observed as well as any measurements or calculations that you made. You may also want to draw sketches or take photos of your experiment.

_____

_____

_____

_____

_____

_____

Results and Conclusions

What was the final result of your experiment? Was it what you expected? Why or why not?

_____

_____

_____

_____

_____

What's Next?

How could you improve on this experiment? Did the results make you think of any other questions that you could investigate with new experiments?

_____

_____

_____

_____

Wet Air

PURPOSE

To demonstrate the use of hair in measuring humidity.

Materials

cellophane tape

straight strand of hair about 5 in. (12 cm) long

flat toothpick

marker

pencil

large glass jar

glue

Procedure

1. Use a small piece of tape to secure one end of the strand of hair to the center of the toothpick.

2. Color the pointed end of the toothpick with the marker.

3. Tape the free end of the hair strand to the center of the pencil.

4. Place the pencil across the mouth of the jar with the toothpick hanging inside the jar. If the toothpick does not hang horizontally, add a drop of glue to the light end to balance the toothpick.

5. Place the jar where it will be undisturbed.

6. Observe the directions that the toothpick points for 1 week.

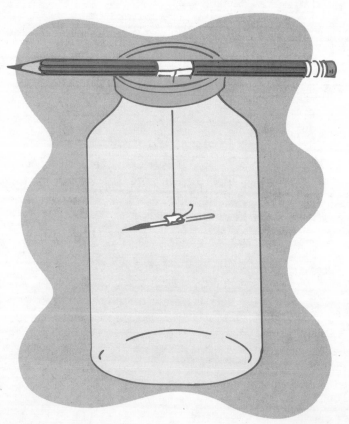

Wet Air

Observations and Data

What happens during the experiment? Write down what you observed as well as any measurements or calculations that you made. You may also want to draw sketches or take photos of your experiment.

_____

_____

_____

_____

_____

_____

Results and Conclusions

What was the final result of your experiment? Was it what you expected? Why or why not?

_____

_____

_____

_____

_____

What's Next?

How could you improve on this experiment? Did the results make you think of any other questions that you could investigate with new experiments?

_____

_____

_____

_____

Wet Bulb

PURPOSE

To determine how a psychrometer measures relative humidity.

Materials

2 thermometers
1 cotton ball
tap water
fan

Procedure

1. Place both thermometers on a table.

2. Record the temperature on both thermometers.

3. Wet the cotton ball with water and place it over the bulb of one of the thermometers.

4. Place the fan so that it blows across both bulbs.

5. Record the temperature of the two bulbs after 5 minutes.

Wet Bulb

Observations and Data

What happens during the experiment? Write down what you observed as well as any measurements or calculations that you made. You may also want to draw sketches or take photos of your experiment.

_____

_____

_____

_____

_____

_____

Results and Conclusions

What was the final result of your experiment? Was it what you expected? Why or why not?

_____

_____

_____

_____

_____

What's Next?

How could you improve on this experiment? Did the results make you think of any other questions that you could investigate with new experiments?

_____

_____

_____

_____

Dew Point

PURPOSE

To determine the temperature at which dew forms.

Materials

drinking glass
ice
tap water
thermometer

Procedure

1. Fill the glass with ice.

2. Add enough water to cover the ice.

3. Place the thermometer in the glass of icy water.

4. Watch the outside of the glass and record the temperature when water is observed on the outside of the glass.

5. Perform this experiment several times, selecting days that have different humidities.

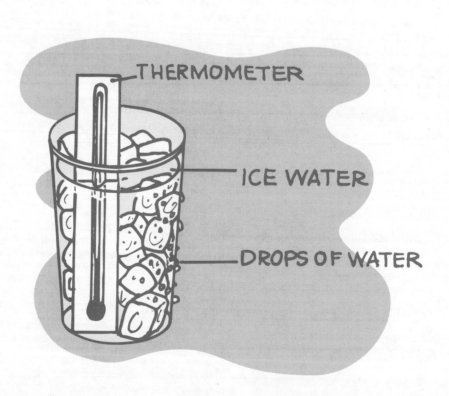

THERMOMETER

ICE WATER

DROPS OF WATER

Dew Point

Observations and Data

What happens during the experiment? Write down what you observed as well as any measurements or calculations that you made. You may also want to draw sketches or take photos of your experiment.

_____

_____

_____

_____

_____

_____

Results and Conclusions

What was the final result of your experiment? Was it what you expected? Why or why not?

_____

_____

_____

_____

_____

What's Next?

How could you improve on this experiment? Did the results make you think of any other questions that you could investigate with new experiments?

_____

_____

_____

_____

Spurt

PURPOSE

To demonstrate what causes magma (liquid rock) to move.

Materials

½-empty tube of toothpaste

Procedure

1. Hold the tube of toothpaste in your hands.

2. With the cap screwed on tight, press against the tube with your thumbs and fingers.

3. Move your fingers and press in different places on the tube.

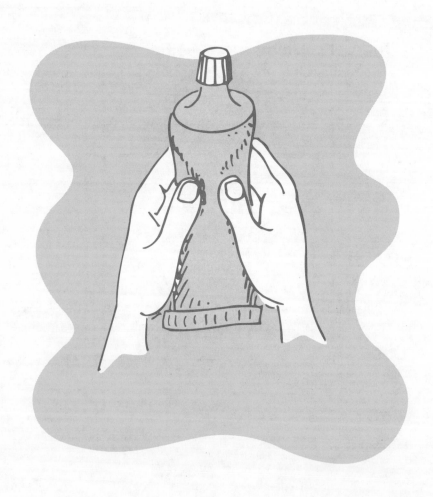

Spurt

Observations and Data

What happens during the experiment? Write down what you observed as well as any measurements or calculations that you made. You may also want to draw sketches or take photos of your experiment.

_____

_____

_____

_____

_____

_____

Results and Conclusions

What was the final result of your experiment? Was it what you expected? Why or why not?

_____

_____

_____

_____

_____

What's Next?

How could you improve on this experiment? Did the results make you think of any other questions that you could investigate with new experiments?

_____

_____

_____

_____

Line Up

PURPOSE

To demonstrate that some minerals have a definite cleavage line.

Materials

paper towels

Procedure

1. Try to rip a single sheet of a paper towel from top to bottom.

2. Turn another sheet of paper towel and try to tear it from side to side.

Line Up

Observations and Data

What happens during the experiment? Write down what you observed as well as any measurements or calculations that you made. You may also want to draw sketches or take photos of your experiment.

_____

_____

_____

_____

_____

Results and Conclusions

What was the final result of your experiment? Was it what you expected? Why or why not?

_____

_____

_____

_____

_____

What's Next?

How could you improve on this experiment? Did the results make you think of any other questions that you could investigate with new experiments?

_____

_____

_____

_____

Spoon Pen

PURPOSE

To demonstrate a mineral streak test.

Materials

metal spoon (stainless steel)
unglazed porcelain tile (The back of any
porcelain tile will work.)

Procedure

1. Rub the handle of the spoon across the
   back of the porcelain tile.

2. Write your name on the back of the tile
   with the spoon handle.

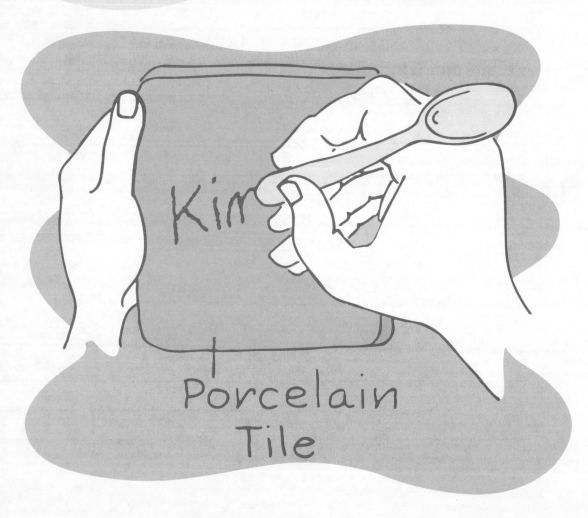

Kim

Porcelain
Tile

Spoon Pen

Observations and Data

What happens during the experiment? Write down what you observed as well as any measurements or calculations that you made. You may also want to draw sketches or take photos of your experiment.

_____

_____

_____

_____

_____

_____

Results and Conclusions

What was the final result of your experiment? Was it what you expected? Why or why not?

_____

_____

_____

_____

What's Next?

How could you improve on this experiment? Did the results make you think of any other questions that you could investigate with new experiments?

_____

_____

_____

_____

Tasty

PURPOSE

To determine the taste of ocean water.

Materials

two 9-ounce (180-ml) cups
tap water
¼ teaspoon (0.63 ml) table salt
spoon
marking pen

NOTE: Never taste anything in a laboratory setting unless you are sure that it does not contain chemicals or materials.

Procedure

1. Fill each cup half full with water.
2. Add the salt to one of the cups of water and stir.
3. Label the cup containing the salt S.
4. Taste the water in each cup.

Tasty

Observations and Data

What happens during the experiment? Write down what you observed as well as any measurements or calculations that you made. You may also want to draw sketches or take photos of your experiment.

_____

_____

_____

_____

_____

_____

Results and Conclusions

What was the final result of your experiment? Was it what you expected? Why or why not?

_____

_____

_____

_____

_____

What's Next?

How could you improve on this experiment? Did the results make you think of any other questions that you could investigate with new experiments?

_____

_____

_____

_____

Salty Water

PURPOSE

To determine how the ocean gets its salt.

Materials

pencil
2 paper cups
coffee filter
1 tablespoon (15 ml) soil
1 tablespoon (15 ml) table salt
spoon
sheet of black construction paper
plate
modeling clay
tap water

Procedure

1. Use the pencil to punch 6 holes in the bottom of one of the paper cups.

2. Place the coffee filter inside the cup.

3. In the other cup, mix the soil and the salt together.

4. Pour the soil–salt mixture into the cup with the coffee filter.

5. Place the paper on the plate.

6. Use the clay to make short legs to support the cup above the paper.

7. Add spoonfuls of water until water starts to drain out of the cup.

8. Allow the water to drain. Then let the paper dry.

Salty Water

Observations and Data

What happens during the experiment? Write down what you observed as well as any measurements or calculations that you made. You may also want to draw sketches or take photos of your experiment.

_____

_____

_____

_____

_____

_____

Results and Conclusions

What was the final result of your experiment? Was it what you expected? Why or why not?

_____

_____

_____

_____

_____

What's Next?

How could you improve on this experiment? Did the results make you think of any other questions that you could investigate with new experiments?

_____

_____

_____

_____

Drops

PURPOSE

To determine how raindrops form.

Materials

tap water
quart (liter) jar with lid
ice cubes

Procedure

1. Pour enough water into the jar to cover the bottom.

2. Turn the jar lid upside down and set it over the mouth of the jar.

3. Put 3 or 4 ice cubes inside the lid.

4. Observe the underside of the lid for 10 minutes.

Ice

Water

Drops

Observations and Data

What happens during the experiment? Write down what you observed as well as any measurements or calculations that you made. You may also want to draw sketches or take photos of your experiment.

_____

_____

_____

_____

_____

_____

Results and Conclusions

What was the final result of your experiment? Was it what you expected? Why or why not?

_____

_____

_____

_____

_____

What's Next?

How could you improve on this experiment? Did the results make you think of any other questions that you could investigate with new experiments?

_____

_____

_____

_____

Bigger

PURPOSE

To determine how tiny water droplets in clouds grow into raindrops.

Materials

eyedropper
tap water
clear plastic lid (coffee can lid)
pencil

Procedure

1. Fill the eyedropper with water.

2. Hold the plastic lid in your hand, bottom side up.

3. Squeeze as many separate drops of water as will fit on the lid.

4. Quickly turn the lid over.

5. Use the point of a pencil to move the tiny drops of water together.

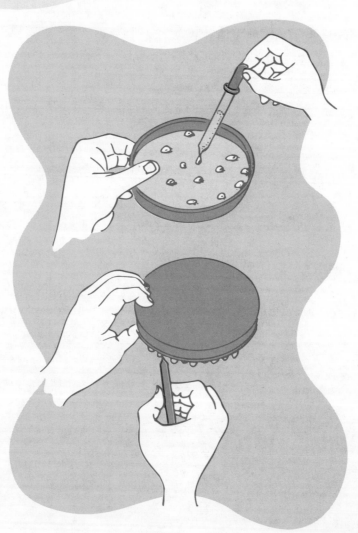

Bigger

Observations and Data

What happens during the experiment? Write down what you observed as well as any measurements or calculations that you made. You may also want to draw sketches or take photos of your experiment.

_____

_____

_____

_____

_____

_____

Results and Conclusions

What was the final result of your experiment? Was it what you expected? Why or why not?

_____

_____

_____

_____

What's Next?

How could you improve on this experiment? Did the results make you think of any other questions that you could investigate with new experiments?

_____

_____

_____

_____

Crunch

PURPOSE

To demonstrate the formation of metamorphic rocks.

Materials

20 flat toothpicks
table
book

Procedure

1. Snap the toothpicks in half, but leave them connected.

2. Pile the toothpicks on a table.

3. Place the book on top of the toothpick pile and press down.

4. Remove the book.

Crunch

Observations and Data

What happens during the experiment? Write down what you observed as well as any measurements or calculations that you made. You may also want to draw sketches or take photos of your experiment.

_____

_____

_____

_____

_____

_____

Results and Conclusions

What was the final result of your experiment? Was it what you expected? Why or why not?

_____

_____

_____

_____

_____

What's Next?

How could you improve on this experiment? Did the results make you think of any other questions that you could investigate with new experiments?

_____

_____

_____

_____

Sedimentary Sandwich

PURPOSE

To demonstrate a sedimentary rock formation.

Materials

2 slices of bread
crunchy peanut butter
jelly
knife, for spreading
plate

Procedure

NOTE: Do this before lunch.

1. Lay one slice of bread on a plate.

2. Use the knife to spread a layer of peanut butter on the slice of bread.

3. Add a layer of jelly on top of the peanut butter layer.

4. Place the second slice of bread on top of the jelly layer.

5. Eat the sandwich.

CAUTION: Never taste anything in a laboratory setting unless you are sure that there are no harmful chemicals or materials. This experiment is safe.

Sedimentary Sandwich

Observations and Data

What happens during the experiment? Write down what you observed as well as any measurements or calculations that you made. You may also want to draw sketches or take photos of your experiment.

_____

_____

_____

_____

_____

_____

Results and Conclusions

What was the final result of your experiment? Was it what you expected? Why or why not?

_____

_____

_____

_____

What's Next?

How could you improve on this experiment? Did the results make you think of any other questions that you could investigate with new experiments?

_____

_____

_____

_____

Ticker

PURPOSE

To demonstrate how sound is used to find petroleum.

Materials

2 sheets of typing paper
transparent tape
timer
hardcover book
index card
helper

Procedure

1. Roll and tape the sheets of paper to form two large tubes. Set the timer for 5 or more minutes and place it in the end of one of the tubes.

2. Tape the index card to the table as shown.

3. Position and tape the tubes to the table so that they lie along the sides of the index card with the empty tube extending about 1 inch (2.5 cm) past the edge of the table.

4. Place your ear next to the open tube and note the sound of the ticking timer.

5. While listening to the timer, ask your helper to stand the book next to the open ends of the tubes.

Ticker

Observations and Data

What happens during the experiment? Write down what you observed as well as any measurements or calculations that you made. You may also want to draw sketches or take photos of your experiment.

_____

_____

_____

_____

_____

_____

Results and Conclusions

What was the final result of your experiment? Was it what you expected? Why or why not?

_____

_____

_____

_____

_____

What's Next?

How could you improve on this experiment? Did the results make you think of any other questions that you could investigate with new experiments?

_____

_____

_____

_____

Tilt

PURPOSE

To demonstrate the effect of the earth's tilt on seasons.

Materials

2 pencils
ball of modeling clay the size of an apple
flashlight

Procedure

1. Insert a pencil through the ball of clay.

2. Use the second pencil to mark the equator line around the center of the clay ball. This line should be halfway between the top and bottom of the ball.

3. Position the ball on a table so that the pencil eraser is leaning slightly to the right.

4. In a darkened room, place the flashlight about 6 inches (15 cm) from the left side of the ball.

5. Observe where the light strikes the ball.

6. Place the light about 6 inches (15 cm) from the right side of the clay ball.

7. Observe where the light strikes the ball.

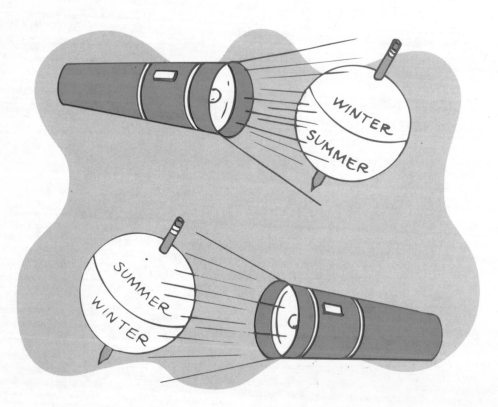

Tilt

Observations and Data

What happens during the experiment? Write down what you observed as well as any measurements or calculations that you made. You may also want to draw sketches or take photos of your experiment.

_____

_____

_____

_____

_____

_____

Results and Conclusions

What was the final result of your experiment? Was it what you expected? Why or why not?

_____

_____

_____

_____

_____

What's Next?

How could you improve on this experiment? Did the results make you think of any other questions that you could investigate with new experiments?

_____

_____

_____

_____

Which Way?

PURPOSE

To determine why the air is cooler in the winter.

Materials

flashlight
1 sheet of dark paper

Procedure

1. In a dark room, hold the flashlight about 6 inches (15 cm) directly above the dark paper.

2. Observe the size and shape of the light pattern formed.

3. Tilt the flashlight and observe the light pattern again.

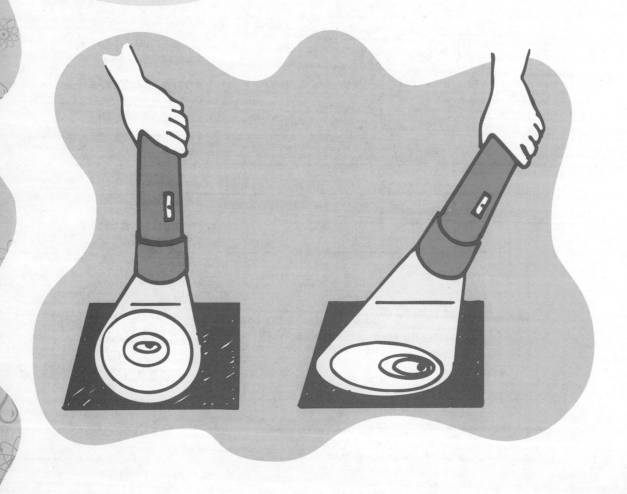

Which Way?

Observations and Data

What happens during the experiment? Write down what you observed as well as any measurements or calculations that you made. You may also want to draw sketches or take photos of your experiment.

_____

_____

_____

_____

_____

_____

Results and Conclusions

What was the final result of your experiment? Was it what you expected? Why or why not?

_____

_____

_____

_____

What's Next?

How could you improve on this experiment? Did the results make you think of any other questions that you could investigate with new experiments?

_____

_____

_____

_____

S-Waves

PURPOSE

To determine how S-waves move through the earth's interior.

Materials

6-foot (2-m) piece of rope

Procedure

1. Tie one end of the rope to a doorknob.
2. Hold the free end of the rope in your hand.
3. Back away from the door until the rope is straight.
4. Gently shake the rope up and down.
5. Gently shake the rope from side to side.

S-Waves

Observations and Data

What happens during the experiment? Write down what you observed as well as any measurements or calculations that you made. You may also want to draw sketches or take photos of your experiment.

_____

_____

_____

_____

_____

_____

Results and Conclusions

What was the final result of your experiment? Was it what you expected? Why or why not?

_____

_____

_____

_____

_____

What's Next?

How could you improve on this experiment? Did the results make you think of any other questions that you could investigate with new experiments?

_____

_____

_____

_____

Clack!

PURPOSE

To determine how earthquake waves (P-waves) are transmitted through the earth.

Materials

scissors
ruler
string
masking tape
5 marbles

Procedure

1. Cut five 12-inch (30-cm) pieces of string.

2. Tape one string to each of the marbles.

3. Tape the free end of each string to the edge of a table. Adjust the position and length of the strings so that the marbles are at the same height and are side by side.

4. Pull one of the end marbles to the side and then release it.

5. Observe any movement of the marbles.

Clack!

Observations and Data

What happens during the experiment? Write down what you observed as well as any measurements or calculations that you made. You may also want to draw sketches or take photos of your experiment.

_____

_____

_____

_____

_____

_____

Results and Conclusions

What was the final result of your experiment? Was it what you expected? Why or why not?

_____

_____

_____

_____

What's Next?

How could you improve on this experiment? Did the results make you think of any other questions that you could investigate with new experiments?

_____

_____

_____

_____

Slower

PURPOSE

To determine why seismic waves move slowly through sand.

Materials

paper towel
paper core from roll of paper towels
uncooked rice
rubber band

Procedure

1. Cover the end of the paper core with one paper towel.

2. Secure the paper towel to the tube with the rubber band.

3. Fill the tube with rice.

4. Use your fingers to push down on the rice. Try to push the rice down and out through the paper towel.

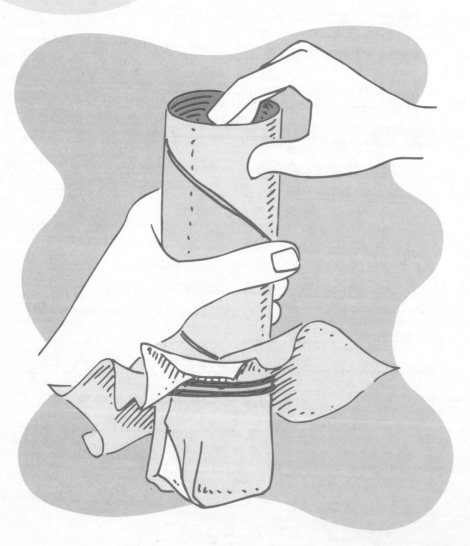

Slower

Observations and Data

What happens during the experiment? Write down what you observed as well as any measurements or calculations that you made. You may also want to draw sketches or take photos of your experiment.

_____

_____

_____

_____

_____

_____

Results and Conclusions

What was the final result of your experiment? Was it what you expected? Why or why not?

_____

_____

_____

_____

_____

What's Next?

How could you improve on this experiment? Did the results make you think of any other questions that you could investigate with new experiments?

_____

_____

_____

_____

Boom!

PURPOSE

To determine what causes thunder.

Materials

9-inch (23-cm) round balloon
glove
straight pin

Procedure

1. Inflate the balloon and make a knot.
2. Lay the inflated balloon on a table.
3. Place the glove on one hand.
4. Hold the pin with the gloved hand.
5. Stand at arm's length from the balloon.
6. Stick the pin into the balloon.

Boom!

Observations and Data

What happens during the experiment? Write down what you observed as well as any measurements or calculations that you made. You may also want to draw sketches or take photos of your experiment.

_____

_____

_____

_____

_____

_____

Results and Conclusions

What was the final result of your experiment? Was it what you expected? Why or why not?

_____

_____

_____

_____

_____

What's Next?

How could you improve on this experiment? Did the results make you think of any other questions that you could investigate with new experiments?

_____

_____

_____

_____

Bang!

PURPOSE

To demonstrate how thunder is produced.

Materials

paper lunch bag

Procedure

1. Fill the bag by blowing into it.

2. Twist the open end and hold it closed with your hand.

3. Quickly and with force hit the bag with your free hand.

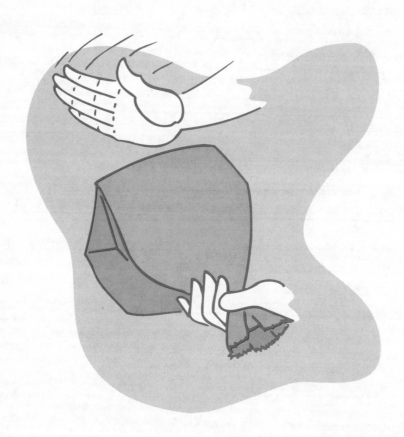

Bang!

Observations and Data

What happens during the experiment? Write down what you observed as well as any measurements or calculations that you made. You may also want to draw sketches or take photos of your experiment.

_____

_____

_____

_____

_____

_____

_____

Results and Conclusions

What was the final result of your experiment? Was it what you expected? Why or why not?

_____

_____

_____

_____

_____

What's Next?

How could you improve on this experiment? Did the results make you think of any other questions that you could investigate with new experiments?

_____

_____

_____

_____

Slosh!

PURPOSE

To determine how the shape of shorelines affects the height of tides.

Materials

square baking pan
pie pan
round baking pan
outdoor water source

Procedure

NOTE: This is an outdoor activity.

1. Fill each container to overflowing with water.

2. Pick up one pan at a time and walk forward with the container held in front of you.

Slosh!

Observations and Data

What happens during the experiment? Write down what you observed as well as any measurements or calculations that you made. You may also want to draw sketches or take photos of your experiment.

_____

_____

_____

_____

_____

_____

Results and Conclusions

What was the final result of your experiment? Was it what you expected? Why or why not?

_____

_____

_____

_____

_____

What's Next?

How could you improve on this experiment? Did the results make you think of any other questions that you could investigate with new experiments?

_____

_____

_____

_____

Tides

PURPOSE

To determine the effect of centrifugal force on tides.

Materials

pencil
7-ounce (210-ml) paper cup
24-inch (60-cm) piece of string
tap water

Procedure

1. Use the pencil to punch 2 holes across from each other beneath the top rim of the paper cup.

2. Tie the ends of the string through each hole in the cup.

3. Fill the cup one-fourth full with water.

4. Take the cup outside.

5. Hold the string and swing the cup around in a horizontal circle above your head several times.

Tides

Observations and Data

What happens during the experiment? Write down what you observed as well as any measurements or calculations that you made. You may also want to draw sketches or take photos of your experiment.

_____

_____

_____

_____

_____

_____

Results and Conclusions

What was the final result of your experiment? Was it what you expected? Why or why not?

_____

_____

_____

_____

_____

What's Next?

How could you improve on this experiment? Did the results make you think of any other questions that you could investigate with new experiments?

_____

_____

_____

_____

Twister

PURPOSE

To demonstrate the shape of a tornado.

Materials

two 2-liter soda bottles

tap water

paper towel

flat metal washer with the same
circumference as the mouth of the bottles

duct tape

adult helper

Procedure

1. Ask an adult to remove the plastic rings left
   on the necks of the bottles when the caps
   are removed.

2. Fill one bottle half full with water.

3. Dry the mouth of the bottle with the paper
   towel and place the washer over the mouth
   of the bottle.

4. Place the second bottle upside down on top
   of the washer.

5. Secure the bottles together with tape.

6. Turn the bottles upside down so that the
   bottle with the water is on top. Stand the
   bottles on a table.

7. Place one hand around the lower bottle and
   the other hand on top of the upper bottle.

8. Support the lower bottle while quickly
   moving the top of the upper bottle in a
   small counterclockwise circle.

9. Stand the bottles upright, with the empty
   bottle remaining on the bottom.

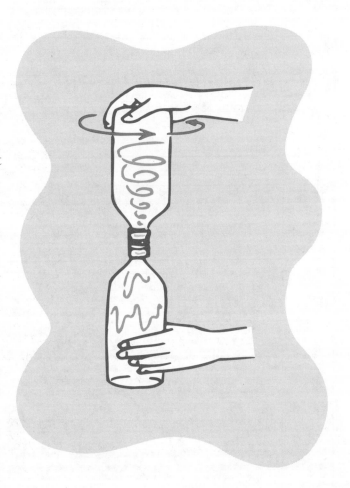

Twister

Observations and Data

What happens during the experiment? Write down what you observed as well as any measurements or calculations that you made. You may also want to draw sketches or take photos of your experiment.

_____

_____

_____

_____

_____

_____

_____

Results and Conclusions

What was the final result of your experiment? Was it what you expected? Why or why not?

_____

_____

_____

_____

_____

What's Next?

How could you improve on this experiment? Did the results make you think of any other questions that you could investigate with new experiments?

_____

_____

_____

_____

Low Pressure

PURPOSE

To demonstrate the formation and effect of low pressure.

Materials

two 9-inch (23-cm) balloons
ruler
sewing thread
cellophane tape
pencil

Procedure

1. Inflate each balloon to the size of an apple and tie a knot.

2. Attach a 12-inch (30-cm) thread to the top of each balloon.

3. Tape the ends of each thread to the pencil so that the balloons hang about 3 inches (7.5 cm) apart.

4. Hold the pencil level with the balloons about 3 inches (7.5 cm) from your face.

5. Direct your exhaled breath between the balloons.

Low Pressure

Observations and Data

What happens during the experiment? Write down what you observed as well as any measurements or calculations that you made. You may also want to draw sketches or take photos of your experiment.

_____

_____

_____

_____

_____

_____

Results and Conclusions

What was the final result of your experiment? Was it what you expected? Why or why not?

_____

_____

_____

_____

_____

What's Next?

How could you improve on this experiment? Did the results make you think of any other questions that you could investigate with new experiments?

_____

_____

_____

_____

Tilting

PURPOSE

To determine how a tiltmeter gives clues to when a volcanic eruption is likely to occur.

Materials

pencil
two 5-ounce (150-ml) paper cups
drinking straw
modeling clay
shallow baking pan
tap water

Procedure

1. Use the pencil to make a hole through the side of each paper cup near the bottom edge. The holes must be small enough so that the straw will fit tightly.

2. Insert about ½ inch (1.25 cm) of one end of the straw into each hole and seal with the clay.

3. Set the pan on a table and place the connected cups in the center of the pan.

4. Fill both cups half full with water.

5. Lift one end of the pan so that it is about 2 inches (5 cm) above the table. Observe the contents of each cup.

Tilting

Observations and Data

What happens during the experiment? Write down what you observed as well as any measurements or calculations that you made. You may also want to draw sketches or take photos of your experiment.

_____

_____

_____

_____

_____

_____

_____

Results and Conclusions

What was the final result of your experiment? Was it what you expected? Why or why not?

_____

_____

_____

_____

_____

What's Next?

How could you improve on this experiment? Did the results make you think of any other questions that you could investigate with new experiments?

_____

_____

_____

_____

Squirt!

PURPOSE

To demonstrate the action of a shield volcano.

Materials

pencil
half-empty tube of toothpaste

Procedure

1. Use the point of a pencil to make a hole in the tube near the cap.

2. Hold the toothpaste tube in your hands.

3. With the cap screwed on tight, push against the tube to force the toothpaste toward the capped end.

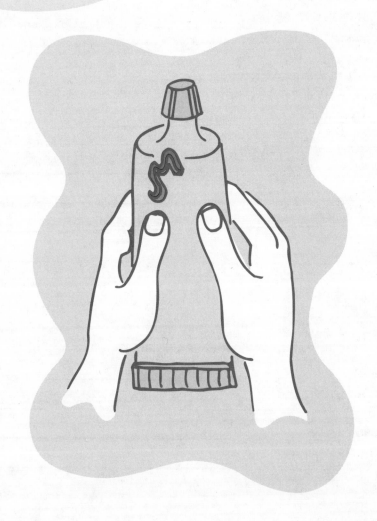

Squirt!

Observations and Data

What happens during the experiment? Write down what you observed as well as any measurements or calculations that you made. You may also want to draw sketches or take photos of your experiment.

_____

_____

_____

_____

_____

_____

Results and Conclusions

What was the final result of your experiment? Was it what you expected? Why or why not?

_____

_____

_____

_____

_____

What's Next?

How could you improve on this experiment? Did the results make you think of any other questions that you could investigate with new experiments?

_____

_____

_____

_____

Erupting Volcano

PURPOSE

To simulate a volcanic eruption.

Materials

soda bottle
baking pan
moist soil
1 tbsp (15 ml) baking soda
1 cup (250 ml) vinegar
red food coloring

Procedure

1. Place the soda bottle in the pan.

2. Shape moist soil around the bottle to form a mountain. Do not cover the bottle's mouth and do not get dirt inside the bottle.

3. Pour 1 tablespoon (15 ml) of baking soda into the bottle.

4. Color 1 cup (250 ml) of vinegar with the red food coloring, and pour the liquid into the bottle.

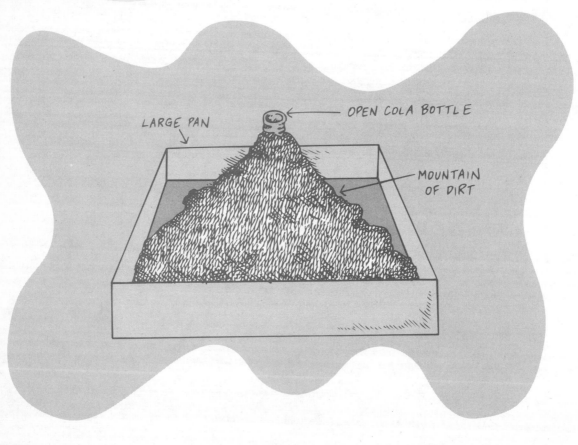

LARGE PAN

OPEN COLA BOTTLE

MOUNTAIN OF DIRT

Erupting Volcano

Observations and Data

What happens during the experiment? Write down what you observed as well as any measurements or calculations that you made. You may also want to draw sketches or take photos of your experiment.

_____

_____

_____

_____

_____

_____

Results and Conclusions

What was the final result of your experiment? Was it what you expected? Why or why not?

_____

_____

_____

_____

What's Next?

How could you improve on this experiment? Did the results make you think of any other questions that you could investigate with new experiments?

_____

_____

_____

_____

Block Out

PURPOSE

To determine how volcanic clouds can lower atmospheric temperature.

Materials

white poster board
ruler
clear plastic report cover
8 paper cups
cardboard, the size of the report cover
2 thermometers
timer

Procedure

1. At midday on a sunny day, lay the poster board on a table outdoors or on the ground.

2. Set the paper cups, upside down, on the poster board. Space them so that one cup sits under each corner of the plastic sheet and cardboard, as shown.

3. Read and record the temperature on both thermometers. Then place one thermometer under each cover.

4. After 15 minutes, read the thermometers again.

Block Out

Observations and Data

What happens during the experiment? Write down what you observed as well as any measurements or calculations that you made. You may also want to draw sketches or take photos of your experiment.

_____

_____

_____

_____

_____

_____

Results and Conclusions

What was the final result of your experiment? Was it what you expected? Why or why not?

_____

_____

_____

_____

_____

What's Next?

How could you improve on this experiment? Did the results make you think of any other questions that you could investigate with new experiments?

_____

_____

_____

_____

Up and Down

PURPOSE

To demonstrate the motion of water waves.

Materials

6-foot (2-m) rope or strong cord

Procedure

1. Tie one end of the rope to a doorknob.

2. Hold the other end of the rope in your hand and stretch the rope between you and the door.

3. Gently move the rope up and down several times.

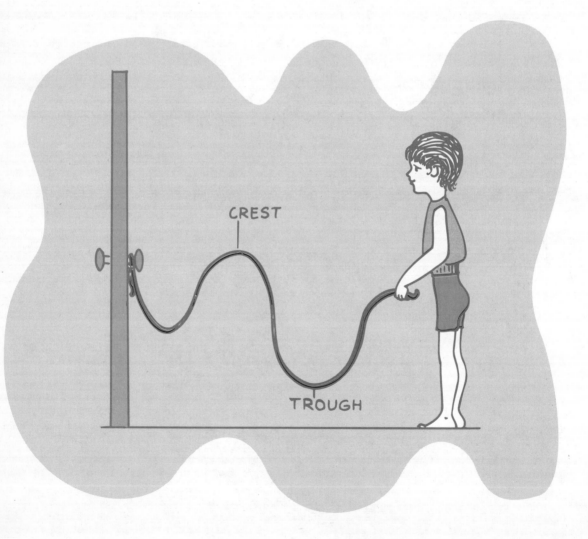

CREST

TROUGH

Up and Down

Observations and Data

What happens during the experiment? Write down what you observed as well as any measurements or calculations that you made. You may also want to draw sketches or take photos of your experiment.

_____

_____

_____

_____

_____

_____

_____

Results and Conclusions

What was the final result of your experiment? Was it what you expected? Why or why not?

_____

_____

_____

_____

What's Next?

How could you improve on this experiment? Did the results make you think of any other questions that you could investigate with new experiments?

_____

_____

_____

_____

Bump!

PURPOSE

To demonstrate the forward movement of wave energy.

Materials

book
6 marbles

Procedure

1. Lay the book on a flat surface such as a table or the floor.

2. Open the book and place 5 of the marbles in the book's groove. Push the marbles tightly together and position the group in the center of the book.

3. Place the free marble about 1 in. (3 cm) from the group of marbles, and thump it with your finger so that it moves forward and bumps into the end marble of the group.

Bump!

Observations and Data

What happens during the experiment? Write down what you observed as well as any measurements or calculations that you made. You may also want to draw sketches or take photos of your experiment.

_____

_____

_____

_____

_____

_____

Results and Conclusions

What was the final result of your experiment? Was it what you expected? Why or why not?

_____

_____

_____

_____

_____

What's Next?

How could you improve on this experiment? Did the results make you think of any other questions that you could investigate with new experiments?

_____

_____

_____

_____

Break Down

PURPOSE

To demonstrate how water, with and without sediment in it, wears away a solid.

Materials

3 tablespoons (45 ml) dirt
small glass bowl
spoon
white school glue
paper towel
2 plastic bowls of equal size with lids
tap water
1 teaspoon (5 ml) aquarium gravel

Procedure

1. Place the dirt in the bowl.

2. Stir in enough glue to make a stiff mixture.

3. Shape the mixture into two balls of equal size.

4. Wipe the glass bowl clean with a paper towel and place the balls of dirt inside the bowl.

5. Place the glass bowl in a sunny area and allow the dirt balls to harden for several days.

6. Fill each plastic bowl half full with water.

7. Add the gravel to one of the plastic bowls.

8. Place one dirt ball in each bowl and secure the lid.

9. Shake each bowl vigorously 10 times.

10. Open the lids and observe the shape of each dirt ball.

11. Close the lid. Shake and observe three more times.

Break Down

Observations and Data

What happens during the experiment? Write down what you observed as well as any measurements or calculations that you made. You may also want to draw sketches or take photos of your experiment.

_____

_____

_____

_____

_____

_____

Results and Conclusions

What was the final result of your experiment? Was it what you expected? Why or why not?

_____

_____

_____

_____

What's Next?

How could you improve on this experiment? Did the results make you think of any other questions that you could investigate with new experiments?

_____

_____

_____

_____

Splitter

PURPOSE

To determine how ice can split rocks.

Materials

small plastic bowl with a tight-fitting lid
cold tap water

Procedure

1. Fill the plastic bowl to overflowing with water.
2. Secure the lid.
3. Place the closed container in the freezer.
4. After 24 hours, remove the bowl.

Splitter

Observations and Data

What happens during the experiment? Write down what you observed as well as any measurements or calculations that you made. You may also want to draw sketches or take photos of your experiment.

_____

_____

_____

_____

_____

_____

_____

Results and Conclusions

What was the final result of your experiment? Was it what you expected? Why or why not?

_____

_____

_____

_____

_____

What's Next?

How could you improve on this experiment? Did the results make you think of any other questions that you could investigate with new experiments?

_____

_____

_____

_____

PHYSICS

Upward

PURPOSE

To determine why the shape of an airplane's wing is important for flight.

Materials

scissors

ruler

typing paper

Procedure

1. Cut a 2-inch × 10-inch (5-cm × 25-cm) strip from the paper.

2. Hold one end of the paper against your chin, just below your bottom lip.

3. Blow just above the top of the paper.

4. Observe the movement of the paper strip.

Upward

Observations and Data

What happens during the experiment? Write down what you observed as well as any measurements or calculations that you made. You may also want to draw sketches or take photos of your experiment.

_____

_____

_____

_____

_____

_____

_____

Results and Conclusions

What was the final result of your experiment? Was it what you expected? Why or why not?

_____

_____

_____

_____

_____

What's Next?

How could you improve on this experiment? Did the results make you think of any other questions that you could investigate with new experiments?

_____

_____

_____

_____

Paper Flop

PURPOSE

To demonstrate the effect of speed on air pressure.

Materials

2 books of equal size
ruler
1 sheet of notebook paper
1 drinking straw

Procedure

1. Position the books 4 in. (10 cm) apart on a table.

2. Lay the sheet of paper across the space between the books.

3. Place the end of the straw just under the edge of the paper.

4. Blow as hard as you can through the straw.

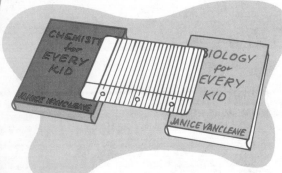

Paper Flop

Observations and Data

What happens during the experiment? Write down what you observed as well as any measurements or calculations that you made. You may also want to draw sketches or take photos of your experiment.

_____

_____

_____

_____

_____

_____

Results and Conclusions

What was the final result of your experiment? Was it what you expected? Why or why not?

_____

_____

_____

_____

_____

What's Next?

How could you improve on this experiment? Did the results make you think of any other questions that you could investigate with new experiments?

_____

_____

_____

_____

Divers

PURPOSE

To determine how the buoyancy of ocean diving vessels changes.

Materials

drinking glass
seltzer or club soda
raisins

Procedure

1. Fill the drinking glass ¾ full with seltzer.

2. Immediately add 5 raisins to the glass, one at a time.

3. Wait and watch.

Divers

Observations and Data

What happens during the experiment? Write down what you observed as well as any measurements or calculations that you made. You may also want to draw sketches or take photos of your experiment.

_____

_____

_____

_____

_____

_____

Results and Conclusions

What was the final result of your experiment? Was it what you expected? Why or why not?

_____

_____

_____

_____

_____

What's Next?

How could you improve on this experiment? Did the results make you think of any other questions that you could investigate with new experiments?

_____

_____

_____

_____

Floating Boat

PURPOSE

To determine how a heavy ship floats.

Materials

scissors
ruler
aluminum foil
20 paper clips
small bucket
tap water

Procedure

1. Cut two 12-inch (30-cm) squares from the aluminum foil.

2. Wrap one of the metal squares around 10 paper clips and squeeze the foil into a tight ball.

3. Fold the four edges of the second aluminum square up to make a small boat.

4. Place 10 paper clips in the boat.

5. Fill the bucket with water.

6. Set the boat on the water's surface in the bucket.

7. Place the metal ball on the water's surface.

Floating Boat

Observations and Data

What happens during the experiment? Write down what you observed as well as any measurements or calculations that you made. You may also want to draw sketches or take photos of your experiment.

_____

_____

_____

_____

_____

_____

Results and Conclusions

What was the final result of your experiment? Was it what you expected? Why or why not?

_____

_____

_____

_____

_____

What's Next?

How could you improve on this experiment? Did the results make you think of any other questions that you could investigate with new experiments?

_____

_____

_____

_____

Up Hill

PURPOSE

To determine the effect that an object's center of gravity has on motion.

Materials

2 yardsticks (meter sticks)
3 books, each at least 1 in. (2.5 cm) thick
masking tape
2 funnels of equal size

Procedure

1. Put two books 30 in. (90 cm) apart on the floor.

2. Place the remaining book on top of one of the other books.

3. Position the yardsticks on top of the books to form a V shape with the open part of the letter on the double book stack.

4. Tape the bowls of the funnels together.

5. Place the joined funnels at the bottom of the track formed by the yardsticks.

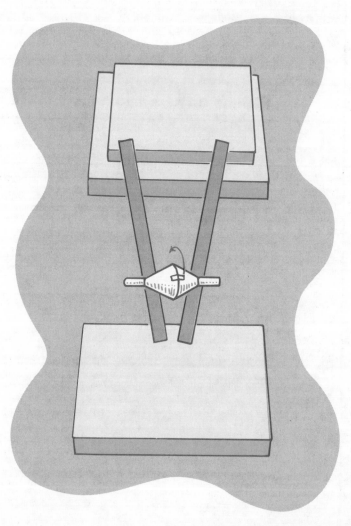

Up Hill

Observations and Data

What happens during the experiment? Write down what you observed as well as any measurements or calculations that you made. You may also want to draw sketches or take photos of your experiment.

_____

_____

_____

_____

_____

_____

_____

Results and Conclusions

What was the final result of your experiment? Was it what you expected? Why or why not?

_____

_____

_____

_____

What's Next?

How could you improve on this experiment? Did the results make you think of any other questions that you could investigate with new experiments?

_____

_____

_____

_____

Over the Edge

PURPOSE

To demonstrate that the center of gravity is the balancing point of an object.

Materials

string, 12 in. (30 cm)

yardstick (meter stick)

hammer (wooden-handled hammer works best)

Procedure

1. Hold the ends of the string together and tie a knot about 2 in. (5 cm) from the ends.

2. Insert the hammer and yardstick through the loop.

3. Position the end of the yardstick on a table's edge.

4. The handle of the hammer must touch the yardstick and the head of the hammer will extend under the table.

5. Change the position of the hammer until the whole unit—yardstick, string, and hammer—balances.

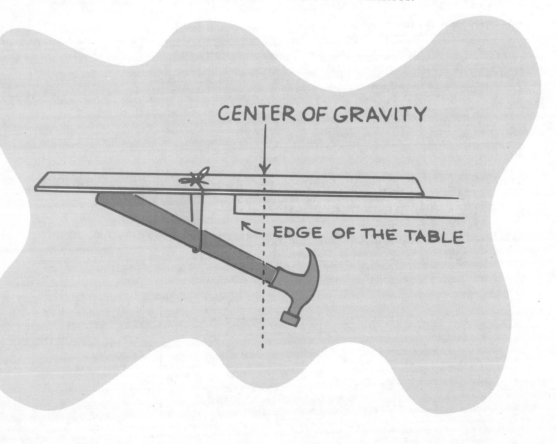

CENTER OF GRAVITY

EDGE OF THE TABLE

Over the Edge

Observations and Data

What happens during the experiment? Write down what you observed as well as any measurements or calculations that you made. You may also want to draw sketches or take photos of your experiment.

_____

_____

_____

_____

_____

_____

Results and Conclusions

What was the final result of your experiment? Was it what you expected? Why or why not?

_____

_____

_____

_____

_____

What's Next?

How could you improve on this experiment? Did the results make you think of any other questions that you could investigate with new experiments?

_____

_____

_____

_____

Balancing Point

PURPOSE

To locate an object's center of gravity.

Materials

scissors
manilla folder
paper hole punch
12-inch (30-cm) piece of string
washer
push pin
tackboard
ruler
pen

Procedure

1. Cut one side of the manilla folder into an irregular shape.

2. Punch five randomly spaced holes in the edge of the paper with the paper hole punch.

3. Tie one end of the string to the washer and the other end to the push pin.

4. Stick the push pin through one of the holes in the paper and into the tackboard.

5. Allow the paper and string to swing freely.

6. Use the ruler and pen to mark a line on the paper next to the string.

7. Move the push pin to the other holes and mark the position of the hanging string each time. Do this for the remaining four holes.

8. Place the paper on the end of your index finger. Your finger is to be below the point where the lines cross.

Balancing Point

Observations and Data

What happens during the experiment? Write down what you observed as well as any measurements or calculations that you made. You may also want to draw sketches or take photos of your experiment.

_____

_____

_____

_____

_____

_____

Results and Conclusions

What was the final result of your experiment? Was it what you expected? Why or why not?

_____

_____

_____

_____

_____

What's Next?

How could you improve on this experiment? Did the results make you think of any other questions that you could investigate with new experiments?

_____

_____

_____

_____

Flashlight

PURPOSE

To determine how a flashlight works.

Materials

flashlight that holds 2 size D batteries
16-inch (40-cm) aluminum foil strip
duct tape
2 size D batteries

Procedure

1. Unscrew the top section (which holds the bulb) from the flashlight.

2. Wrap one end of the foil strip around the base of the bulb holder.

3. Tape the two batteries together with the positive terminal of one touching the negative terminal of the other.

4. Stand the flat, negative terminal of the battery column on the free end of the foil strip.

5. Press the metal tip at the bottom of the flashlight bulb against the positive terminal of the battery, as shown in the diagram.

Flashlight

Observations and Data

What happens during the experiment? Write down what you observed as well as any measurements or calculations that you made. You may also want to draw sketches or take photos of your experiment.

_____

_____

_____

_____

_____

_____

Results and Conclusions

What was the final result of your experiment? Was it what you expected? Why or why not?

_____

_____

_____

_____

What's Next?

How could you improve on this experiment? Did the results make you think of any other questions that you could investigate with new experiments?

_____

_____

_____

_____

Galvanometer

PURPOSE

To construct a galvanometer.

Materials

inexpensive compass
cardboard box to fit the compass
thin, insulated wire, 22 gauge
D cell battery
adult helper

Procedure

1. Construct a galvanometer by following these steps. Place the compass in the box.

2. Wind the wire around the box, about 50 times, leaving about 12 inches (30 cm) free on both ends.

3. Ask an adult helper to scrape about 2 inches (10 cm) of the insulation from the ends of the wires.

4. Turn the galvanometer so that the compass needle and wire wrapped around the box both point in a north-to-south direction.

5. Touch one end of the wire to the top of the battery and the other end of the wire to the bottom.

6. Watch the compass needle as you hold one wire against the end of the battery and alternately touch the other wire to the battery and remove it several times.

7. Disconnect the wires from the battery and keep the galvanometer for Experiment 190.

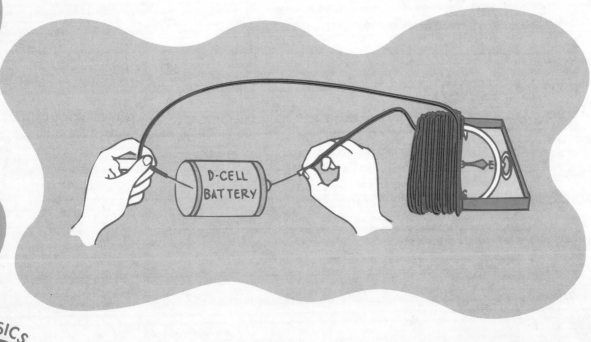

Galvanometer

Observations and Data

What happens during the experiment? Write down what you observed as well as any measurements or calculations that you made. You may also want to draw sketches or take photos of your experiment.

_____

_____

_____

_____

_____

_____

Results and Conclusions

What was the final result of your experiment? Was it what you expected? Why or why not?

_____

_____

_____

_____

_____

What's Next?

How could you improve on this experiment? Did the results make you think of any other questions that you could investigate with new experiments?

_____

_____

_____

_____

Battery

PURPOSE

To produce an electric current.

Materials

aluminum-foil baking cup
tap water
2 teaspoons (10 ml) of table salt
galvanometer (from Experiment 189)
paper clip
metal washer

Procedure

1. Fill the aluminum-foil baking cup ¾ full with water.

2. Add the salt to the water and stir.

3. Connect one end of the wire to the cup with a paper clip.

4. Turn the galvanometer so that the compass needle is parallel with the wire wrapped around the box.

5. Press the other end of the wire against the washer and dip it into the salt solution close to, but not touching, the paper clip.

6. Alternately dip and raise the washer from the solution as you watch the compass needle.

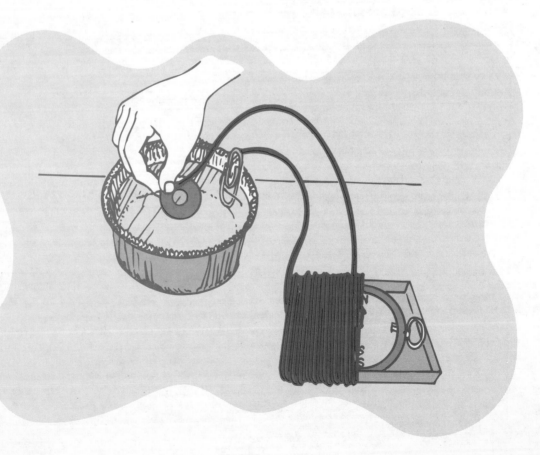

Battery

Observations and Data

What happens during the experiment? Write down what you observed as well as any measurements or calculations that you made. You may also want to draw sketches or take photos of your experiment.

_____

_____

_____

_____

_____

_____

Results and Conclusions

What was the final result of your experiment? Was it what you expected? Why or why not?

_____

_____

_____

_____

What's Next?

How could you improve on this experiment? Did the results make you think of any other questions that you could investigate with new experiments?

_____

_____

_____

_____

Electromagnet

PURPOSE

To demonstrate that an electric current produces a magnetic field.

Materials

wire, 18-gauge, insulated, 1 yd. (1 m)
long iron nail
paper clips
6-volt battery
adult helper

Procedure

1. Wrap the wire tightly around the nail, leaving about 6 in. (15 cm) of free wire on each end.

2. Have an adult strip the insulation off both ends of the wire.

3. Secure one end of the wire to one pole of the battery.

4. Touch the free end of the wire to the other battery pole while touching the nail to a pile of paper clips.

5. Lift the nail while keeping the ends of the wire on the battery pole.

6. When the nail starts to feel warm, disconnect the wire end you are holding against the battery pole.

Electromagnet

Observations and Data

What happens during the experiment? Write down what you observed as well as any measurements or calculations that you made. You may also want to draw sketches or take photos of your experiment.

_____

_____

_____

_____

_____

_____

Results and Conclusions

What was the final result of your experiment? Was it what you expected? Why or why not?

_____

_____

_____

_____

_____

What's Next?

How could you improve on this experiment? Did the results make you think of any other questions that you could investigate with new experiments?

_____

_____

_____

_____

Line Up

PURPOSE

To demonstrate how electricity and magnetism are related.

Materials

long iron nail

piece of cardboard, 6 inches (15 cm) square

1 yard (1 m) 18-gauge insulated wire

roll of masking tape

6-volt battery

iron filings (purchase at
a teacher-supply store)

adult helper

Procedure

1. Ask an adult to use the nail to punch a hole through the center of the cardboard.

2. Wrap the wire tightly around the nail, leaving about 6 inches (15 cm) of free wire on each end.

3. Ask your helper to strip the insulation off both ends of the wire and to insert the wire-wrapped nail through the hole in the cardboard.

4. Make the cardboard sit flat by placing it on the roll of the tape. Then attach one end of the wire to either battery terminal.

5. Sprinkle a thin layer of iron filings on the cardboard around the coiled wire.

6. Attach the free wire to the open battery terminal.

7. Observe the pattern made by the iron filings.

CAUTION: The nail and wires will get hot if left connected to the battery. Be sure to interrupt the circuit by disconnecting one wire from one pole.

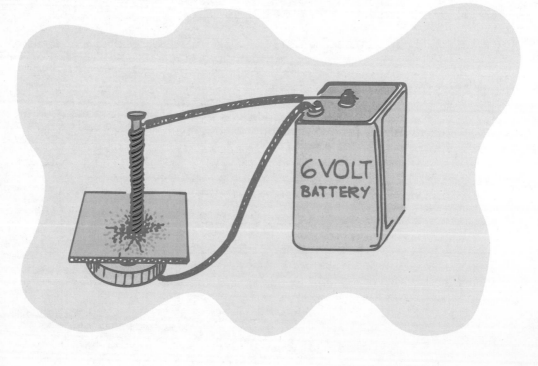

Line Up

Observations and Data

What happens during the experiment? Write down what you observed as well as any measurements or calculations that you made. You may also want to draw sketches or take photos of your experiment.

_____

_____

_____

_____

_____

_____

Results and Conclusions

What was the final result of your experiment? Was it what you expected? Why or why not?

_____

_____

_____

_____

What's Next?

How could you improve on this experiment? Did the results make you think of any other questions that you could investigate with new experiments?

_____

_____

_____

Moving On

PURPOSE

To demonstrate how friction affects inertia.

Materials

shoe box
scissors
adult helper
ruler
10 round marking pens
balloon, 9 in. (20 cm)
table

Procedure

1. Ask an adult to cut a hole about ½ inch (1 cm) square in the center of the end of a shoe box.

2. Lay the balloon inside the box with its mouth sticking out through the square hole in the end of the box.

3. Inflate the balloon and hold the mouth of the balloon shut between your fingers.

4. Place 10 round marking pens under the bottom of the shoe box on a table.

5. Release the balloon.

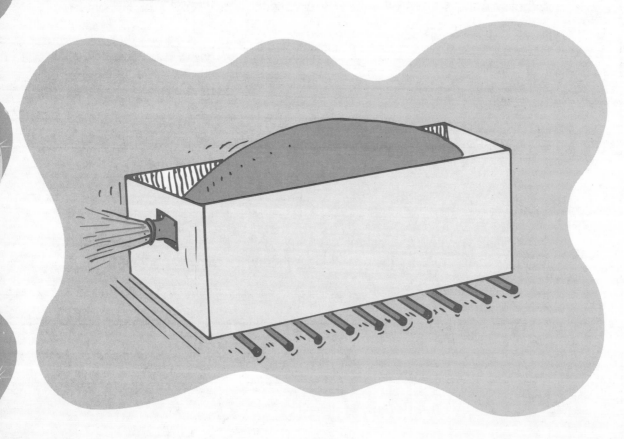

193

Moving On

Observations and Data

What happens during the experiment? Write down what you observed as well as any measurements or calculations that you made. You may also want to draw sketches or take photos of your experiment.

_____

_____

_____

_____

_____

_____

Results and Conclusions

What was the final result of your experiment? Was it what you expected? Why or why not?

_____

_____

_____

_____

What's Next?

How could you improve on this experiment? Did the results make you think of any other questions that you could investigate with new experiments?

_____

_____

_____

_____

Air Car

PURPOSE

To demonstrate how friction affects motion.

Materials

scissors
ruler
cardboard
empty thread spool
glue
notebook paper
9-inch (23-cm) balloon
pencil
adult helper

Procedure

1. Cut a 4-inch (10-cm) square from the cardboard.

2. Ask an adult to punch a hole equal in size to the hole in the thread spool through the center of the cardboard square.

3. Glue the empty thread spool over the hole in the cardboard. Be sure the hole in the spool lines up with the hole in the cardboard.

4. Place a bead of glue around the base of the spool.

5. Cut and glue a circle of paper over the top end of the thread spool. Allow the glue to dry for several hours.

6. Use a pencil to punch a hole in the paper circle to line up with the hole in the spool.

7. Inflate the balloon and twist the end.

8. Stretch the mouth of the balloon over the top of the spool.

9. Untwist the balloon and give the cardboard a little push. Observe its motion.

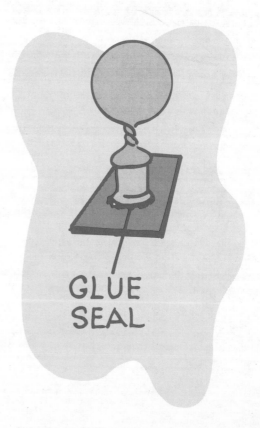

GLUE SEAL

Air Car

Observations and Data

What happens during the experiment? Write down what you observed as well as any measurements or calculations that you made. You may also want to draw sketches or take photos of your experiment.

_____

_____

_____

_____

_____

_____

Results and Conclusions

What was the final result of your experiment? Was it what you expected? Why or why not?

_____

_____

_____

_____

What's Next?

How could you improve on this experiment? Did the results make you think of any other questions that you could investigate with new experiments?

_____

_____

_____

_____

Roller

PURPOSE

To determine how different surfaces affect friction.

Materials

2 books
24-inch (60-cm) string
rubber band
ruler
10 round marking pens

Procedure

1. Stack the books on a table.

2. Tie the string around the bottom book.

3. Attach the string to the rubber band.

4. Move the stack of books by pulling on the rubber band.

5. Measure how far the rubber band stretches.

6. Place the 10 marking pens under the stack of books.

7. Move the books by pulling on the rubber band.

8. Observe how far the rubber band stretches.

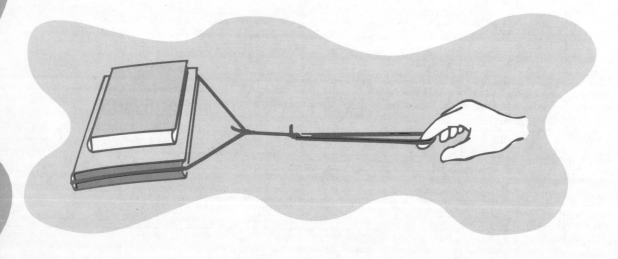

Roller

Observations and Data

What happens during the experiment? Write down what you observed as well as any measurements or calculations that you made. You may also want to draw sketches or take photos of your experiment.

_____

_____

_____

_____

_____

_____

Results and Conclusions

What was the final result of your experiment? Was it what you expected? Why or why not?

_____

_____

_____

_____

_____

What's Next?

How could you improve on this experiment? Did the results make you think of any other questions that you could investigate with new experiments?

_____

_____

_____

_____

Energy Change

PURPOSE

To demonstrate the effect that height has on the energy of a moving object.

Materials

scissors

8-ounce (236-ml) paper cup

ruler with a center groove

pencil

marble

book

Procedure

1. Cut a 1½-inch (3.75-cm) square section from the top of the paper cup.

2. Place the cup over the ruler. The end of the ruler should touch the back edge of the cup.

3. Raise the opposite end of the ruler and rest it on the pencil.

4. Place the marble in the center groove of the ruler at the ruler's highest end.

5. Release the marble and observe the cup.

6. Raise the end of the ruler and rest it on the edge of the book.

7. Again, position the marble in the groove at the ruler's highest end.

8. Release the marble and observe the cup.

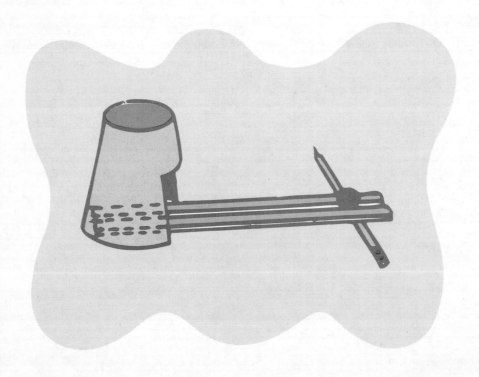

Energy Change

Observations and Data

What happens during the experiment? Write down what you observed as well as any measurements or calculations that you made. You may also want to draw sketches or take photos of your experiment.

_____

_____

_____

_____

_____

_____

Results and Conclusions

What was the final result of your experiment? Was it what you expected? Why or why not?

_____

_____

_____

_____

_____

What's Next?

How could you improve on this experiment? Did the results make you think of any other questions that you could investigate with new experiments?

_____

_____

_____

_____

Bonk!

PURPOSE

To determine how energy can change its form.

Materials

scissors
ruler
string
book
duct tape
2 small rubber balls of equal size

Procedure

1. Cut a 24-inch (60-cm) piece of string.

2. Insert one end of the ruler into a book.

3. Lay the book on the edge of a table so the ruler sticks over the edge of the table.

4. Tie the center of the string around the end of the ruler.

5. Use very small pieces of tape to attach the hanging ends of the string to the balls. The tape sticks best if the balls are clean and oil-free.

6. The strings on the balls must be the same length.

7. Pull the balls away from each other and release them.

Bonk!

Observations and Data

What happens during the experiment? Write down what you observed as well as any measurements or calculations that you made. You may also want to draw sketches or take photos of your experiment.

_____

_____

_____

_____

_____

_____

Results and Conclusions

What was the final result of your experiment? Was it what you expected? Why or why not?

_____

_____

_____

_____

_____

What's Next?

How could you improve on this experiment? Did the results make you think of any other questions that you could investigate with new experiments?

_____

_____

_____

_____

Hanging Bubbles

PURPOSE

To discover how gravity affects the shape of soap bubbles.

Materials

small bowl
¼ cup (60 ml) dishwashing liquid
¼ cup (60 ml) water
1 teaspoon (5 ml) sugar
spoon
large empty thread spool

Procedure

1. Place the bowl on a table outdoors. Add the dishwashing liquid, water, and sugar to the bowl.

2. Dip one end of the spool into the mixture.

3. Place your mouth against the dry end of the spool, and gently blow through the hole in the spool.

4. Blow a large bubble, but do not allow it to break free from the spool. Then, place your finger over the hole you blew through to prevent the air from leaking out of the soap bubble, as shown.

5. Study the bubble's shape.

Hanging Bubbles

Observations and Data

What happens during the experiment? Write down what you observed as well as any measurements or calculations that you made. You may also want to draw sketches or take photos of your experiment.

_____
_____
_____
_____
_____
_____

Results and Conclusions

What was the final result of your experiment? Was it what you expected? Why or why not?

_____
_____
_____
_____

What's Next?

How could you improve on this experiment? Did the results make you think of any other questions that you could investigate with new experiments?

_____
_____
_____
_____

Toys and Gravity

PURPOSE

To determine how gravity affects playing paddleball.

Materials

paddleball toy

Procedure

1. Hold the paddle in one hand and the ball in the other hand.

2. Pull the ball straight out horizontally from the paddle as far as your outstretched arms or the elastic will allow.

3. Release the ball.

4. Observe the path of the returning ball.

5. Again, pull the ball straight out from the paddle as far as your outstretched arms or the elastic will allow. Raise the ball about 1 foot (30 cm) from its horizontal position.

6. Release the ball and observe its path.

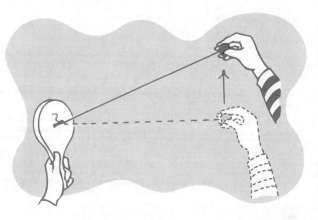

7. Continue to change the position of the ball until its returning path directs it to the center of the paddle.

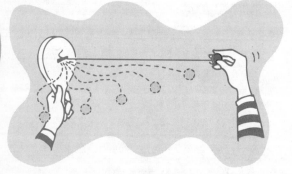

Toys and Gravity

Observations and Data

What happens during the experiment? Write down what you observed as well as any measurements or calculations that you made. You may also want to draw sketches or take photos of your experiment.

_____

_____

_____

_____

_____

_____

Results and Conclusions

What was the final result of your experiment? Was it what you expected? Why or why not?

_____

_____

_____

_____

_____

What's Next?

How could you improve on this experiment? Did the results make you think of any other questions that you could investigate with new experiments?

_____

_____

_____

_____

Snap!

PURPOSE

To demonstrate that an object remains stationary due to inertia.

Materials

scissors

ruler

typing paper

unopened can of soda

Procedure

1. Cut a 4-inch × 10-inch (10-cm × 25-cm) strip of paper.

2. Lay the paper strip on a clean, dry table.

3. Place the soda can over one end of the paper.

   NOTE: Be sure that the bottom of the can is clean and dry.

4. Hold the other end of the paper and push it close to the can.

5. Quickly snap the paper away from the can in a straight line.

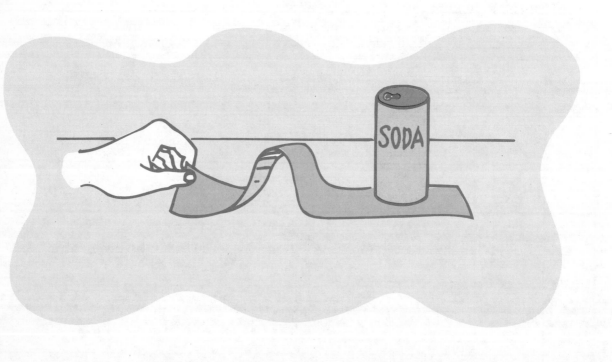

Snap!

Observations and Data

What happens during the experiment? Write down what you observed as well as any measurements or calculations that you made. You may also want to draw sketches or take photos of your experiment.

_____

_____

_____

_____

_____

_____

_____

Results and Conclusions

What was the final result of your experiment? Was it what you expected? Why or why not?

_____

_____

_____

_____

_____

What's Next?

How could you improve on this experiment? Did the results make you think of any other questions that you could investigate with new experiments?

_____

_____

_____

_____

Crash!

PURPOSE

To demonstrate that moving objects have inertia.

Materials

1 ruler
1 book, about 1 inch (2.5 cm) thick
masking tape
pencil
piece of modeling clay, size of a walnut
small toy car that can roll on the ruler

Procedure

1. Raise one end of the ruler and place it on the edge of the book.

2. Tape the other end of the ruler to a table.

3. Tape the pencil perpendicular to, and about 2 toy car lengths from, the end of the ruler.

4. Make a clay figure similar to a snowman.

5. Flatten the bottom of the clay figure and gently rest it on the hood of the toy car. You want the clay figure to fall off the car easily, so do not press the clay against the car.

6. Position the car with its clay figure at the top of the raised ruler.

7. Release the car and allow it to roll down the ruler and collide into the pencil.

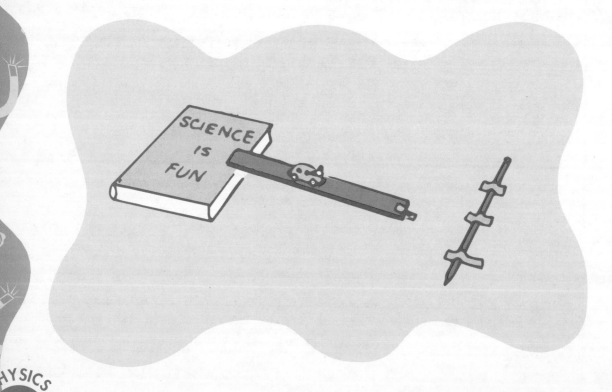

Crash!

Observations and Data

What happens during the experiment? Write down what you observed as well as any measurements or calculations that you made. You may also want to draw sketches or take photos of your experiment.

_____

_____

_____

_____

_____

_____

Results and Conclusions

What was the final result of your experiment? Was it what you expected? Why or why not?

_____

_____

_____

_____

What's Next?

How could you improve on this experiment? Did the results make you think of any other questions that you could investigate with new experiments?

_____

_____

_____

_____

Spool Racer

PURPOSE

To demonstrate the transformation of energy.

Materials

rubber band (slightly longer
than a thread spool)

empty thread spool

2 round toothpicks

masking tape

metal washer (diameter must be
smaller than that of the spool)

Procedure

1. Insert the rubber band through the hole in the spool.

2. Put one toothpick through the loop formed by the rubber band at one end of the spool.

3. Center the toothpick on the end of the spool, and secure the toothpick to the spool with tape.

4. At the other end of the spool, thread the rubber band through the hole in the washer.

5. Put the second toothpick through the loop in the rubber band. Do not attach it to the spool.

6. Hold the spool steady with one hand, and with the index finger of your other hand turn the unattached toothpick around and around in a clockwise direction to wind the rubber band tightly.

7. Place the spool on a flat, smooth surface such as the floor, and let go.

8. Observe the movement of the spool, rubber band, and toothpicks.

Spool Racer

Observations and Data

What happens during the experiment? Write down what you observed as well as any measurements or calculations that you made. You may also want to draw sketches or take photos of your experiment.

_____

_____

_____

_____

_____

_____

Results and Conclusions

What was the final result of your experiment? Was it what you expected? Why or why not?

_____

_____

_____

_____

_____

What's Next?

How could you improve on this experiment? Did the results make you think of any other questions that you could investigate with new experiments?

_____

_____

_____

_____

Straight

PURPOSE

To demonstrate that light travels in a straight line.

Materials

scissors
ruler
cardboard
modeling clay
flashlight
index card

Procedure

1. Cut three 6-inch (15-cm) squares from the cardboard.

2. Cut 1-inch (2.5-cm) square notches from the center of one edge of each of the three cardboard squares.

3. Use the clay to position the square about 4 inches (10 cm) apart with the notches aligned in a straight line.

4. Lay the flashlight behind the column of cards.

5. Use clay to position the index card like a screen at the other end of the column.

6. Darken the room and observe any light pattern on the paper screen.

7. Move the cardboard so that the notches are not in a straight line.

8. Observe any light pattern on the paper screen.

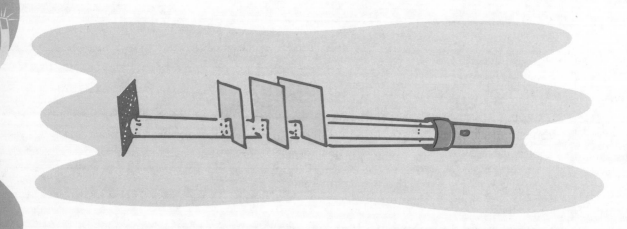

Straight

Observations and Data

What happens during the experiment? Write down what you observed as well as any measurements or calculations that you made. You may also want to draw sketches or take photos of your experiment.

_____

_____

_____

_____

_____

_____

Results and Conclusions

What was the final result of your experiment? Was it what you expected? Why or why not?

_____

_____

_____

_____

_____

What's Next?

How could you improve on this experiment? Did the results make you think of any other questions that you could investigate with new experiments?

_____

_____

_____

_____

Starburst

PURPOSE

To demonstrate how a diffraction grating affects light.

Materials

lamp
cotton handkerchief

Procedure

1. Remove the shade from the lamp.

2. Stand about 6 feet (2 m) from the glowing bulb.

3. Hold the handkerchief at eye level and stretch it with both hands.

4. Look at the light through the stretched cloth.

Starburst

Observations and Data

What happens during the experiment? Write down what you observed as well as any measurements or calculations that you made. You may also want to draw sketches or take photos of your experiment.

_____

_____

_____

_____

_____

_____

_____

Results and Conclusions

What was the final result of your experiment? Was it what you expected? Why or why not?

_____

_____

_____

_____

_____

What's Next?

How could you improve on this experiment? Did the results make you think of any other questions that you could investigate with new experiments?

_____

_____

_____

_____

Belted

PURPOSE

To make a model of belted wheels.

Materials

hammer
large 8-penny nail
2 metal jar lids of equal size
wooden board, 2 by 4 by 12 inches
(5 by 10 by 30 cm)
ruler
2 small 6-penny nails
rubber band
marking pen
adult helper

Procedure

1. Ask an adult to use the hammer and nail to make a hole in the center of each lid.

2. Ask your adult helper to attach the lids to the board with the nails, as shown, leaving enough space between the lids and the heads of the nails so that the lids turn easily.

3. Connect the two lids by stretching the rubber band around the outer rims of both lids.

4. Use the marking pen to mark lines on the tops of the lids directly across from each other.

5. Use your hand to turn one lid clockwise so that it makes one complete turn. Observe the marks.

Belted

Observations and Data

What happens during the experiment? Write down what you observed as well as any measurements or calculations that you made. You may also want to draw sketches or take photos of your experiment.

_____

_____

_____

_____

_____

_____

Results and Conclusions

What was the final result of your experiment? Was it what you expected? Why or why not?

_____

_____

_____

_____

_____

What's Next?

How could you improve on this experiment? Did the results make you think of any other questions that you could investigate with new experiments?

_____

_____

_____

_____

Flag Raiser

PURPOSE

To determine what a fixed pulley is, and how it makes work easier.

Materials

pencil (must be small enough to slide through the hole in the thread spool)

large, empty thread spool

6-foot (2-m) piece of string

blue and red crayons

index card

masking tape

helper

Procedure

1. Place the pencil through the hole in the spool. The spool must turn easily on the pencil.

2. Tie the ends of the string together.

3. Draw and color a flag on the index card.

4. Tape the side with the flag to the string.

5. Place the loop of string over the spool, with the flag hanging at the bottom of the loop.

6. Ask your helper to hold the ends of the pencil, one in each hand, at arm's length over his or her head.

7. Pull down on the string opposite the flag.

8. Observe the distance the string is pulled down and the distance and direction the flag moves.

Flag Raiser

Observations and Data

What happens during the experiment? Write down what you observed as well as any measurements or calculations that you made. You may also want to draw sketches or take photos of your experiment.

_____

_____

_____

_____

_____

_____

Results and Conclusions

What was the final result of your experiment? Was it what you expected? Why or why not?

_____

_____

_____

_____

_____

What's Next?

How could you improve on this experiment? Did the results make you think of any other questions that you could investigate with new experiments?

_____

_____

_____

_____

Threads

PURPOSE

To determine how a screw is like an inclined plane.

Materials

pencil
ruler
sheet of typing paper
scissors
marking pen
transparent tape

Procedure

1. Draw a right triangle with a base of 4 inches (10 cm) and a height of 6 inches (15 cm) on the paper.

2. Cut out the triangle.

3. Color the diagonal edge of the paper triangle with the marking pen.

4. Tape the triangle to the pencil with the colored edge facing up, as shown in the diagram.

5. Rotate the pencil to wrap the paper tightly around the pencil.

6. Tape the end of the wrapped paper to itself.

7. Count the number of diagonal stripes made by the colored edge of the triangle that is wrapped around the pencil.

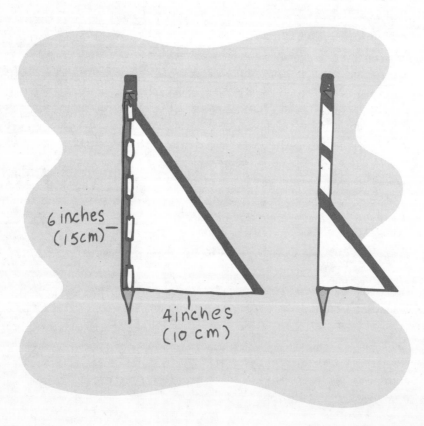

6 inches (15cm)

4 inches (10 cm)

Threads

Observations and Data

What happens during the experiment? Write down what you observed as well as any measurements or calculations that you made. You may also want to draw sketches or take photos of your experiment.

_____

_____

_____

_____

_____

_____

Results and Conclusions

What was the final result of your experiment? Was it what you expected? Why or why not?

_____

_____

_____

_____

What's Next?

How could you improve on this experiment? Did the results make you think of any other questions that you could investigate with new experiments?

_____

_____

_____

_____

Levers

PURPOSE

To demonstrate the effectiveness of a lever.

Materials

4 books
2 pencils

Procedure

1. Stack the books on a table.
2. Put your little finger under the edge of the bottom book in the stack and try to lift the books.

3. Place one pencil under the edge of the bottom book in the stack.
4. Place the second pencil under the first pencil near the book.
5. Push down on the end of the second pencil with your little finger and try to lift the books.

Levers

Observations and Data

What happens during the experiment? Write down what you observed as well as any measurements or calculations that you made. You may also want to draw sketches or take photos of your experiment.

_____

_____

_____

_____

_____

Results and Conclusions

What was the final result of your experiment? Was it what you expected? Why or why not?

_____

_____

_____

_____

What's Next?

How could you improve on this experiment? Did the results make you think of any other questions that you could investigate with new experiments?

_____

_____

_____

_____

Stickers

PURPOSE

To discover what materials are attracted to a magnet.

Materials

testing materials: aluminum foil, copper wire, glass marble, iron nail, paper, steel BBs, wooden match

bar magnet

Procedure

1. Lay the testing materials on a wooden table.

2. Touch the magnet to, and slowly move the magnet away from, each material.

3. Observe and record which materials cling to the magnet.

Stickers

Observations and Data

What happens during the experiment? Write down what you observed as well as any measurements or calculations that you made. You may also want to draw sketches or take photos of your experiment.

_____

_____

_____

_____

_____

_____

_____

Results and Conclusions

What was the final result of your experiment? Was it what you expected? Why or why not?

_____

_____

_____

_____

_____

What's Next?

How could you improve on this experiment? Did the results make you think of any other questions that you could investigate with new experiments?

_____

_____

_____

_____

Magnetic Strength

PURPOSE

To determine the strength of a magnetic field.

Materials

masking tape
bar magnets, several different sizes
box of small paper clips

Procedure

1. Tape the magnet to a table with part of the magnet extending over the edge of the table.

2. Bend open the end of a paper clip and touch it to the bottom of the part of the magnet that extends over the table's edge.

3. Add paper clips one at a time to the open clip until the clips pull loose from the magnet and fall.

Magnetic Strength

Observations and Data

What happens during the experiment? Write down what you observed as well as any measurements or calculations that you made. You may also want to draw sketches or take photos of your experiment.

_____

_____

_____

_____

_____

_____

_____

Results and Conclusions

What was the final result of your experiment? Was it what you expected? Why or why not?

_____

_____

_____

_____

What's Next?

How could you improve on this experiment? Did the results make you think of any other questions that you could investigate with new experiments?

_____

_____

_____

_____

More Muscle

PURPOSE

To determine what part of a magnet has the strongest attracting ability.

Materials

scissors

ruler

string

bar magnet

masking tape

box of about 100 small paper clips

large bowl

Procedure

1. Cut two 3-foot (1-m) pieces of string.

2. Tie one end of each string to each end of the magnet.

3. Tape the free ends of the strings to the top of a door frame.

4. Adjust the length of the strings so that the magnet hangs in a level position and is at a height that is easy for you to reach.

5. Spread the paper clips in the bottom of the bowl.

6. Raise the bowl so that the magnet touches the paper clips.

7. Slowly lower the bowl.

8. Observe where the clips cling to the magnet.

Straight Through

Observations and Data

What happens during the experiment? Write down what you observed as well as any measurements or calculations that you made. You may also want to draw sketches or take photos of your experiment.

_____

_____

_____

_____

_____

_____

Results and Conclusions

What was the final result of your experiment? Was it what you expected? Why or why not?

_____

_____

_____

_____

_____

What's Next?

How could you improve on this experiment? Did the results make you think of any other questions that you could investigate with new experiments?

_____

_____

_____

_____

Paddle Boat

PURPOSE

To demonstrate Newton's Law of Action and Reaction.

Materials

cardboard
rubber band
scissors
container of water at least
4 in. (10 cm) deep
ruler

Procedure

1. Measure and cut a 4-in. (10-cm) square from the cardboard.

2. Shape the boat by cutting one side into a point and cutting out a 2-in. (5-cm) square from the opposite end.

3. Cut a paddle from the cardboard. Make it 1 in. × 2 in. (2.5 cm × 5 cm).

4. Loop the rubber band over the ends of the boat.

5. Insert the paddle between the sides of the rubber band.

6. Turn the cardboard paddle toward you to wind the rubber band.

7. Place the boat in the container of water and release the paddle.

8. Wind the rubber band in the opposite direction by turning the paddle away from you.

9. Place the boat in the water and release the paddle.

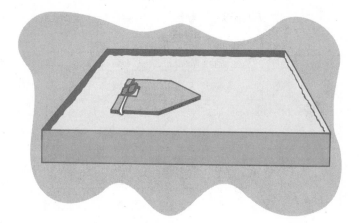

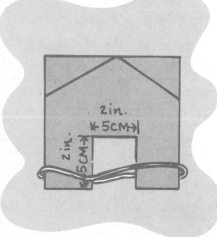

213

Paddle Boat

Observations and Data

What happens during the experiment? Write down what you observed as well as any measurements or calculations that you made. You may also want to draw sketches or take photos of your experiment.

_____

_____

_____

_____

_____

_____

Results and Conclusions

What was the final result of your experiment? Was it what you expected? Why or why not?

_____

_____

_____

_____

_____

What's Next?

How could you improve on this experiment? Did the results make you think of any other questions that you could investigate with new experiments?

_____

_____

_____

_____

Balloon Rocket

PURPOSE

To demonstrate how unbalanced forces produce motion.

Materials

yardstick (meter stick)
drinking straw
scissors
string
2 chairs
balloon, 9 in. (23 cm)
masking tape

Procedure

1. Measure and cut a 4-in. (10-cm) piece from the drinking straw.

2. Cut about 3½ ft. (4.5 m) of string.

3. Thread the end of the string through the straw piece.

4. Position the chairs about 4 ft. (4 m) apart.

5. Tie the string to the backs of the chairs. Make the string as tight as possible.

6. Inflate the balloon and twist the open end.

7. Move the straw to one end of the string.

8. Tape the inflated balloon to the straw.

9. Release the balloon.

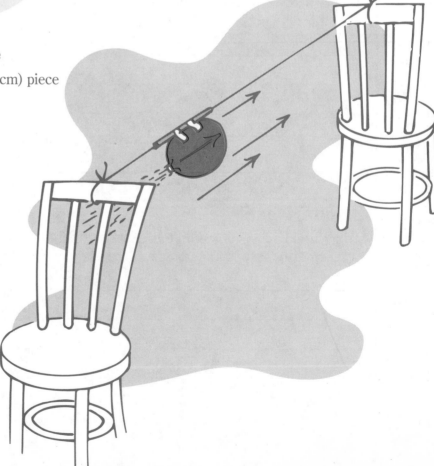

Balloon Rocket

Observations and Data

What happens during the experiment? Write down what you observed as well as any measurements or calculations that you made. You may also want to draw sketches or take photos of your experiment.

_____

_____

_____

_____

_____

_____

Results and Conclusions

What was the final result of your experiment? Was it what you expected? Why or why not?

_____

_____

_____

_____

_____

What's Next?

How could you improve on this experiment? Did the results make you think of any other questions that you could investigate with new experiments?

_____

_____

_____

_____

Helicopter

PURPOSE

To determine how weight affects the rotation speed of a paper helicopter.

Materials

notebook paper
scissors
ruler
pencil
3 paper clips

Procedure

1. Fold and cut one sheet of paper in half lengthwise.

2. Fold one of the halves in half lengthwise.

3. Use a ruler to draw a triangle on one edge of the paper. The base will be 1 in. (3 cm) long and one side will be between the 4-in. and 6-in. (9-cm and 14-cm) marks on the ruler. See the diagram.

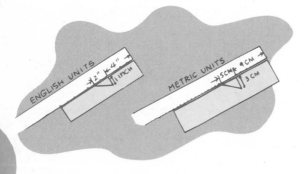

4. Cut out the triangle. Cut through both layers of the paper.

5. Open the paper and cut up the center fold to the point indicated on the diagram. This forms the two wings.

6. Fold the tabs toward the center and attach a paper clip to the bottom.

7. Fold the wings in opposite directions.

8. Hold the helicopter above your head and drop it.

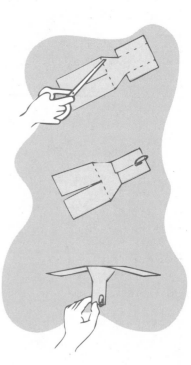

9. Add different numbers of paper clips one at a time and drop the plane after each addition. Save paper helicopter for Experiment 216.

Helicopter

Observations and Data

What happens during the experiment? Write down what you observed as well as any measurements or calculations that you made. You may also want to draw sketches or take photos of your experiment.

_____

_____

_____

_____

_____

_____

Results and Conclusions

What was the final result of your experiment? Was it what you expected? Why or why not?

_____

_____

_____

_____

What's Next?

How could you improve on this experiment? Did the results make you think of any other questions that you could investigate with new experiments?

_____

_____

_____

_____

Right or Left?

PURPOSE

To determine how wing position affects the direction of a paper helicopter's rotation.

Materials

paper helicopter from Experiment 215

Procedure

1. Hold the helicopter above your head and drop it.

2. Observe the direction that the helicopter spins.

3. Bend the wings in the opposite direction and again drop the helicopter from above your head.

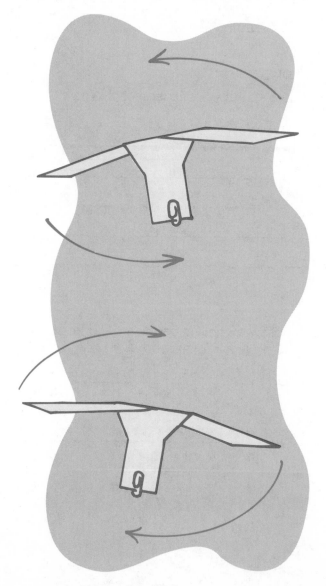

Right or Left?

Observations and Data

What happens during the experiment? Write down what you observed as well as any measurements or calculations that you made. You may also want to draw sketches or take photos of your experiment.

_____

_____

_____

_____

_____

_____

Results and Conclusions

What was the final result of your experiment? Was it what you expected? Why or why not?

_____

_____

_____

_____

What's Next?

How could you improve on this experiment? Did the results make you think of any other questions that you could investigate with new experiments?

_____

_____

_____

_____

Twang

PURPOSE

To demonstrate the effect that length has on the sound of a vibrating material.

Materials

ruler
table

Procedure

1. Place the ruler on a table with about 10 inches (25 cm) of the ruler hanging over the edge of the table.

2. Press the end of the ruler against the table with your hand.

3. With your other hand, push the free end of the ruler down and then quickly release it.

4. As the ruler moves, slide it quickly onto the table.

5. Listen to the sounds produced.

Twang

Observations and Data

What happens during the experiment? Write down what you observed as well as any measurements or calculations that you made. You may also want to draw sketches or take photos of your experiment.

_____

_____

_____

_____

_____

_____

_____

Results and Conclusions

What was the final result of your experiment? Was it what you expected? Why or why not?

_____

_____

_____

_____

_____

What's Next?

How could you improve on this experiment? Did the results make you think of any other questions that you could investigate with new experiments?

_____

_____

_____

_____

Bottle Organ

PURPOSE

To demonstrate how frequency affects the pitch of sound.

Materials

tap water

6 small-mouth glass bottles of comparable size

metal spoon

Procedure

1. Pour different amounts of water in each bottle.

2. Gently tap each bottle with the metal spoon.

3. Note the difference in the pitch produced.

Bottle Organ

Observations and Data

What happens during the experiment? Write down what you observed as well as any measurements or calculations that you made. You may also want to draw sketches or take photos of your experiment.

_____

_____

_____

_____

_____

_____

_____

Results and Conclusions

What was the final result of your experiment? Was it what you expected? Why or why not?

_____

_____

_____

_____

_____

What's Next?

How could you improve on this experiment? Did the results make you think of any other questions that you could investigate with new experiments?

_____

_____

_____

_____

Sound Blaster

PURPOSE

To demonstrate stereophonic sound.

Materials

36-inch (1-m) piece of string
wire coat hanger
metal spoon
helper

Procedure

1. Wrap the ends of the string around your index fingers.

2. Place your fingers in your ears.

3. Hang the hook of the hanger in the middle.

4. Lean over so that the hanger hangs freely.

5. Ask your helper to use the spoon to tap the hanger several times.

Sound Blaster

Observations and Data

What happens during the experiment? Write down what you observed as well as any measurements or calculations that you made. You may also want to draw sketches or take photos of your experiment.

_____

_____

_____

_____

_____

_____

Results and Conclusions

What was the final result of your experiment? Was it what you expected? Why or why not?

_____

_____

_____

_____

What's Next?

How could you improve on this experiment? Did the results make you think of any other questions that you could investigate with new experiments?

_____

_____

_____

_____

Cup Telephone

PURPOSE

To demonstrate how sound travels.

Materials

pencil
two 7-ounce (210-ml) paper cups
9-yard (8-m) piece of string
helper

Procedure

1. Use the pencil to make a small hole in the bottom of each cup.

2. Thread the ends of the string through the holes in the cups.

3. Knot each end of the string to keep them from pulling through the holes.

4. Have your helper hold one cup while you hold the other. Hold the cups by placing your thumb and index finger on the rim.

5. Walk away from your helper until the string is stretched tightly between you.

6. Hold the cup to your ear while your helper speaks softly into the other cup.

Cup Telephone

Observations and Data

What happens during the experiment? Write down what you observed as well as any measurements or calculations that you made. You may also want to draw sketches or take photos of your experiment.

_____

_____

_____

_____

_____

_____

Results and Conclusions

What was the final result of your experiment? Was it what you expected? Why or why not?

_____

_____

_____

_____

_____

What's Next?

How could you improve on this experiment? Did the results make you think of any other questions that you could investigate with new experiments?

_____

_____

_____

_____

Streamers

PURPOSE

To charge an object with static electricity.

Materials

scissors
ruler
tissue paper
comb

Procedure

1. Measure and cut a strip of tissue paper about 3 in. × 10 in. (7.5 cm × 25 cm).

2. Cut long, thin strips in the paper, leaving one end uncut (see diagram).

3. Quickly move the comb through your hair several times. Your hair must be clean, dry, and oil-free.

4. Hold the teeth of the comb near, but not touching, the cut end of the paper strips.

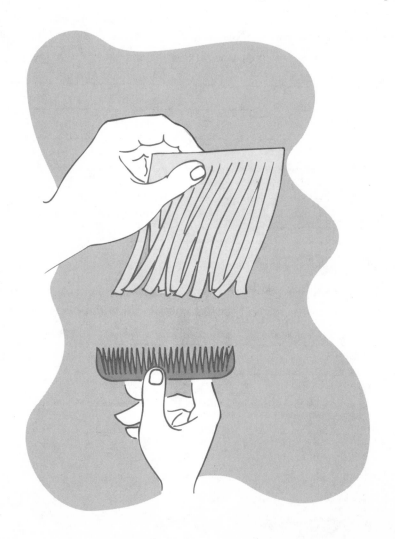

221

Streamers

Observations and Data

What happens during the experiment? Write down what you observed as well as any measurements or calculations that you made. You may also want to draw sketches or take photos of your experiment.

_____

_____

_____

_____

_____

_____

_____

Results and Conclusions

What was the final result of your experiment? Was it what you expected? Why or why not?

_____

_____

_____

_____

_____

What's Next?

How could you improve on this experiment? Did the results make you think of any other questions that you could investigate with new experiments?

_____

_____

_____

_____

Snap

PURPOSE

To demonstrate how static charges produce sound.

Materials

clear plastic sheet
scissors
ruler
modeling clay
large paper clip
piece of wool: a scarf, coat,
or sweater made of 100% wool will work

Procedure

1. Measure and cut a plastic strip about 1 in. × 8 in. (2.5 cm × 20 cm).

2. Use the clay to stand the paper clip upright on a table.

3. Wrap the wool around the plastic strip and quickly pull the plastic through the cloth. Do this quickly at least three times.

4. Immediately hold the plastic near the top of the paper clip.

Snap

Observations and Data

What happens during the experiment? Write down what you observed as well as any measurements or calculations that you made. You may also want to draw sketches or take photos of your experiment.

_____

_____

_____

_____

_____

_____

Results and Conclusions

What was the final result of your experiment? Was it what you expected? Why or why not?

_____

_____

_____

_____

_____

What's Next?

How could you improve on this experiment? Did the results make you think of any other questions that you could investigate with new experiments?

_____

_____

_____

_____

Fly Away

PURPOSE

To demonstrate the effect of static electricity.

Materials

scissors
ruler
newspaper

Procedure

NOTE: This experiment works best when the air is dry and cool.

1. Cut two strips of newspaper 1 inch × 12 inches (1.25 cm × 30 cm).

2. Hold the two strips of paper together at one end.

3. Put the middle finger of your other hand between the strips.

4. Squeeze the papers lightly between your fingers and quickly pull your hand down the strips.

Fly Away

Observations and Data

What happens during the experiment? Write down what you observed as well as any measurements or calculations that you made. You may also want to draw sketches or take photos of your experiment.

_____

_____

_____

_____

_____

_____

_____

Results and Conclusions

What was the final result of your experiment? Was it what you expected? Why or why not?

_____

_____

_____

_____

_____

What's Next?

How could you improve on this experiment? Did the results make you think of any other questions that you could investigate with new experiments?

_____

_____

_____

_____

Attracters

PURPOSE

To demonstrate the attraction between unlike charges.

Materials

two 9-inch (23-cm) round balloons
marking pen
two 1-yard (1-m) pieces of thread
masking tape
clean, dry, oil-free hair

Procedure

NOTE: This experiment works best on a cool, dry day.

1. Inflate both balloons and tie their ends. Use the marking pen to label one balloon A and the other balloon B.

2. Tie one thread to the end of each balloon.

3. Tape the free ends of the threads to the top of a door frame so that the balloons hang about 8 inches (20 cm) apart.

4. Stroke balloon A on your hair about 10 times, then gently release it.

NOTE: Leave the balloons hanging for Experiment 225.

Attracters

Observations and Data

What happens during the experiment? Write down what you observed as well as any measurements or calculations that you made. You may also want to draw sketches or take photos of your experiment.

_____

_____

_____

_____

_____

_____

Results and Conclusions

What was the final result of your experiment? Was it what you expected? Why or why not?

_____

_____

_____

_____

_____

What's Next?

How could you improve on this experiment? Did the results make you think of any other questions that you could investigate with new experiments?

_____

_____

_____

_____

Repellers

PURPOSE

To demonstrate the repulsion between like charges.

Materials

hanging balloons from Experiment 224
clean, dry, oil-free hair
helper

Procedure

NOTE: This experiment works best on a cool, dry day.

1. Stroke balloon A on your hair 10 times.

2. Hold your balloon as your helper rubs balloon B on your hair 10 times.

3. Gently release the balloons.

Repellers

Observations and Data

What happens during the experiment? Write down what you observed as well as any measurements or calculations that you made. You may also want to draw sketches or take photos of your experiment.

_____

_____

_____

_____

_____

_____

Results and Conclusions

What was the final result of your experiment? Was it what you expected? Why or why not?

_____

_____

_____

_____

What's Next?

How could you improve on this experiment? Did the results make you think of any other questions that you could investigate with new experiments?

_____

_____

_____

_____

Answer Key

Note: Circled numbers indicate experiment numbers.

Astronomy

1

Where Is It?

Results   The angle reading varies with the time of day.
Why   Each day the sun appears to rise from below the eastern horizon (a line where the earth and sky appear to meet). It then moves across the sky and sinks below the western horizon. The altitude (height) of the sun changes during the day. At sunrise and sunset, the altitude is zero degrees. Each day the greatest altitude is around noon. During the year, the sun's greatest altitude is during the summer. Its lowest altitude is during the winter.

2

How High?

Results   The angle increases as the height of the object increases.
Why?   To see the tops of the distant objects, the protractor had to be elevated. The hanging string remains perpendicular to the ground because gravity continues to pull it toward the center of the earth. As the protractor turns, the string has a different angle in relation to the straw. This instrument is called an astrolabe and can be used to compare the apparent distances between stars, since the distance increases as the angle increases.

3

Mirage

Results   The coin is visible and appears to be in a different position in the bowl.
Why?   Light from the coin changes direction as it leaves the water and enters the air. This makes the coin appear to be in a different place. This change in the direction of light is called refraction. The earth's atmosphere refracts light in a similar way, causing the image of the sun to appear before the actual sun rises above the horizon at sunrise and lingers after the sun moves below the horizon at sunset.

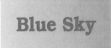

4

Blue Sky

Results   The light passes through the clear water, but the milky water has a pale blue-gray look.
Why?   The waves of color in white light all have a different size. The particles of milk in the water separate and spread the small blue waves from the light throughout the water, causing the water to appear blue. Nitrogen and oxygen molecules in the earth's atmosphere, like the milk particles, are small enough to separate out the small blue light waves from sunlight. The blue light spreads out through the atmosphere, making the sky look blue from the earth and giving the entire planet a blue look when it is observed from space. The color in the glass is not a bright blue because more than just the blue light waves are being scattered by large particles in the milk. This happens in the atmosphere when large quantities of dust or water vapor scatter more than just the blue light waves. Clean, dry air produces the deepest blue sky color because the blue waves in the light are scattered the most.

5

Eclipse

Results   Your shadow crossed the circle at different points during the day.
Why?   A shadow is a dark shape cast upon a surface when something blocks light. You cast a shadow because your body blocks the sun's light. During an eclipse, one object passes through the shadow of another. A solar eclipse occurs when the earth moves into the moon's shadow. At such times, the moon lies between the sun and the earth. The moon's shadow, like your shadow, falls on different areas of the earth because the earth rotates.

6 Darker

Results The shadow is darker in the center than on the outside.

Why? Your hand casts a shadow because light traveling in a straight line from the flashlight is blocked by your hand. Light cannot pass through your hand; therefore, a dark shape or shadow appears on the paper. A shadow has two parts—the umbra and the penumbra. The umbra is the dark inner part of a shadow where the light is completely cut off. During a solar eclipse, the umbra of the moon's shadow falls on a small part of the earth. The penumbra is the outer, lighter part of the shadow where the light is only partly cut off. The penumbra of the moon's shadow falls on a larger part of the earth during a solar eclipse.

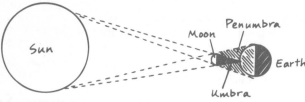

7 Blocked

Results A dark shadow from the baseball falls across the golf ball as the golf ball moves behind the baseball.

Why? A lunar eclipse occurs when the moon moves into the earth's shadow. At such times, the earth lies between the sun and the moon. In this experiment, the baseball represents the earth, the flashlight represents the sun, and the golf ball represents the moon. As the moon moves into the shadow of the earth, the part of the moon covered by the shadow is no longer visible. Finally, the entire moon seems to disappear. The reverse happens as the moon moves out of the earth's shadow.

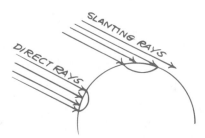

8 Direct

Results The thermometer facing the sun has a higher temperature.

Why? The black paper facing the sun receives more direct rays of sunlight than the sheet on the opposite side of the book. Areas that receive direct light rays from the sun are much hotter. The earth's equator receives about 2½ times as much heat during the year as does the area around the poles. Mars, like the earth, has colder pole areas. Both of these planets are slightly tilted in their relationship to the sun, causing the equator to receive more direct solar light rays than do the poles.

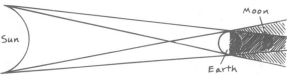

9 Slanted

Results The dots made by the slanted markers are further apart.

Why? The standing markers represent direct rays from the sun and the leaning markers represent slanting solar rays. Just like the marks left by the pen, the distance between slanting solar rays is greater. Areas that receive direct rays from the sun are much hotter. Mars, like the earth, has colder pole areas. Both of these planets are slightly tilted from the path of the sun's rays, causing the surface at the equator to receive more direct solar rays than do the poles.

10 Hidden

Results The print cannot be read on the pencil, and the color of the pencil is difficult to determine.

Why? The light behind the pencil is so bright that it is difficult to see the surface of the pencil. In a similar way, the glare of the sun behind the planet Mercury makes it difficult to study the planet's surface. Mercury is less than half the size of the earth and the closest planet to the sun. From the earth, astronomers are looking almost directly into the sun when they view Mercury. The first photographs of one-third of the planet's surface were taken in 1974 and 1975 when the Mariner 10 space probe flew about 200 miles (320 km) from the surface of Mercury.

11

Peeper

Results The dot is easily seen when it is to the side of the bulb and the basketball blocks out the light from the bulb.
Why? The planet Mercury can be seen from the earth with your naked eye just before the sun rises in the morning and sets below the horizon in the afternoon. The basketball in this experiment repre- sents the horizon of the earth, the dot is Mercury, and the light bulb is the sun. The position of these materials demonstrates that only when the sun's blinding light is below the earth's horizon can the planet Mercury peep above the horizon and be seen easily.

12

Blasters

Results The ball sinks into the flour and some flour dust flies upward from its surface.
Why? The surface of the moon is pitted with craters (holes) ranging in size from tiny pits called craterlets to large basins many miles across called walled plains. Most craters were probably caused by high-speed meteorites (stony or metallic objects from space that reach the surface of a celestial body) crashing onto the moon. The baseball represents a meteorite crash- ing into the surface of the moon (the flour). Unlike the baseball, the high-speed mete- orites explode on impact and scatter over a large area leaving only a large hole behind.

13

Plop!

Results The rock made a larger impression on the foil lying on the soft carpet.
Why? The rock sank into the softer car- pet surface, which allowed more of the ball to be pressed against the paper. Like the rock, a meteorite (a stony or metallic object from space that falls through an atmos- phere and strikes the surface of a celestial body) makes a larger imprint when it strikes a soft surface. Bowl-shaped holes called craters are best formed when mete- orites strike soft, powdery surfaces such as the surface of the moon.

14

Moving Target

Results The paper wads hit the washer when aimed at a point in front of the swing- ing washer.
Why? It takes time for the paper wads to move through the air. While they move, the washer moves to another position. Astronauts have the same problem when aiming their spacecraft at the moon because the moon, like the washer, is con- stantly changing positions. The paper wads and the spacecraft must be directed to a point in front of the moving target so that they arrive at the same place at the same time.

15

Face Forward

Results Facing the X-marked paper resulted in different parts of your body pointing toward the paper marked EARTH as you revolved around the earth. Continuing to face the earth allowed only your front side to point toward the earth during the revolution.
Why? You had to turn your body slightly in order to continue to face the earth as you moved around it. In order for the same side of the moon to always face the earth, the moon also has to turn slowly on it's axis as it moves around the earth. The moon rotates one complete turn on its own axis during the 28 days it takes to revolve around the earth.

16

Changes

Results The ball is dark when you face the door. Part of the ball lightens as you turn and it is fully illuminated when your back is to the door. The ball starts to darken as you turn toward the door.
Why? The light from the doorway lights up one side of the ball at a time—the side facing the lamp. As you turn, more of the lighted side faces you. The moon behaves like the ball. Moonlight is a reflection of the sun's light, and only one side of the moon faces the sun. The moon has phases because as the moon travels around the earth, different parts of its bright side are seen.

17
Quicker

Results The ruler hits the surface first.
Why? The clay ball on the yardstick has farther to fall than does the ball on the ruler. This is similar to the movement of the planets, which are continuously "falling" around the sun. Mercury, with the shortest distance from the sun, 36 million miles (57.96 million km), takes only 88 earth days to make its voyage around the sun. Pluto has a much longer path to follow—it is 3,688 million miles (5,901 million km) away from the sun and requires 248 earth years to complete its period of

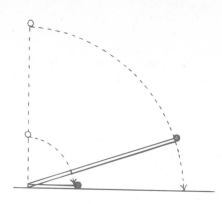

18
Speedy

Results As the length of the string decreases, the washer must be spun around more times in order to keep the string taut.
Why? The washer seems to move sluggishly around in its circular path when attached to a long string, while on a shorter string, it zips around quickly. This is also true about planets, which differ in their distance from the sun. As the planet's distance from the sun increases, the pull toward the sun, called gravity (the force that pulls celestial bodies toward each other), decreases. With less pull toward the sun, the orbiting speed of the planet decreases. Mercury, the closest planet to the sun, has the fastest orbiting speed and Pluto, the furthermost planet, has the slowest orbiting speed. (Twirling the washer on the string is not a true simulation of how planets move around the sun, because planets are not attached to the sun by a cord and do not move in a circular path.)

19
On the Move

Results The marble rolls in a circular path. It rolls farther and faster without the paper lining in the pan.
Why? Inertia is the resistance that all objects have to any change in motion. Inertia causes stationary objects to remain at rest and moving objects to continue to move in a straight line, unless some force acts on them. The marble stopped moving more quickly in the paper-lined pan because of friction. When the friction between the pan and the marble was reduced, the marble rolled for a longer time. The planets continue to move around the sun because their movement through space is not restricted by friction.

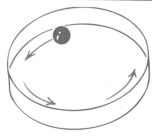

20
Back Up

Results At first, you are looking forward to view the background past your helper, but as you take the lead you must look backward to see your helper and the objects beyond.
Why? Your helper is not going backward; you are simply looking from a different position. Mars was thought by early observers to move forward, stop, go backward, and then go forward again. Actually the planet was continuing forward on its orbit around the sun while the earth was zipping around the sun in one-half the time of Mars' trip. Earth speeds ahead of Mars during part of the time, giving Mars the appearance of moving backward. Mars appears to move forward when the earth races around the orbit and approaches Mars from behind. This apparent change in the direction of Mars is called retrograde motion.

21
In and Out

Results The spoon spins in a circular path with only the weight of the tape pulling on the attached string.
Why? Any circling object, spoon or satellite, has a centripetal force (force directed toward the center) keeping it in its circular path. Moons that orbit planets and planets that orbit the sun are all pulled toward the celestial body that they orbit. Their own forward speed keeps them from being pulled into the body that they orbit, and the centripetal force acting on the orbiting bodies keeps them from moving off into space.

22

Orbiter

Results The marble remains inside the jar as long as the jar is spun. The marble continues to spin for a short time after you stop moving the jar, but finally the marble slows and falls out of the jar.

Why? The jar pushes on the marble and provides an inward force that keeps the marble moving in a circular path. This force toward the center is called a centripetal force. The word centripetal means "seeking the center." If the bottle were suddenly removed, the marble would fly off in a straight line because of its forward speed. Any object moving in a circular path—the marble, a moon, or an artificial satellite—has a forward speed and a centripetal force pulling it inward. The earth's natural and artificial satellites are pulled toward the earth's surface by gravity, but their own forward speed keeps them from being pulled into the earth. Satellites, like the marble, fall when their forward speed decreases.

23

Tumbler

Results The astronaut and spacecraft rotate around three different axes.

Why? The three different movements are called roll, pitch, and yaw. Turning around Axis A is called a roll. When the craft turns around Axis B, the movement is called pitch. Turning around Axis C is called yaw. Roll, pitch, and yaw are terms used to describe the motion of a spacecraft. These same terms are also used to describe the movements of airplanes and boats.

24

Rings

Results As your helper turns the cardboard circle, the pencil points push the salt to the side, forming two cleared paths.

Why? Saturn's rings are made of icy particles. Just as the pencil points move through the salt crystals in this experiment, astronomers believe that Saturn's moons move through the icy particles, pushing them into separate bands. These moons are called shepherd satellites (a small body orbiting a larger body). The moons are given this name because they herd the icy particles in the rings.

25

See Through

Results Two black rings are seen, but you can see through the spinning blades.

Why? Your eyes blend the color on the paper strips as they spin, producing what appears to be solid rings. The rings around Saturn are made of chunks of ice and rock. Their movement makes them appear to be a continuous surface as does the movement of the black marks on the spinning paper.

Spreader

Results The light pattern becomes brighter and smaller as the flashlight nears the wall.

Why? Light moves away from the flashlight in a straight line. If the beam of light leaves the light source at an angle, it continues to spread out until it hits an object. Other light sources, such as stars, behave in the same manner. Two stars giving off the same amount of light, but at different distances from the earth, will appear to have different apparent magnitude (the measure of how bright a celestial object appears to be as observed from earth). The spreading of the light from the most distant star results in less light hitting the earth. Thus, the distant star appears dimmer, as did the light when the flashlight was farthest from the wall.

27 · Hazy

Results The separate circles can be seen when standing close to the paper, but at a distance, the circles blend together to form one large white shape.

Why? Due to the inability of our eye to distinguish discrete points of light that are too close together, the separate circles blend together as does the light from distant stars. Using binoculars or a telescope helps our eyes to see stars more clearly. Part of the Milky Way galaxy (a group of stars and other celestial bodies including our solar system) appears as a milky haze in the night sky. This haze is actually light from billions of stars. This haziness is partly due to the inability of our eyes to separate distant light sources, but great amounts of galactic dust also scatter and block the starlight from the Milky Way.

28 · Twinkling Star

Results Light reflecting from the foil appears to twinkle.

Why? The up-and-down movement of the water causes the depth of the water to vary. Light rays reflecting from the foil twinkle because they refract, or bend, differently as they pass through different depths of water. To an observer on earth, light rays from distant stars appear to twinkle because they also refract differently as they move through different densities (how close together the particles in a material are) of air in the earth's atmosphere. This twinkling or motion of starlight is called scintillation.

29 · Brightest Star

Results What appears to be a very bright star is usually seen in the morning before sunrise or in the evening after sunset. Sometimes the star is not visible.

Why? The brightest star in the sky is not really a star, but the planet Venus. It appears as a bright star because the dense, unbroken clouds surrounding the planet reflect about 75 percent of the incoming sunlight back into space. The movement of the planet around the sun, as seen from the earth, makes it appear as an "evening" or "morning" star. It appears in the evening in the western sky when moving toward the earth. It is in the eastern sky in the morning after it has passed between the sun and the earth and begins moving away from the earth. As viewed from earth, if Venus is too close to the sun, the brightness of the sun blocks out the light from Venus and it cannot be seen.

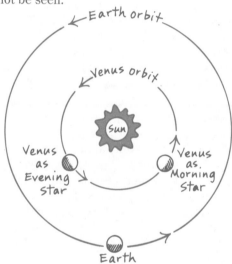

30 · Box Planetarium

Results An enlarged pattern of the holes made in the paper is projected onto the wall.

Why? As light beams shine through the tiny holes, they spread outward, producing larger circles of light on the wall. A planetarium presentation showing the entire night sky uses a round sphere with holes spaced in the positions of single stars and constellations. A constellation is a group of stars whose arrangement appears to form an imaginary figure. A bright light in the center of the sphere projects light spots on a curved ceiling, representing the sky. As the ball rotates, different star groups are seen. Because of the earth's revolution around the sun, different stars are viewed in the sky at different times of the year.

31 · Star Projector

Results An enlarged pattern of the holes in the paper is projected onto the ceiling.

Why? Light shining through the holes spreads out, producing larger circles of light on the ceiling. The stars projected on the ceiling are in the correct order as seen in the sky. The star pattern is the constellation (grouping of stars that appears to form the outline of an object or figure) called Draco.

Results The position of the group of stars called the Big Dipper is drawn on the paper and Polaris, the North Star, is plotted on the star chart.

Why? As your finger moves from one star to the next, the free hanging nail moves to a new position, thus plotting the position of the stars. Polaris, the star that the earth's imaginary axis points to, is also called the North Star. This star can be found by following the two pointer stars, Dubhe and Merak, in the bowl of the Big Dipper.

Results The steel wool pieces form a pattern on the paper above the magnet.

Why? A magnetic field is the area around a magnet in which the force of the magnet affects the movement of other magnetic objects, such as steel wool. This area is made up of invisible lines of magnetic force. The small pieces of steel wool follow the lines of force, allowing you to "see" the magnetic field. Magnetic fields exist on the sun. Dark spots on the sun where gases are cooler are called sunspots. Like magnets, the sunspots are surrounded by magnetic fields that attract magnetic materials.

Results The iron filings form curved lines around the magnet. Adding the vinegar makes the iron in the filings rust. When the filings are shaken off, the rust leaves marks on the paper where the filings were.

Why? Every magnet has an invisible magnetic field around it. This field is made up of lines of force that attract magnetic material such as iron filings. The magnetic field of the sun, like the bar magnet in this experiment, has a north and south pole. It is thought that the sun's magnetic field may extend out of its north pole to the outer limits of our solar system (the orbit of Pluto) where it bends around and returns to the sun's magnetic south pole.

Results The plate is turned so the letters on the plate point in the general compass directions of north, south, east, and west.

Why? When you point the end of the pencil straight at the sun, no shadow appears on the paper. The sun appears to move in a general direction from east to west. As it moves toward the west, the sun's light hits the pencil, forming a shadow pointing toward the east. Rotating the plate so that the letter E lines up with the shadow places all the letters in line with the compass directions of north, south, east, and west. Any general direction can then be determined from the shadow compass. (If you had performed the experiment before noon, you would have rotated the plate so that the letter W lined up with the shadow.)

Results North will be halfway between the shadow and the number 12 on your paper clock. *NOTE: Use a compass to check the accuracy of your clock compass.*

Why? This compass is most accurate March 21 and September 23 when the sun rises in the east and sets in the west. On these dates, the shadow of the pin approaches due north as noon nears. At other times of the year, the clock compass loses accuracy, but the general direction of north can be found.

Results Flickering rainbow-colored flames appear on the white paper.

Why? The layer of water between the mirror and the surface of the water acts like a prism. A prism is a triangle-shaped piece of glass that bends the rays of light passing through it so that the light breaks into its separate colors, called a spectrum. The white light of the sun can be separated by a prism into a spectrum of seven colors always appearing in the same order: red, orange, yellow, green, blue, indigo, violet. The moving water changes the direction of the light, causing the colors to appear like flickering flames.

38 Rainbow

Results   A rainbow can be seen only when the sun is behind you.

Why?   A rainbow is an arc of colors in the sky. To see a rainbow, there must be water droplets in the air in front of you and the sun must be shining behind you. When sunlight passes through a raindrop, it is refracted or bent, and the light separates into seven colors: red, orange, yellow, green, blue, indigo, and violet. All rainbows are part of a circle, but only part of the circle is visible, because the earth is in the way.

39 Inverted

Results   The image produced on the wall is turned upside down.

Why?   Light travels in a straight line, but when it hits the lens, it changes direction, causing the image to be upside down. Refractive telescopes have lenses similar to the one used in this experiment, and so stars viewed through a refractive telescope appear upside down.

MAGNIFYING LENS

40 Sky Gazer

Results   A small, inverted image of the objects outside the window is projected onto the paper. This image is larger when seen through both lenses.

Why?   A refracting telescope has two lenses, an objective lens (the lens closer to the object being viewed) and an eyepiece (the lens closer to your eye). The two magnifying lenses in this activity represent the objective lens and eyepiece in a refracting telescope. The objective lens collects light from distant objects and brings it into focus in front of the eyepiece. This image can be projected onto a screen, such as the paper. When you look through the magnifying lens eyepiece or a real eyepiece in a telescope, you see the same image, but it is magnified.

41 How Far?

Results   Cooling the plastic folder caused it to become cloudy. It was easy to see through the plastic before it was cooled.

Why?   The moisture in the air condensed (changed from a gas to a liquid) on the surface of the cool plastic folder causing it to look cloudy. Clouds form in the earth's atmosphere because of the condensing of water vapor similar to the cloudy covering on the plastic. There is no appreciable atmosphere on the moon to form clouds so the view of distant objects is always unobstructed.

42 Details

Results   The two holes appear as one beam of light from a distance.

Why?   Resolution measures the ability to see details. This is true with your eyes as well as with telescopes. The resolving power of a telescope lens indicates the lens's ability to distinguish between the images of two points. The greater the resolution, the better one can see the object studied. The resolving power of a lens increases with the diameter of the lens. Atmospheric conditions also affect resolving power.

43 Thick

Results   The light looks blurred through the paper.

Why?   The light rays bend and bounce off the wax paper. This is similar to the way sunlight bends and bounces off the thick clouds that surround Venus, which are not particularly dark, just very thick. In their thickest part, the visibility is about 0.6 miles (1 km) or less. This low visibility would result in the closing of most airports on earth.

44 Bent

Results   The penny in the cup filled with air disappears from view first, while you can still see the penny in the cup filled with water.

Why?   You see the penny in the water at a greater distance because light enters the cup, reflects from the penny, hits the surface of the water, and is refracted (bent) toward your eye. The water is thicker than the air and thicker materials refract the light more. A change in thickness of the earth's atmosphere (the gases around a planet) due to pollution, increases the refraction of light. Venus' thick atmosphere refracts light much more than does the earth's atmosphere. An observer on Venus would see many mirages (optical illusions due to atmospheric conditions) and distortions because of this.

Results The temperature inside the closed jar is higher than outside the jar.
Why? The glass jar is used to simulate the trapping of infrared light waves by gases in the atmosphere around planets. The thick atmosphere around Venus allows short wave radiation through, but blocks long wave radiation. The trapped long wave infrared light warms the planet's surface to about 800 degrees Fahrenheit (427°C).

Biology

Results The bag and the feather both can be closed.
Why? Both the bag and the feather have edges that fit together. The vane of the feather is made of barbs with a rolled edge on one side and tiny hooks on the other side. These edges interlock when pressed together, just as the edges of the bag interlock. Birds press the barbs together with their beaks to keep their feathers smooth.

Results Water pours out of the straw into the vase.
Why? The straw is long enough to reach and remove water in the vase. Hummingbirds have long, slender, hollow bills like the straw. The long, slender shape of their bills makes it easier for them to probe flowers for nectar.

Results It is easy for the foot and hand to perform the same pattern of movement, but difficult to move them simultaneously in two different patterns.
Why? When the patterns for hand and foot are the same, repetitive movement is easy. Up-and-down or circular patterns are easily done, but only when one pattern at a time is being processed by the brain. It takes much concentration and practice to successfully accomplish both patterns simultaneously.

Results It is easy for the hands to perform the same pattern of movement, but much concentration is necessary to successfully move the hands simultaneously in two different patterns.
Why? Through repetition of motion, you become proficient at moving the hands in the same pattern. Your brain is programmed to do this. Back-and-forth motions or circular motions are easily done, but only one pattern at a time. Both types of motion are in the brain's many programs, but it takes much concentration to activate the two programs at the same time.

Results Usually people only see the black and orange fish.
Why? The newspaper fish are an example of camouflage. Camouflage occurs when an animal's color blends into the color of its environment (the natural surroundings of an organism). Camouflage makes it difficult for an animal to be seen by a predator (an animal that lives by killing and eating other animals).

Results Some colors are easily found and others are more difficult. All of the pieces were not found.
Why? If the grass is the same shade of green as the colored pieces, it is difficult to distinguish between the two. Colors that look alike are harder to find. Some of the darker colored pieces blend in with the shadows of the grass. A white bunny is hard to see when sitting on a field of snow, and green snakes blend in very well on a lawn of green grass. Thus, they are protected from their predators (animals that prey on other animals).

52 Earthworm Farm

Results   The worms start wiggling and burrow into the soil. Tunnels are seen in the soil after a few days. The apple peelings disappear and pellets appear on the surface of the soil.

Why?   An earthworm does not have jaws or teeth, but a muscle draws soil particles into its mouth. The worm extracts food from the soil, and the remaining part of the soil passes through the worm's body unchanged. Waste pellets called casts contain undigested soil and are deposited by the worm on the surface of the soil.

53 Night Crawlers

Results   The worms crawl away from the white light and under the paper partition where it is darker.

Why?   Earthworms have no obvious sense organs such as eyes, but the worms respond to white light. Earthworms often surface at night and, therefore, are referred to as night crawlers.

54 Vanishing Ball

Results   The left dot vanishes when the paper is about 1 foot (30 cm) away from your face.

Why?   The light-sensitive layer on the back of the eyeball is called the retina. Images are directed to this area by the eye's lens and the optic nerve carries the message of the image from the retina to the brain. The optic nerve enters the eyeball at the back and makes a break in the retina. If an image is projected to the spot where the optic nerve enters the retina the image is not seen because no message is sent to the brain. The spot where the optic nerve enters the eye is called the "blind spot."

55 Blinking

Results   Your helper will blink, and possibly jerk or raise a hand, to protect his or her eyes.

Why?   The sudden unexpected approach of the cotton ball causes your helper's eyes to blink. Blinking is a reflex action. Like other reflex actions, it is not controlled by thinking about it. The involuntary movement of the eyelids, head, and hand happens because nerve cells in the eyes send messages to nerve cells in the brain and spinal cord. The instructions are then quickly passed on to the muscles, resulting in the protective movements of blinking, jerking the head, and raising the hand in front of the face.

56 Eye Lens

Results   A small, colored, inverted image forms on the paper.

Why?   Just like the light passing through the lens in the human eye, the light changes direction as it passes through. The light hits the paper in the same way that light hits the retina when it passes through the lens of an eye and forms an inverted image. Nerves on the retina send the message of the inverted image to the brain, which turns the image right side up again.

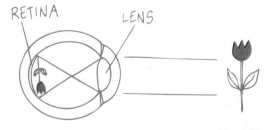

57 Fish Rings

Results   The number of wide bands equals the age of the fish in years.

Why?   Like rings on a tree trunk, fish scales form rings with each year of growth. The rings grow fastest in warm weather when there is an abundance of food. During this growing season, the growth band is lighter in color and much wider than during the colder months of winter. The winter growth produces dark slim bands because the growth is so very slow. The ring pattern varies in design from one species to another.

Results The fish breathes more often when the water temperature is warmer. **Why?** Fish lose heat, thus losing energy, when the temperature around them is cold. Their body movements slow down to conserve energy. With slower body movements, the fish also breathes more slowly.

Results It sounds like a church bell. **Why?** The metal in the spoon starts to vibrate when struck. These vibrations are transmitted up the string to the ears. The ability to hear is due to one's ability to detect vibrations. Objects must vibrate to produce a sound. The vibrating object causes the air around it to move. Vibrating air molecules enter the ear and strike the eardrum, causing it to vibrate. These vibrations continue to travel through bones and fluids in the ear until they reach a nerve that sends the message to the brain.

Results By random chance, some of the answers will be correct, but if enough trials are made, it will be obvious that the person cannot tell where the sound is coming from. **Why?** The direction of sound is not always clear unless it is coming from a point directed toward the ear. If the sound is in the center of the head at the front, top, or back, one cannot tell the exact direction of the sound source. This confusion is due to the fact that in these areas the sound is received with equal intensity by both ears.

Results Within a few days, maggots can be seen crawling around. Later, small capsules replace the maggots, and finally, new flies emerge. **Why?** The fruit flies are attracted to the smell of the ripening fruit. The flies laid eggs on the fruit, and the eggs developed into the larvae, called maggots. The maggots go through a resting stage called the pupae. Pupae are similar to the cocoon formed by caterpillars. The last stage is the emerging adult fly and the cycle starts over again.

STOCKING

RUBBER BAND

MAGGOTS

Results A buzzing sound is heard. **Why?** Sound is produced when objects vibrate (move quickly back and forth). The pitch is the property of sound that makes it high or low. A high-pitched sound, such as the buzzing of the paper, is produced when an object vibrates many times per second. The same high-pitched buzzing sound is produced by the rapid back-and-forth movement of an insect's wings.

Results When the pencil is held against the finger and both are rubbed, it feels as if part of your finger is numb. **Why?** When you rub your finger, mechanoreceptors (cells that are stimulated by pressure, touch, or sound) on both sides of the touched finger send messages to the brain. Mechanoreceptors on the finger and thumb of the hand doing the rubbing are also sending messages. These messages are analyzed by the brain, which sends an output message that results in the sensation that you are rubbing both sides of your finger. When the pencil is rubbed instead of the finger's underside, a message is missing. The brain interprets the missing information to mean that the finger is numb on one side. The brain takes in and puts out information based on what the sensory receptors tell it. Even though you know better, the output message is that your finger is numb.

64

How Do You Feel?

Results   The helper feels only one point on the forearm, and two points are felt on the finger or thumb tip.

Why?   The nerve endings in the arm and other parts of the body are too few to allow one to distinguish the separate pressures from the pencil points. The extra number of nerve endings in the finger and thumb tips allows one to make more accurate identifications. There is an increase in the pain experienced in areas with more nerve endings.

65

Food Producers

Results   Dark areas appear on the leaf.

Why?   Photosynthesis is an energy-producing reaction that occurs in the leaves of plants. Starch is indirectly one of the products of this reaction. Soaking the leaf in alcohol removes the waxy coating on the leaf and partially dissolves out the green pigment used in the photosynthesis reaction, chlorophyll. It is easier to see the results of the starch test without the presence of the green chlorophyll. Iodine combines with starch particles to form a dark purple to black color.

66

Independence

Results   Periodically, drops of water will be seen on the inside of the jar. The plant continues to grow.

Why?   The water drops come from the moisture in the soil and from the plant leaves. Plants use the sugar in their cells plus oxygen from the air to produce carbon dioxide, water, and energy. This is called the respiration reaction. They can use the carbon dioxide, water, chlorophyll, and light energy in their cells to produce sugar, oxygen, and energy. This process is called photosynthesis. Notice that the products of the respiration reaction fuel the photosynthesis reaction and vice versa. Plants continue to make their own food. They eventually die in the closed bottle because the nutrients in the soil are used up.

WATER DROPS

67

Light Seekers

Results   The leaves of the plant turn toward the window. Rotating the plant changes the direction of the leaves, but within three days they turn back toward the light.

Why?   Plants contain a chemical called auxin that promotes the lengthening of plant cells. A buildup of auxin occurs on the dark side of the plant stem. The extra auxin causes the cells on the dark side to grow longer, forcing the stems to bend toward the light. This movement toward light is called phototropism. Photo means light and tropism means movement.

68

Flower Maze

Results   The plant winds around the obstacles and out the hole in the lid.

Why?   The plant grows toward the light. This growth of a plant in response to light is called phototropism. A buildup of auxin occurs on the dark side of the stem. Auxin causes stem cells to grow longer on the dark side, which forces the stem to bend toward light.

Results In 10 to 14 days, a plant shoot will emerge from the soil.
Why? A potato is an underground stem called tuber. The potato eyes are the organs of vegetative reproduction. Each eye will grow into a new potato plant. The production of a new plant from parts of an old plant is one way that potatoes propagate (reproduce).

POTATO PLANT — SOIL

69 Eyes Up

Results Tiny roots start to grow.
Why? Many house plants and especially ivy will easily form roots on cut stems. This is one way in which plants propagate, or produce new plants other than by seed growth. For the plant top to continue to grow, it must be planted in soil or nutrients must be added to the water.

ROOTS

70 Cuttings

Results No matter in which direction the bean is planted, the roots grow downward.
Why? Plants contain auxin, a chemical that changes the speed of plant growth. Gravity causes the auxin to collect in the lower part of the plant. Root cells grow faster on the side where there is a smaller amount of auxin, causing this section to bend downward. The result is that auxin causes roots to grow down.

71 Grow a Bean

Results The beans at room temperature have started to grow, but the ones in the refrigerator are unchanged.
Why? Seeds need a specific temperature to grow, and pinto beans require warmth. Very few seeds sprout during the colder months. Most are dormant (inactive) during the cold parts of the year and start to grow when the ground warms.

ROOM TEMPERATURE   COLD

72 Growing Season

Results The patterns on each fingerprint are the same.
Why? The inner layer of skin, called the dermis, has projections. The outer skin layer, the epidermis, fits over these projections, thus taking on the same pattern. Each person has a fingerprint unique to that individual. These personal signatures form five months before birth and never change.

73 Fingerprints

Results The coins are easily picked up when the glove is right side out, but are difficult or impossible to pick up when the glove is inside out.
Why? The fingertips are rough when the glove is on properly and smooth when the glove is inside out. The textured tips of the glove act like the ridged skin on the tips of your fingers, the ridges that cause fingerprints. The ridges in the rubber, as well as in your skin, increase friction and allow you to pick up objects more easily. Friction is the resistance to motion between two surfaces that are touching each other. Without the ridges on your fingertips, your fingers would tend to slide over objects, making it difficult to pick them up, just as it was difficult with the smooth tips of the inside-out glove.

74 Gripper

481

75 Skin Color

Results The skin color is much lighter where it was covered by the bandage.
Why? Special cells in animals contain dark brown grains called melanin. In the absence of light, the grains group together, producing skin with a light appearance. Melanin responds to light by spreading out, causing the skin to be much darker. People with dark skin have more melanin. Albinos have no melanin in their skin. The skin of albinos is white.

76 Stronger

Results The smell of the vanilla is stronger when you take a good sniff than when you breathe normally.
Why? In normal breathing, some of the air carrying the vanilla molecules (smallest particles of a substance) fills the nasal cavity but most of the air passes through the nasal cavity and into the back of the throat. When you take a good sniff, currents of air are drawn upward, flowing over the chemoreceptors (cells that are stimulated by smell or taste) located high up at the back of your nose. Sniffing also brings in more air containing the vanilla molecules.

77 Fooling Your Tongue

Results Before you smell the vanilla, the apple has a regular apple taste. While smelling the vanilla, however, the apple seems to taste like vanilla.
Why? The nerve endings on the tongue allow you to identify only four different basic tastes: sweet, sour, salty, and bitter. Other taste sensations are due to your sense of smell. The apple's smell influences how it seems to taste. When the apple's smell is masked by the strong smell of the vanilla extract, the apple tastes like what you smell: vanilla.

78 Geometric Designs

Results The web designs vary.
Why? Spiders of the same species do build webs of the same geometric design, but the design changes from one species to another. The web shown is a basic orb web design.

79 Telegraph Lines

Results You will be able to feel the varying degrees of vibrations of the string with your fingertips.
Why? When the string is plucked at one end, it causes the entire string to vibrate. A gentle touch produces a weak vibration (back-and-forth movement of material) and a more aggressive plucking causes the entire string to vibrate briskly. Spiders feel the vibration of their web. The web acts like a telegraph line. When the web shakes, the spider senses the movement because it has sensory hair on its legs. If the vibration is very weak, the spider ignores it. Very large vibrations could mean a prey that would injure the spider so it often hides or cuts a strand. A medium vibration lets the spider know that the intruder is small enough to catch for dinner and it rushes toward the source of vibration. The spider quickly wraps the trapped visitor in strands of silk before it can escape from the sticky web.

80 Hummer

Results You can hum as long as your mouth and/or nose is open, but if both are closed, you cannot hum.
Why? When you hum or make any other sounds, air passes between the vocal cords in your throat and causes them to vibrate. When your mouth and nose are closed, the air flow stops. Thus, the vibrations stop and the sound stops along with them.

Results The song sounds natural without the paper, but with it you hear a strange vibrating tune. The wax paper also tickles your lips.

Why? Sound is produced by vibrating materials. Humming causes the wax paper to vibrate. Snoring, is nothing more than the vibration of soft tissue within the mouth. As you sleep, gravity pulls your tongue, uvula (the hanging piece of skin at the top of your throat), and other soft tissue in the mouth down, causing the airway to be partially blocked. As you inhale, air moves through the small passage and causes the soft parts of the mouth to vibrate. This vibrating sound is called snoring.

Results The red color moves slowly through the leaf, first following the pattern made by the leaf's veins (the bundles of vascular tubes forming the framework through which liquids flow) and then throughout the rest of the leaf.

Why? The leaf is part of a vascular plant. Like all vascular plants, the leaf has two main vascular tubes, xylem tubes and phloem tubes. Xylem tubes transport water and minerals upward from the roots through the plant. The xylem tubes also provide support for the plant because their walls are thick. Phloem tubes transport food manufactured in the plant's leaves upward and downward to other parts of the plant. In this activity, you saw colored water moving through xylem tubes.

Scientists believe that leaves are responsible for the upward movement of water through xylem tubes against the pull of gravity (the force that pulls things toward the center of the earth). Xylem tubes from the roots to the leaves are believed to be filled with water. Some of the water in xylem tubes evaporates (changes from a liquid to a gas) during transpiration, a process by which water vapor is lost through leaves. As water is lost from the xylem tubes, the column of water in the tube is pulled upward. This is because water molecules (the smallest particles of a substance that retain the properties of the substance) hold tightly to each other. As the water molecules in the xylem tubes move upward, water from the soil is pulled into the roots.

Results Droplets of water collect on the inside of the plastic bag. The inside of the bag may appear cloudy due to the water in the air.

Why? Plants absorb water from the soil through their roots. This water moves up the stem to the leaves, where 90 percent is lost through the pores of the leaf (stomata). Some trees lose as much as 15,000 pounds (6,818 kg) of water within a 12-hour period. Plants can greatly affect the temperature and humidity of a heavily vegetated area. This loss of water through the stomata of the leaves is called transpiration.

Results After 48 hours, the flower will have changed color. One side will be red and the other blue.

Why? Tiny tubes, called xylem, run up the stalk to the flower petals. The colored water moves through the xylem allowing the color to be distributed throughout the cells in the petals, causing their color to change. Minerals in the soil are carried to plant cells in this way providing nutrients to the flowers and leaves. The minerals dissolve in water (as did the red and blue coloring) and the solution is carried up through the xylem, from the plant's roots, to the leaves and flowers, and the rest of the plant.

85 Desert Plants

Results   The flat towel is dry. The rolled towel is dry on the ends, but has damp spots inside. The waxed paper-coated towel is damp all over.

Why?   The more surface area that is exposed to the air, the faster the water evaporates. Evaporation is the changing of a liquid to a gas by increasing the heat content of the liquid. The speed that the water evaporates is called the evaporation rate. Desert plants have thick and/or round leaves to help prevent water loss. The surface of the leaves is waxy, further restricting water loss. The shape, thickness, and covering of desert plant leaves cause them to have a very slow rate of evaporation.

86 Stand Up

Results   The celery leaves become a blue-green color, and the stalk is firm and crisp.

Why?   A fresh cut across the bottom insures that the celery cells are not closed off or dried out. Water enters into the water-conducting tubes called xylem. These tubes run the length of the stalk of the celery. Water leaves the xylem tubes and enters the cells up and down the celery stalk. Plants usually stand erect and return to their original position when gently bent. This happens because each plant cells is normally full of water. The water makes each cell firm, and all the cells together cause the plant to be rigid. A plant wilts when it is deprived of water, and like half-filled balloons, the cells collapse, causing leaves and stems to droop. The pressure of the water inside the plant cell is called turgor pressure.

— STALK FIRM

AFTER 24 HOURS

87 Morning Glory

Results   The petals rise and the entire flower opens and floats on the surface of the water.

Why?   The pressure of water inside the cells of plants is called turgor pressure. Morning glories are among a few types of flowers that open and close because of changes in the amount of water inside their cells. Turgor movements are usually rapid, occurring within 1 to 2 seconds or, at the most, 30 minutes. Water movement through the petals of morning glories as in the paper flower of this experiment causes the structure to spread open.

88 Retainer

Results   The fish appears to be inside the bowl.

Why?   You see each picture as it passes in front of your eyes. Your mind retains the image of each picture for about 1/16 of a second. The image of the bowl is still being retained when the fish image is projected to the brain. This causes an overlapping of the pictures in your mind, and thus the fish appears to be inside the bowl.

89 Winker

Results   The mirror image of the turning disk looks like a face with one eye blinking again and again.

Why?   Looking through the slits allows you to see each face for only a fraction of a second until the rotating disk brings another drawing into view. Your brain holds on to each image for about 1/16 of a second, by which time the image of another face has spun into view. This is called persistence of vision. Because one eye's position is slightly changed in each drawing, the overlapping of the images of the face gives you the illusion that the eye on the faces is blinking.

90 Night Vision

Results   The brown letter is harder to see at a distance than is the white letter.

Why?   Contrasting colors are those colors that stand out against their background. The white letter has a high contrast against the black paper, and the brown letter has a low contrast with the black paper. In dim light or at night you have more difficulty viewing low contrasts, such as brown on black.

Results   The water level is lower in the bowl that held the paper diaper.
Why?   The paper diaper contains a chemical called sodium polyacrylate. This chemical can absorb (take in or swallow up) large amounts of water. Thus, paper diapers with sodium polyacrylate are more absorbent than cloth diapers without the chemical.

91 Soakers

Results   The contents of the bag marked "USED" smell like an onion.
Why?   Baking soda is adsorbent (other chemicals stick to its surface). Being adsorbent is different from being absorbent. A sponge absorbs or picks up water by taking the water into the material of the sponge. When the baking soda adsorbs the gases given off by the cut onion, the gas molecules stick to the surface of the baking soda. The more the baking soda is spread out, the greater is its surface area and the more adsorbing it is. Baking soda is often placed inside refrigerators to adsorb odors.

92 Stick On

Results   The juice from the cabbage is purple.
Why?   The blender breaks open the cells of the cabbage, and the colored chemicals inside the cells mix with the water. The juice that forms can be used to indicate the presence of an acid (substance that turns cabbage indicator a pink-to-red color) or a base (substance that turns cabbage indicator a blue-to-green color).

93 Cabbage Indicator

Results   The cabbage indicator changes from purple to red when mixed with pickle juice.
Why?   Cabbage indicator always turns a pink-to-red color when mixed with an acid. Pickle juice contains vinegar, which is an acid. The chemical name for vinegar is acetic acid.

94 Acid Testing

Results   The cabbage indicator changes from purple to blue or green when mixed with the antacid tablet.
Why?   Cabbage indicator turns a blue-to-green color when mixed with a base. Thus, the antacid tablet is a base. The colors blue and green indicate the amount of base. Green indicates a greater amount.

95 Base Testing

Results   A few bubbles appear on the surface of the mixture after 30 minutes. As time passes, more bubbles are seen and the surface of the mixture rises in the bowl.
Why?   Making bread involves a chemical reaction (the changing to new substances). One of the ingredients in making bread is a tiny, one-celled living fungus called yeast. This hungry plant eats the sugar and changes it into carbon dioxide gas, alcohol, and energy. The bubbles observed in this experiment are carbon dioxide; they produce holes as they rise through the flour mixture. This same gas causes bread to rise during baking as the bubbles push the dough outward. Holes made by pockets of gas can be seen in slices of baked bread.

96 Holes

Results   Soapsuds form in both jars, but they rise higher in the jar without the Epsom salts.
Why?   Saying that water is "hard" does not mean that it is a solid, but that it contains calcium, magnesium, and/or iron salts. Epsom salt is a magnesium salt. Water without these salts is called "soft." Hard water does not make suds as well as soft water because the salts and the soap chemically react, forming a slimy film called soap scum.

97 Hard Water

98 Lumpy

Results The milk separates into white solid lumps mixed with a thin, watery liquid. Most of the lumps sink to the bottom of the bowl.

Why? Milk contains particles of casein (milk protein). The casein particles are negatively charged. Vinegar is an acid; like all acids, it contains positively charged hydrogen particles. Negative and positive charges are attracted to each other. Thus, the negatively charged casein particles and the positively charged hydrogen particles combine, forming white lumps. Allowing milk to become warm produces the same results that adding vinegar does. The sugar in the milk changes into an acid. The positive hydrogens in the acid attract the negative casein. In both cases, the milk is sour (acidic) and separates into white lumps called curds (the solid part of sour milk) and a thin watery liquid called whey (the liquid part of sour milk).

99 Drinkable Iron

Results Dark particles are seen in the pineapple juice after 20 minutes. Particles are seen in the cranberry and white grape juices after 2 hours. No particles form in the apple juice.

Why? A chemical change takes place that is evident by the solid particles that form. The particles are not the color of the juices—another indication that something new has been produced. Iron in the juices combines with chemicals in the tea to form the dark particles. More particles formed in a faster time in the pineapple juice because it contains more iron. The quantity and speed of the formation of the dark particles indicates the quantity of the iron in the juice.

100 Needles

Results Long, slender, needle-shaped crystals form on the paper.

Why? A crystal is a solid made up of atoms arranged in an orderly, regular pattern; a recognizable shape that results from the repetition of the same combination of atomic particles. Epsom salt crystals are long and slender. The particles in the box have been crushed for packaging and do not have a slender shape. As the water evaporates from the solution, small, unseen crystals start to stack together. Further evaporation increases the building process and long, needle-shaped crystals are produced.

101 Lace

Results Lacy crystals may be seen at the top and sides of the paper after several days. More lace develops the longer the jar sits.

Why? The salty water moves up the paper and onto the glass where it spreads out. The water evaporates, leaving microscopic bits of salt on the glass. This continues until visible crystals of salt are seen. The water continues to evaporate, producing layers of lacy crystals around the inside of the jar.

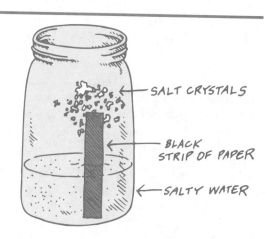

SALT CRYSTALS

BLACK STRIP OF PAPER

SALTY WATER

102 Dripper

Results Water drips from the center of the loop onto the paper. A hard white crust forms on the string and grows down as time passes. A mound of white crystals builds up on the paper beneath the string.

Why? Water containing Epsom salts moves through the string. As the water evaporates, crystals of Epsom salts are deposited. The Epsom salt formations are models of how crystal deposits form in caves. Stalactites are icicle-shaped crystals that hang from a cave's roof. Stalagmites are crystals that build up from the floor of the cave.

Results   The egg has large craters on its surface.

Why?   Tangled strings of some proteins (the large molecules made up of chains of smaller molecules that are essential to all living cells) get wrapped around the fibers in clothes, causing stains. For these stains to be removed, the proteins must be broken into smaller pieces. Enzymes, like those in the detergent used in this experiment, are biological catalysts (chemicals that change the rate of a chemical reaction without being changed themselves). They cut the long strands of proteins (as they did on the surface of the egg) without affecting the cloth fibers. These cut pieces slip out of the cloth and are washed away with the dirt.

Results   The untreated section turns brown, but the section treated with vitamin C is unchanged.

Why?   Apples and other fruit, such as pears and bananas, discolor when bruised or peeled and exposed to air. This discoloration is caused by chemicals called enzymes. The enzymes are released by the damaged cells and react with oxygen to digest the cells of the fruit. Rapid color and taste changes occur because of the reaction with oxygen. Vitamin C prevents the darkening by reacting with the enzyme before it can start digesting the cell tissue.

Results   The water drop spreads out and flattens on the clean surface of the glass. The drop of water on the oiled surface is more ball-like in shape.

Why?   The shape of the water drops is due to two different forces, cohesion and adhesion. Cohesion is the force of attraction between like molecules, such as water molecules. The water molecules pull on each other, which gives the drops of liquid a spherical (ball-like) shape. Adhesion is the force of attraction between different kinds of molecules, such as glass and water molecules. Glass strongly attracts the water molecules, which causes the water drop to flatten and spread out. Water is said to "wet" a surface if it spreads out on the material. The wetting ability of water depends on the adhesive force between the surface molecules and the water molecules. The adhesion between an oily surface and water molecules is very small, and thus a drop of water on an oily surface retains its spherical shape.

Results   One long strip is formed.

Why?   The powder is used to cover the cement so that the pieces do not stick together. When the sharp edges of the scissors cut the paper, the pressure applied by the blades pushes a small amount of rubber cement along the cut surface. The adhesion between the cement molecules is great. These molecules are able to bridge the gap between the cut pieces and hold them together.

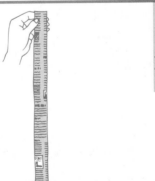

Results   Within seconds, the coin starts to make a clicking sound as it rises and falls.

Why?   Cooling causes matter to contract. The air in the bottle contracts and takes up less space. This allows more cold air to flow into the bottle. When it is removed from the freezer, this cold air starts to heat up and expand. The gas exerts enough pressure on the coin to cause it to rise on one side. The coin falls when the excess gas escapes. This process continues until the temperature inside the bottle equals that outside.

NOTE: The coin will also stop clicking if it falls into a position that leaves a space for the gas to escape through. Try repositioning the coin.

108 Bubbler

Results A soap bubble forms at the top of the straw.

Why? The wet tissue tears and the baking soda and vinegar mix, forming carbon dioxide gas. The gas fills the bottle and goes up the straw. The pressure of the gas pushes against the thin soap film across the straw's opening, stretching it outward to form a bubble.

109 Hotter

Results A very thick, cool liquid forms at first. As the liquid hardens, its temperature increases.

Why? The plaster of paris gives off energy in the form of heat as it hardens. A chemical reaction that gives off energy is called an exothermic reaction. Plaster of paris is made by grinding glassy-looking gypsum crystals into a powder. The powder is then heated to remove its moisture. This dry powder changes back into a crystal structure when water is added. Heat is given off during the reforming of the crystal. (Note that the chalky-looking crystal structure does not look like the original glassy structure.)

110 Colder

Results The temperature of the water lowers.

Why? The reaction of the antacid tablets with water requires energy. A reaction that absorbs energy is called endothermic reaction. The energy for this reaction is absorbed from the water; consequently, the water gets colder.

111 No Room

Results The balloon expands only slightly.

Why? Air, like all gases, is an example of matter (anything that has weight and takes up space). The bottle is filled with air. Blowing into the balloon causes the air molecules inside the bottle to move closer together, but only slightly. The air is in the way of the balloon, thus preventing it from inflating.

112 Blow Up

Results The balloon inflates and air is felt coming out of the straw.

Why? The air surrounding the bottle, like all gases, is in constant motion. This moving gas enters, spreads out, and fills the open bottle and straw. As you inflate the balloon inside the bottle, it pushes against the air inside the bottle. The pressure from the balloon forces the air in the bottle out the straw.

113 Dry Paper

Results The paper is dry.

Why? The glass is filled with paper and air. The air prevents the water from entering the glass, thus keeping the paper dry.

114 Stretchy

Results The cup rises slightly when the rubber band is heated.

Why? Heating the rubber band causes the rubber molecules to vibrate. The moving molecules separate slightly and slip past each other, causing the rubber band to thicken and become shorter.

115 In Motion

Results The gelatin dissolves quickly in the warm water, but most of it sinks to the bottom of the cold water.

Why? Heat causes the molecules of water to move faster. Thus, in the warm water, the water molecules bump into the particles of gelatin. This bumping motion quickly mixes the warm water and gelatin. The gelatin in the cold water will eventually mix because even in cold water, the molecules are in motion; they just move much more slowly.

116

Glob

Results Kneading quickly dries the glob and results in a piece of soft pliable material that bounces slightly when dropped. It snaps if pulled quickly, but stretches if pulled slowly.
Why? This most unusual material is an example of a non-Newtonian fluid. Fluids (anything that can flow) have a property called viscosity (the thickness of a fluid or its resistance to flowing). In the 1600s, Sir Isaac Newton stated that only a change in temperature could change the viscosity of a fluid. Fluids that change viscosity due to temperature changes are called Newtonian fluids. Non-Newtonian fluids' ability to flow, however, can also be changed by applying a force. Pushing or pulling on the piece of glob makes it thicker and less able to flow.

117

Sticky Sand

Results Your hand slowly sinks into the cornstarch mixture, but cannot be pulled out easily. The bowl rises as you lift your hand.
Why? A non-Newtonian fluid is a fluid (material that can flow) whose viscosity (thickness) increases when pressure is applied to it. Pushing or pulling on the mixture makes it so thick and firm that it is difficult to pull your hand out.

Faded

Results A light red or pink star shape is in the center of the red paper.
Why? The energy from the sunlight causes some color pigments to fade (get lighter in color). Different chemical reactions occur when sunlight is absorbed by a substance. The fading of colors is generally the result of the combination of oxygen in the air with the color pigment. (The combination of oxygen with a substance is called oxidation.) This fading happens very slowly without the sunlight, but with the sunlight, it occurs quickly.

119

Chemical Heating

Results The temperature rises.
Why? The vinegar removes any protective coating from the steel wool, allowing the iron in the steel to rust. Rusting is a slow combination of iron with oxygen, and heat energy is always released. The heat released by the rusting of the iron causes the liquid in the thermometer to expand and rise in the thermometer tube.

Super Chain

Results The shape of the paper changed from a rectangle to an open chain-like structure.
Why? Cutting the paper results in a physical change (a change that does not produce a new substance). The zigzag structure allows the paper to stretch out into a large super chain.

Frosty

Results The glass looks frosty, and a very thin layer of soft ice seems to be stuck to the outside of the glass.
Why? Frost forms when water vapor changes directly to a solid—ice. The glass is cold enough to cause the water vapor in the air to cool so quickly that it sublimes (changes from a gas to a solid without forming a liquid). Sublimation is a physical change.

122
Tasty Solution

Results Moving the candy around and chewing it decrease the time necessary for dissolving.

Why? The candy dissolves in the saliva in your mouth to form a liquid solution. Solutions contain two parts, a solute and a solvent. The solvent is the saliva and the solute is the candy. The solute dissolves by spreading out evenly throughout the solvent. The candy can quickly dissolve when it is crushed by chewing and stirred by moving it around with the tongue.

123
Speedy Soup

Results The solid cube dissolved more quickly when placed in warm water and stirred.

Why? Dissolving means that the solute breaks apart and moves evenly throughout the solvent. The bouillon cube is the solute and the water is the solvent. Heat causes the molecules of water to move faster; thus, the water molecules hit the cube, causing pieces to break off. Stirring increases the breaking process. The cube will finally dissolve in the cold water, but it takes a much longer period of time. Stirring the cold water will help speed up the dissolving.

124
Cooler

Results The temperature under the pot is lower than outside the pot.

Why? Evaporation occurs when a liquid absorbs enough heat energy to change from a liquid to a gas. As the water evaporates from the clay pot, it takes energy away; thus, the air underneath the pot is cooler than the air outside. Water from the bowl is soaked up by the pot, and so the evaporation and cooling process continues.

125
Frozen Orange Cubes

Results The liquid orange juice and water both change to solids. The frozen cube of orange juice is not as firm as the cube of ice. It is easy to eat the cube of orange juice.

Why? The liquids both lost energy and changed from liquids to solids. The orange juice does not become as firm as the water because all the materials in the juice are not frozen. Many liquids freeze at a lower temperature than water does. Most of the frozen material in the juice is water. The juice cube is a combination of frozen and unfrozen material that makes it easy to eat.

126
Crystal Ink

Results The message appears as white, shiny crystals on a black background.

Why? The water evaporates, leaving dry salt crystals on the paper. Evaporation is the process by which a material changes from a liquid to a gas. Liquid molecules are in constant motion, moving at different speeds and in different directions. When the molecules reach the surface with enough speed, they break through and become gas molecules. Heating the paper speeds up the evaporation process.

127
A Different Form

Results The mixture starts to bubble and the balloon inflates.

Why? A chemical change occurs when the vinegar and baking soda mix together. The balloon inflates because it becomes filled with the carbon dioxide gas produced. The starting materials were in the solid and liquid form, and one of the products from the reaction is in the gas form.

128
Suspended

Results The glass of flour and water looks brighter than the glass of water alone.

Why? A suspension is a mixture of two or more materials that separate on standing. The flour and water suspension is a mixture of a solid and a liquid in which the solid material doesn't dissolve in the liquid but temporarily stays suspended until gravity pulls it down. Light hits the bits of flour floating in the water and is reflected, or bounced back. The water alone does not reflect the light. Reflection of light by suspended particles is called the Tyndall effect, named after the British scientist John Tyndall.

Results At first it appears that the liquids have dissolved, but in only seconds three layers start to form. In only minutes, two layers are present. Liquid bubbles are present in all the layers.

Why? Oil and water are immiscible, meaning they do not mix. A combination of immiscible liquids is called an emulsion (a suspension of two or more liquids). Shaking the jar causes the oil and water to be mixed together, but they immediately start to separate. The heavier water sinks to the bottom, carrying with it trapped bubbles of oil. The center layer has an even distribution of oil and water, making it heavier than the oil but lighter than water. The top layer is mostly oil with trapped bubbles of water in it. It takes about 8 hours for all the oil to rise and all the water to sink. Since only the water is colored, the food coloring has to be water soluble.

Results Small pools of oil spotted with tiny spheres of color float on the surface of the water. Individual spheres of color appear to explode outward, producing flat circles of color on the surface of the water with streams of color that sink down through the water.

Why? Oil and water are immiscible. Immiscible means they do not mix and will separate into layers. Because the food coloring is water based (it dissolves in water but not in oil), it remains in tiny spheres throughout the oil on the water's surface. The round, colored spheres sink through the oil layer and dissolve in the water layer below. At the moment the tiny drops of color touch the water, they quickly flatten on the surface, and long streamers of color begin their descent.

Results The number of swings varies with how fast the bucket is spun, but with enough swings, the solution clears.

Why? Flour and water form a suspension. If it is left standing, gravity would eventually cause the flour particles to separate from the water. Spinning speeds the separation process by producing a strong centrifugal force (an outward force exerted by an object moving through a curved path). This force pushes the floating flour particles to the bottom of the bucket.

Results The food coloring forms colored balls on the powdered surface.

Why? Food coloring is colored water. Water forms beads on certain surfaces because of the surface tension of liquids. Surface tension is the tendency of molecules to cling together at the surface of a liquid to form a skinlike film. The surface molecules tend to pull inward on each other to form a sphere. This occurs when water molecules are more attracted to each other than to the surface they touch.

Results The beads break open and spread out.

Why? The detergent molecules in the dishwashing liquid move between the water molecules that make up the surface of the colored beads. The presence of the detergent molecules decreases the strong attractive forces between the water molecules. Thus, the surface tension of the water decreases, and the beads break apart.

Results The sticks quickly move away from each other.

Why? The surface of water acts as if a thin skin were stretched across it. This allows objects to float on top. Detergent breaks the attraction between the molecules where it touches, causing the water molecules to move outward and taking the floating sticks with them. This outward movement occurs because the water molecules are pulling on each other. It is almost as if the molecules were all playing tug-of-war, and any break causes the "tuggers" to fall backward.

135
Moving Drop

Results The drop moves toward the toothpick.

Why? Water molecules have an attraction for each other. This attraction is strong enough to cause the water drop to move toward the water on the toothpick. The attraction of the water molecules for each other is due to the fact that each molecule has a positive and a negative side. The positive side of one molecule attracts the negative side of another molecule.

Earth Science

136
Push Up

Results The water remains inside the glass.

Why? The air pushing down on the surface of the water outside the glass extends upward hundreds of miles (km). The pressure of this air is called atmospheric pressure. This pressure is great enough to support the weight of the water inside the glass. Thus, the water level inside the glass remains higher than the water level in the bowl.

137
Spacer

Results The liquid quickly pours out of can A, no liquid pours out of can B, and the liquid dribbles out of can C.

Why? Water, like all liquids, takes up space, as does air. In order for the water to leave the cans, air must enter and take its place. The shape of the hole in an open soda can is long enough to allow the liquid to pour out the bottom part of the hole and air to enter at the top. Covering three-fourths of the hole prevents air from entering, and the liquid inside seals the hole. Covering only half the hole allows air to enter, but not continuously; some water has to pour out before the air can enter. This causes the water not to flow in a steady stream, but to dribble.

138
Folds

Results The paper has many folds.

Why? Your hands push the sides of the paper toward the center. Parts of the paper fold over so that it fits into the smaller space provided. When forces from opposite directions push against sections of the earth's crust (the outer layer of the earth's surface) the compressed land is squeezed into new shapes called folds. The upper surface of this folded land has a wavelike appearance.

139
Easy Over?

Results The paper becomes more difficult to fold. After the sixth or seventh folding, you will be unable to bend the paper.

Why? With each folding, the amount of paper doubles. After 7 foldings, there are 128 sheets. The earth's crust, like the paper, requires a small amount of pressure to fold thin, lighter layers on the surface. Tremendous amounts of pressure are required to fold over large, denser sections of land.

140
Widening

Results The clay pieces move away from each other.

Why? The clay represents continents bordering the Atlantic Ocean. The rising paper acts like the hot, molten rock moving out of the crack in the mid-ocean ridge. When liquid rock pushes through the ocean floor's surface, it forms a new layer on both sides of the crack. It is believed that this new material pushes against the old floor, causing it to spread apart.

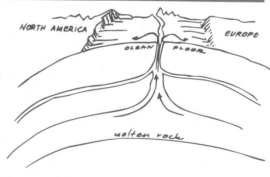

141
Squeezed

Results The sponge "sandwich" folds up and down.

Why? Pushing from opposite directions causes the sponges to be squeezed into shapes representing folds (bends in rock layers). The result is a surface with a wavelike appearance. Forces pushing toward each other from opposite directions are called compression forces. Compression forces within the earth can crush rocks, or can slowly bend rock layers into folds like those of the sponge "sandwich." Folds curving upward are called anticlines and downward curved folds are called synclines.

492

Results While the sphere is spinning, the top and bottom of the strips flatten slightly, and the center bulges.
Why? The spinning sphere has a force that tends to move the paper strips outward, causing the top and bottom to flatten.

The earth, like all rotating spheres, bulges at the center and has some flattening at the poles. The difference between the distance around the earth at the equator and the distance around the earth at the poles is about 27.5 miles (44 km).

Results The water drop swirls around the paper in a clockwise direction.
Why? The free-moving water is thrown forward, and the spinning paper moves out from under the water. Wind and water currents in the Northern Hemisphere are turned toward the right because of the rota-

tion of the earth. Like the spinning paper, the moving earth moves out from under the unattached air and water, causing them to change direction. The deflection in the motion of objects due to the earth's rotation is called the Coriolis effect.

Results The sandpaper-covered blocks temporarily lock together and then move with a jolt.
Why? The lithosphere (solid outer part of the earth) is broken into huge moving pieces referred to as tectonic plates (huge, moving pieces of the lithosphere). Where the edges of two plates push against each other, the crack between the plates is called a fault. Friction causes the plates to be temporarily locked together. Faults that are temporarily locked together are called lock faults. The two blocks of wood represent

two tectonic plates pushing against each other. They temporarily lock together, but as with actual tectonic plates, the friction between the blocks eventually fails, causing a sudden jolt. The bond holding a locked fault in place is under tremendous stress but may last for years before suddenly slipping. Lock faults inevitably and frequently fail, resulting in an explosion of motion that produces powerful earthquakes (shaking of the earth caused by sudden movement of rock beneath the surface).

Results The bottom of the Slinky is pulled to the side. The top section of the Slinky temporarily lags behind, and then springs back into place.
Why? The bottom of the Slinky is pulled to the side by the movement of the paper beneath it. A similar movement occurs during an earthquake, when the ground below a building moves laterally (sideways). These lateral movements are very destruc-

tive, since they cause the walls to bend to one side. Inertia holds the upper part of the Slinky or a building in a leaning position for a fraction of a second, and then the structures snap back into their original shapes. During a typical earthquake lasting only 15 seconds, a building may bend and snap between 15 and 100 times, depending on its structure.

Results More soil washes away from the uncovered soil.
Why? Unprotected soil dissolves in the flowing water and moves down the pan. In nature, leaves, grass, and small twigs provide a protective covering. This covering holds the soil in place and soaks up water

that might wash away the soil. Plants that grow in the soil provide even more protection because their roots help hold the soil in place. The washing away of soil is called erosion (wearing away and removal of materials by moving water, air, or ice).

Results More soil is washed away when the slope of the cookie sheet is increased.
Why? As the slope increases, the water flows more quickly. The faster the water

moves, the more energy it has, and thus the more soil it pushes forward. The process of being worn away by water is called erosion.

148 Wander

Results A winding stream is cut through the soil.

Why? Obstacles that cannot be moved by the water change the direction of the stream. Water is routed around the rocks on the cookie sheet, just as it is routed around rocks in streams. Water moves in the direction of least resistance, and the soft soil is easily moved. The shape of waterways is altered by obstacles, such as rocks, and materials that cannot be moved or dissolved easily by the moving water.

149 Wet Air

Results The toothpick changes direction.

Why? You have made a hair hygrometer. Hygrometers are instruments used to measure humidity, the amount of water in air. The hair stretches when the humidity increases; with a lower humidity, the hair shrinks. The stretching and shrinking of the hair pulls on the toothpick, causing it to move.

150 Wet Bulb

Results The thermometer that has its bulb covered with wet cotton has a lower temperature.

Why? The wet-bulb thermometer is cooled as the water evaporates from the cotton. The faster the water evaporates, the lower the temperature on this thermometer. The dry-bulb thermometer records the air temperature. Low relative humidity (amount of water vapor in the air compared with the amount that the air can hold at that temperature) is indicated by a large difference between the wet and dry bulb reading. The instrument that measures relative humidity is called a psychrometer.

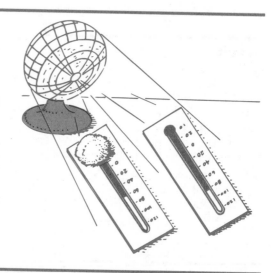

151 Dew Point

Results When the humidity is high, the water collects on the glass at a higher temperature.

Why? Water vapor in the air condenses (changes to a liquid) when it touches the cool surface of the glass. The dew point is the temperature at which water vapor condenses. A high dew point indicates a high humidity (amount of water in the air).

152 Spurt

Results The paste in the tube moves out from under your fingers. Toothpaste bulges around the sides of your fingers.

Why? Liquid rock inside the earth is called magma. Pressure on pools of magma deep within the Earth forces the molten rock toward the surface. Magma cools and hardens as it rises toward the surface. The liquid moves into the closest open space as did the toothpaste when it squeezed between and around the spaces formed by your fingers. Magma that moves up vertically into cracks in the crust and hardens is called a dike. When magma moves horizontally between rock layers, the solid, thin sheet of rock formed is called a sill. This horizontal movement of magma can also form a pool of liquid. This hardened dome-shaped pool is called a laccolith. As the laccolith forms, the layers of rock above it are pushed up, just as the toothpaste was pushed up the tube.

Sill Dike Laccolith

Results The paper will tear easily in one direction but not in the other.

Why? Paper towels are made on a wire screen, creating a straight line in one direction. Pulling on the paper attacks the weakest point. The parallel lines on the paper made by the wire screen are thinner than the rest of the paper, and thus the paper rips easily down one of these lines. Jagged and irregular tears result when the paper is pulled in the opposite direction. This is like cutting minerals, such as diamonds, along cleavage lines. The mineral splits smoothly and easily along the lines where the molecules line up, but it can smash into irregular pieces if hit across the cleavage line (an area where a mineral can be easily split apart).

Results The spoon makes a dark grey mark on the white tile.

Why? A mineral is a single, solid element or chemical compound found in the earth that makes up rock and that has four basic characteristics: (1) it occurs naturally; (2) it is inorganic; (3) it has a definite chemical composition; and (4) it has a crystalline structure. A streak test is made by rubbing a mineral sample across a piece of unglazed porcelain. The color of the streak made is the same as the color of the powdered mineral. Grinding the spoon into a powder would produce the same dark grey color as is seen on the porcelain streak plate. The color of the streak made by a mineral can be an important clue in identifying the mineral.

Results The cup marked S tastes salty.

Why? Ocean water, like the water in cup S, tastes salty because of the salt dissolved in it. A mixture of 1⁄4 teaspoon (0.63 ml) of table salt in 9 ml of water contains about the same amount of salt as ocean water does. Sodium chloride is the chemical name for table salt, which is the most abundant salt in seawater.

Results White crystals of salt form on the paper.

Why? As the water flows through the soil, the salt dissolves in it and collects on the black paper. As the water evaporates from the paper, the dry salt

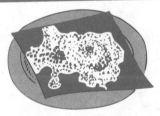

is left behind. In nature, rainwater dissolves salt from the soil. If this water finds its way to rivers that flow into the ocean, the salt is added to the ocean water.

Results The lid looks wet, and finally water drops form on the underside of the lid.

Why? Some of the water in the bottom of the jar evaporates (changes into a gas). The water vapor condenses and then changes back to a liquid when it hits the cool underside of the lid. As the amount of liquid increases, drops form on the underside of the lid. In nature, liquid water evaporates from open water areas such as streams, lakes, and oceans. this vapor rises and condenses as it hits the cooler upper air. Clouds are made of tiny drops of water suspended in the air. The tiny water drops join together, forming larger, heavier drops. The drops start falling when air can no longer support them. Raindrops usually have a diameter larger than 0.02 inch (0.05 cm). Some widely separated drops are smaller. Rain is an example of precipitation (liquid or solid particles that form in the atmosphere and then fall to the earth's surface).

Results Some of the water falls when the lid is inverted, leaving small drops on the lid. The small drops combine, forming larger drops that eventually fall.

Why? Water molecules have an attraction for each other. This attraction is due to the fact that each molecule has a positive and a negative side. The positive side of the molecule attracts the negative side of another molecule. The tiny water droplets on the plastic lid, as well as in clouds, join to form larger, heavier drops, which fall. The falling drops from clouds are called raindrops.

159
Crunch

Results The toothpicks are pressed into flat layers.
Why? Rocks are solids made of one or more minerals. The toothpicks flatten into layers under the pressure of the book. In nature, the weight of rocks at the surface pushes down on rock and dirt beneath, forcing them to flatten into layers. Rocks formed by great pressure are called metamorphic rock.

160
Sedimentary Sandwich

Results A sandwich with a series of layers has been constructed.
Why? Sedimentary rocks are formed from loose particles that have been carried from one place to another and redeposited. These rocks usually are deposited in a series of layers similar to the layers in the sandwich. Each layer can be distinguished by differences in color, texture, and composition. The oldest layer, and lowest bed, is deposited first and the youngest layer is at the top. The layers over a period of time become compacted and cemented together to form solid rock structures.

161
Ticker

Results The ticking is louder with the book in place.
Why? Sound waves can be reflected off solids, such as the book or rock layers. Scientists are able to determine the type and hardness of rock layers beneath the earth's surface by sending down sound waves and listening to the reflected sound. The hardness of rocks can be determined by the loudness of the reflected sound. Scientists know the hardness of rock where petroleum is found, and thus can use this method to find petroleum.

162
Tilt

Results The area below the equator receives the most light when the pencil eraser points away from the light, and the area above the equator is brighter when the pencil eraser points toward the light.
Why? The pencil represents the imaginary axis running through the earth. The Northern Hemisphere, the area above the equator, is warmed most when the earth's axis points toward the sun. This is because more direct light rays hit the area. The Southern Hemisphere, the area below the equator, receives the warming direct light rays when the earth's axis points away from the sun. The direction of the earth's axis changes very slightly during the earth's movement around the sun, causing the Southern and Northern Hemispheres to receive different amounts of light rays. This results in a change of seasons.

163
Which Way?

Results The light coming straight down produces a small, bright circle. Slanting the flashlight produces a larger, less bright pattern on the paper.
Why? In the winter, the sun does not heat the earth as much as it does during other times of the year. The position of the sun in the sky during the winter is not as high in the sky as during other seasons. Winter sunlight comes in at an angle, like the light from the slanted flashlight. This light travels through more of the atmosphere and covers a large area on the surface where it strikes. These slanted rays are spread over a larger area and do not heat as much as when the rays shine straight down.

164
S-Waves

Results Vertical and horizontal S-shaped waves form along the length of the rope.
Why? Earthquakes produce seismic waves (earthquake vibrations) that move through the body of the earth toward its surface. These seismic waves inside the earth are called body waves. The most energetic and fastest body waves are P-waves, which travel at about 5 miles (8 km) per second. S-waves (secondary waves) are slower body waves that travel at about 2 miles (3.2 km) per second beneath the earth's surface, and arrive 5 to 7 minutes after P-waves. Energy from S-waves moves away from the source of vibrations, causing the rock layers to ripple in the same way that the ripples moved along the rope. This up-and-down or side-to-side motion is called a transverse wave.

165

Results The marble swings down, striking the closest marble in its path, and stops moving. The marble on the opposite end swings outward, and strikes its closest neighboring marble when it swings back into its original position. The cycle of the end marbles swinging back and forth continues for a few seconds.

Why? The transfer of energy from one marble to the next simulates the movement of energy from the blow of a seismic P-wave (primary earthquake wave) as it travels through the earth's interior. P-waves move through liquids and solids by compressing (pushing together) the material directly in front of them. Each compressed particle quickly swings back to its original position as soon as the energy moves on. The crust (outer layer of the earth's surface) moves upward as it is hit with the energy of the P-wave, and then settles back into place when the energy moves on.

Clack!

166

Results The rice is not pushed through the bottom of the tube. The rice moves very little.

Why? Sand particles, like the rice, move in all directions when pushed. Vibrations from seismic waves move more slowly through sand because the forward energy of the wave moves in different directions as the sand particles move outward in all directions.

Slower

Results When the pin is inserted into the balloon, the balloon rips. At the same time a loud popping noise is heard.

Why? When your lungs force air inside the balloon, the rubber stretches and the balloon inflates. The air inside the balloon pushes outward. The stretched rubber pushes the air inside the balloon. Sticking the pin into the balloon makes a tiny tear. The stretched rubber immediately starts to pull at the tear. At the same time, the compressed air rushes out and pushes on the tear. The balloon breaks apart. As the compressed air rushes through the tear, it expands (moves apart). This quick expansion of air pushes outward against the air surrounding the balloon. This creates sound waves that reach your ears as a popping sound. Thunder is produced in a similar way. As lightning strikes, it gives off energy that heats the air through which it passes. This heated air quickly expands, then cools and contracts. The fast expansion and contraction of air around lightning causes air molecules to move back and forth, which in turn produces sound waves that you hear as thunder.

Boom!

168

Results The bag breaks and a loud noise is heard.

Why? Hitting the bag causes the air inside to compress so quickly that the pressure breaks the bag. The air that rushes out pushes the air outside away from the bag. The air continues to move forward in a wave. When the moving air reaches your ear, you hear a sound. Thunder is produced in a similar way. As lightning strikes, energy is given off that heats the air through which it passes. This heated air quickly expands, producing energetic waves of air resulting in a sound called thunder.

Bang!

169

Results The water spills more readily out of the square pan than out of the round baking pan or the pie pan.

Why? Tides are the regular rise and fall of ocean waters and the entire ocean is affected from top to bottom. The difference in the rise and fall of the water is observed only along the shorelines. The pans represent shorelines of different shapes. The pie pan has a low, gently sloping side, and the square pan is more irregular than the round containers. Tides on low, gently sloping shores move in and out with little change. Exceptionally high tides occur along irregularly shaped shorelines. The water in the Bay of Fundy in Nova Scotia rises as much as 42 ft (13 m) during its high tide.

Slosh!

170 Tides

Results   The cup turns sideways, but the water stays inside the spinning cup.
Why?   The gravitational pull of the moon causes the ocean water to bulge on the side of the earth facing the moon. There is another bulge of water on the side of the earth opposite the moon. This second bulge results partly from the rotation of the earth. Spinning produces a centrifugal force that causes the turning object to tend to fly away from the center around which it turns. The water

in the cup moves outward because of centrifugal force, but the paper cup prevents it from flying away. The revolution of the earth around the sun produces a centrifugal force. The earth's rotation about its own axis contributes to this force. The result of this spinning, as well as the position of the moon and sun, is a bulging of the ocean waters on the earth, called high tides. The bulging water is prevented from spinning out into space by the earth's gravitational force.

171 Twister

Results   The water inside the upper bottle swirls in a counterclockwise direction, forming a funnel shape as it pours into the lower bottle.
Why?   The funnel formed by the swirling water is called a vortex (a whirling mass of air or water). The vortex formed in the water is the same shape as the vortex formed by a tornado (a violently rotating funnel cloud that touches the ground). A tornado looks like a swirling funnel hanging down from a dark thundercloud.

172 Low Pressure

Results   The balloons move together.
Why?   The fast-moving air between the balloons reduces the air pressure on the insides of the balloons, and the air pressure on the outside pushes the balloons together. The rapidly rising air in a tornado creates a very low pressure area. The tornado acts like a huge vacuum cleaner, sucking in air, dirt, trees, and other materials. These materials are lifted upward and then dropped, generally at some distance from their origin.

173 Tilting

Results   Raising the pan causes the amount of water to decrease in the elevated cup and to increase in the lower cup.
Why?   A volcano is an opening in the earth's crust from which molten rock, steam, ash, and rock fragments are expelled. The cups are a model of a tiltmeter (an instrument that measures the tilting of the ground). Volcanologists (scientists who study volcanoes) place the tiltmeter on a volcano, with one end pointing toward the volcano's cone and the other end pointing away. A swelling in the volcano is detected when the water content in the end pointing toward the cone decreases. An unusually large swelling in a short period of time tells scientists that an eruption is most likely on the way.

174 Squirt!

Results   The toothpaste slowly emerges from the hole and flows down the side of the tube.
Why?   The pressure from your fingers forces the liquid toothpaste out the opening. Tremendous pressure within the earth forces magma out of cracks or weak spots in the earth's surface. The liquid rock is called magma when it is within the earth, but it is called lava once it reaches the surface. The lava cools and hardens on the surface, forming a mound of rock around the opening. A new layer is added to the mound with each eruption. This layered mound of lava is called a shield volcano.

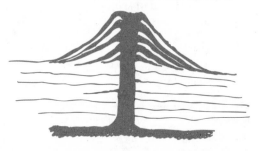

175 Erupting Volcano

Results   Red foam sprays out the top and down the mountain of dirt.
Why?   The baking soda reacts with the vinegar to produce carbon dioxide gas. The gas builds up enough pressure to force the liquid out the top of the bottle. The mixture of the gas and the liquid produces the foam.

Results The thermometer under the clear plastic sheet has a higher temperature.
Why? The clear plastic sheet is transparent, which means it allows light to pass through. The cardboard does not allow light to pass through, making it an opaque object. Normally, the atmosphere of the earth is relatively transparent. The clouds formed by some volcanic eruptions contain opaque ash particles that block out some of the sun's solar rays. This results in a lowering of atmospheric temperature, just as the opaque cardboard blocking the sun's rays resulted in a lower temperature on the thermometer underneath it.

Results Waves move down the rope toward the doorknob, but the rope does not move forward.
Why? Waves that move up and down like those along the rope or on the surface of water are called transverse waves. The top part of the wave is called the crest, and the bottom part is called the trough. The wave moves from one end of the rope to the other just as water waves move outward when you drop a rock into a pond. The water molecules in the pond, like the materials in the rope, do not move forward. Only the energy of each wave moves forward.

Results The thumped marble stops when it strikes the end marble, and the marble on the opposite end of the group moves away from the group.
Why? The thumped marble has kinetic energy (energy of motion). Upon contact, this energy was transferred to the stationary marble, which transferred it to the marble next to it. Each marble transfers the energy to the next marble until the end marble receives it and moves forward. Any one of the marbles would have moved forward had it not been blocked by another marble. Water waves appear to move forward, but actually only the energy is transferred from one water molecule to the next, and each water molecule remains in relatively the same place. Like the end marble, the water near the beach moves forward, since there is nothing holding it back.

Results The shape of both balls changes, but the ball in the bowl with the gravel changes faster.
Why? Land can be worn down by moving water. This change in the land is called weathering (the breaking of rocks into smaller pieces by natural processes). The dirt balls (homemade rocks) in the bowls were weathered by the water and bowl hitting against them. The gravel sped up the weathering process by scraping against the surface of the dirt ball.

Results The water has frozen, expanded, and pushed the lid off the bowl.
Why? Most substances expand when heated and contract when cooled. Water molecules are attracted to each other, forming a flexible chain. This ability to twist around allows liquid water molecules to crowd into smaller spaces. When the water freezes the ice structure that forms is solid and takes up more space than the same number of liquid water molecules. Rocks weather when water seeps into their cracks and freezes. The expanding ice can push hard enough to break the rocks apart.

Physics

Results The paper lifted upward.
Why? The shape of the top of an airplane's wing is more curved than the wing's bottom. Because of this design, air molecules move faster across the wing's top than across its bottom. Bernoulli's principle states that the faster-moving fluids, such as air, exert less pressure than slower-moving fluids. Thus, the air over the top of the wing moves more quickly so the pressure on top of the wing is less than the pressure under the wing. This difference in pressure causes the wing to lift.

182
Paper Flop

Results   The paper flops down toward the table when air is blown under it.
Why?   Air was pushing equally on all sides of the paper before you blew through the straw. As the speed of a flow of air increases, the sideways pressure of the air decreases. Forcing a stream of fast-moving air under the paper reduces the upward pressure on the paper. The air pushing down on the paper is greater than the air pushing up; thus, the paper flops down.

183
Divers

Results   Bubbles collect on the raisins. The raisins rise to the surface, spin over, and fall to the bottom of the glass, where more bubbles start to stick to them again.
Why?   The raisins sink when their weight is greater than the buoyant force (upward force that a liquid exerts on an object in it) exerted by the liquid. The gas bubbles act like tiny balloons that make the raisins light enough to float to the surface. When the bubbles are knocked off at the surface, the raisins sink to the bottom until more bubbles stick to them. Submersibles are ocean research vessels that allow oceanographers to work deep beneath the ocean's surface. The vessels rise and sink in the water, as do the raisins, by changing their buoyancy. The ocean research vessels rise by releasing liquids.

184
Floating Boat

Results   The boat floats and the ball sinks.
Why?   The ball and boat both have the same weight, but the ball takes up a smaller space than does the boat. The amount of water pushed aside by an object equals the force of water pushing upward on the object. The larger boat pushes more water out of its way than does the ball and thus there is enough upward force to cause it to float. Ships are very heavy, but they are large, which increases their buoyancy.

185
Up Hill

Results   The funnels roll up the hill.
Why?   The funnels are not defying the laws of gravity. Actually, as the joined funnels move, their center of gravity (the point where the weight is equally distributed) moves downward. Notice that the center of the joined funnels gets closer to the floor as it moves along the raised yardsticks.

186
Over the Edge

Results   The unit balances with only a small amount of the yardstick touching the table.
Why?   The hammer, string, and yardstick all act as a single unit with a center of gravity. The center of gravity is the point where any object balances. The dashed line in the diagram allows you to visualize the center of gravity. The heavy hammer head counterbalances the weight on the left side of the balancing point.

187
Balancing Point

Results   The paper balances on your finger.
Why?   Center of gravity is the balancing point of an object. The center of gravity of the paper is the point where the five lines cross. Hold your finger under that point and observe the balance.

Results The light glows.
Why? The bulb glows when an electric current (flow of electric charges) flows through the circuit, which includes the battery, foil strip, and fine wire filament inside the flashlight bulb. The movement of the current through the wire filament causes the wire to get hot enough to give off light.

188 Flashlight

Results The needle on the compass moves away from, and then returns to, its north-to-south direction when the wire is touched to and then removed from the battery.
Why? The galvanometer is an instrument used to detect electric current (a flow of electric charges from one place to the other). Electric charges move from the battery through the wire, and back to the battery. An electric current produces a magnetic field. Since the wire is turned in a north-to-south direction, the movement of the current through the wire produces a magnetic field pointing east and west. The needle of the compass will be pulled toward this magnetic field, thus indicating that an electric current is flowing through the wire. The larger the current through the wire, the stronger the magnetic field that is produced.

189 Galvanometer

Results The needle on the compass moves.
NOTE: Add more salt if the needle does not move.
Why? The Italian physicist Alessandro Volta (1745–1827) discovered that electricity could be produced by separating two different metals by an electrical-conducting liquid, such as salt water. The flow of current in this experiment is very small, but it is enough to move the needle on the homemade galvanometer.

190 Battery

Results The paper clips stick to the iron nail.
Why? There is a magnetic field around all wires carrying an electric current. Straight wires have a weak magnetic field around them. The strength of the magnetic field around the wire was increased by coiling the wire into a smaller space, placing a magnetic material—the nail—inside the coil of wire, and increasing the electrical flow through the wire—attaching a battery. The iron nail became magnetized and attracted to the paper clips. A magnet produced because of the flow of an electric current through a wire, usually made by surrounding an iron core with a coil of wire, is called an electromagnet.

191 Electromagnet

Results The iron filings form a starburst pattern around the coil of wire.
Why? There is a magnetic field around all wires carrying an electric current. The iron filings are pulled toward the magnetized nail and form a starburst pattern around the coil of wire.

192 Line Up

Results As the balloon deflates, the box moves forward. It continues to move for a short distance after the balloon deflates.
Why? Newton's First Law of Motion states that an object will not change its motion unless an unbalanced force acts on it. This resistance that an object has to having its motion changed is called inertia. The box stays where you put it unless it is pushed. The deflating balloon gives the box a forward push. This unbalanced force starts the box moving, and it continues to move until a second force, friction, makes the box slow down and then stop. Friction is a force that slows the motion of one surface over another.

193 Moving On

Results As the balloon deflates, the cardboard skims across the table.
Why? The air flowing from the balloon through the holes forms a thin layer of air between the cardboard and table. This air layer reduces friction (a force that tries to stop movement of one surface over another), allowing the cardboard to move quickly across the table.

194 Air Car

195

Roller

Results The rubber band stretches more when the bottom book sits flat against the table than when it is placed on the pens.

Why? The flat surface of the book slides across the table and the round pens roll across the table. Things that roll cause less friction than things that slide. Thus, there is less friction between the pens and the table than between the book and the table.

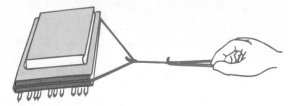

196

Energy Change

Results The cup moves when the marble strikes it. The cup moved farther when the ruler rested on the book.

Why? Objects at rest have potential energy. The higher the object sits above the ground, the greater is its potential energy. When objects fall or roll down an incline, their potential energy changes into kinetic energy—energy of motion. Increasing the height from which the marble rolled gave it more energy, causing it to strike the cup with more force. Therefore, the cup moved farther.

197

Bonk!

Results The balls continue to hit and bounce away from each other until they finally stop moving.

Why? Energy is never lost or created, only changed to another form. Energy in moving things that accomplishes work, in this case moves the balls, is called mechanical energy. When the balls collide, part of the mechanical energy from the balls is changed into heat and sound energy. When all of the mechanical energy has been changed, the balls stop.

198

Hanging Bubbles

Results A bubble that is slightly pointed on the bottom hangs from the spool. Tiny, threadlike streams of liquid quickly swirl down the sides of the bubble and collect at the bottom, where they form drops and fall.

Why? The molecules of dishwashing liquid and water link together to form a thin layer of elastic liquid that stretches to surround the air blown into it. Gravity pulls the spherical bubble downward, forming a slight point at the bottom. The molecules that make up the thin film of the bubble are also pulled downward, causing the bubble's skin to continue to become thinner at the top until it finally breaks.

199

Toys and Gravity

Results The returning ball often misses the paddle when it is stretched straight out from the paddle. Holding the ball at a height higher than the top of the paddle results in the ball striking the center of the paddle.

Why? The string pulls the ball toward the paddle, but gravity pulls the ball straight down. These two forces cause the ball to continue to fall and at the same time move toward the paddle. The result is that the ball moves in a curved path that arches downward. When pulled straight out, the ball's curved path brings it lower than the paddle's handle. The raised ball still moves in a curved path that arches downward, but the new path ends in the center of the paddle.

200

Snap!

Results If you pulled the paper quickly enough, it moved from under the can, but the can remained upright and in the same place.

Why? Inertia is a resistance to any change in motion. An object that is stationary remains that way until some force causes it to move. The can is not attached to the paper. Because of the can's inertia, it remains stationary even though the paper moves forward.

201

Crash!

Results The car with the clay figure moves down the ruler. The car stops when it hits the pencil, but the clay figure continues to move forward for a distance.
Why? The car and clay figure both have inertia, a resistance to a change in motion. Once started, both continue to move until some outside force acts against them, causing them to stop. When the pencil stopped the car's motion, the clay figure continued to move forward. The air molecules slowed the clay figure's forward motion as gravity pulled the clay figure down.

202

Spool Racer

Results As the rubber band unwinds, the spool turns, turning the toothpick taped to the spool. The spool moves forward.
Why? There are two basic forms of energy: kinetic (energy of motion), and potential (stored energy). It took energy stored in the muscles of your body to wind the rubber band. As long as you prevented the rubber band from turning, by holding the stick, the energy was stored (potential). Releasing the stick allowed the rubber band to unwind; thus, the stored energy in the twisted rubber band was transformed into a form of kinetic energy that accomplished work, called mechanical energy.

203

Straight

Results Light appears on the screen only when the notches are in a straight line with each other.
Why? Light travels in a straight line. When the notches were in line, the light rays were able to pass through the openings, but when the notches were out of line, the rays were blocked by the cardboard.

Starburst

Results A starburst of light with dim bands of yellow and orange colors appears around the light.
Why? The cloth acts like a diffraction grating, which disperses light—separates light into the colors of the visible spectrum. Diffraction gratings are made by using a diamond point to cut as many as 12,000 lines per ½ inch (1.25 cm) on a piece of glass or plastic. The spaces between the woven threads in the cloth separate the light, but since the holes in the weave are large, not as many separate colors are seen as one would observe through a diamond-cut grating.

205

Belted

Results Both lids turn clockwise, and the marks return to their original positions at the same time.
Why? The lids and the rubber band act as belted wheels. A belt allows one rotating wheel to turn another distant wheel. Wheels connected by a belt rotate in the same direction. Connected wheels of equal circumference (the distance around the outside of a circle) turn at the same speed.

Flag Raiser

Results The length of string pulled down over the spool equals the distance the flag moves upward.
Why? A pulley is a simple machine that consists of a wheel, usually grooved, that holds a cord. A fixed pulley stays in place; the pulley turns as the cord moves over the wheel, and a load is raised as the cord is pulled. The spool is a fixed pulley that allows you to pull down on the string and raise the flag upward. Placing a fixed pulley at the top of a tall flagpole makes the job of raising a flag easier than if you had to carry the flag up the pole. A fixed pulley makes work easier by changing the direction of the effort force (the push or pull needed to move an object).

207 Threads

Results There are diagonal bands spiraling around the pencil.

Why? A screw is an inclined plane (a sloping or slanting surface) that is wrapped around a cylinder to form spiraling ridges. Screws look like spiral staircases. A common example of a screw is a wood screw. As this screw rotates, it moves into the wood a certain distance. This distance depends on the screw's pitch (the distance between the ridges winding around the screw). Each colored band on the paper around the pencil represents a spiral ridge on a screw, which is called a thread. Screws with a shorter distance between the threads are easier to turn.

208 Levers

Results It is very difficult to lift the books with your finger alone, but easy when two pencils are used.

Why? The pencils form a lever (a rigid bar that rotates around a fixed point). One of the pencils acts as a fulcrum (a point of rotation) for the second pencil. As the distance from where you push down to the fulcrum increases, the easier it is to lift the load on the opposite end. A machine is any object that changes the force a person exerts on it. Different machines change the direction, magnitude, distance, or speed of the force applied. Levers are simple machines that multiply the force that you apply. This makes moving or lifting large objects easier. Inclined planes, wheels and axles, screws, wedges, and pulleys are other types of simple machines.

209 Stickers

Results The iron nail and the BBs are the only materials that cling to the magnet.

Why? One end of a magnet called its north pole is attracted to the earth's magnetic north pole. The other end of the magnet is attracted to the earth's magnetic south pole. All magnetic materials have clusters of atoms that like a magnet are dipolar (have both a north and a south pole). These clusters are called domains. In magnetic materials, many of the domains line up with their north poles pointing in the same direction. The more uniform the arrangement of domains, the stronger the magnetic property of the material. Nonmagnetic materials do not have domains.

210 Magnetic Strength

Results The open paper clip hangs freely under the magnet. It continues to stay attached to the magnet as additional paper clips are added. The number of clips needed to cause the clips to fall will vary with different magnets.

Why? All magnets are surrounded by an area called a magnetic field, made up of invisible lines of force. A weak magnet has a weak magnetic field around it, so its effect on magnetic materials such as paper clips is small. The number of paper clips that your magnet is able to support depends on its magnetic strength. A strong magnet will support more paper clips.

211 More Muscle

Results Most of the clinging paper clips are near the ends of the magnet.

Why? All magnets attract iron, steel, nickel, and cobalt, and they are all surrounded by an area called a magnetic field. This area is made of invisible lines of force coming out of the north pole of the magnet, around each side, and into the south pole of the magnet. The magnetic force lines are closest together at the poles, which give the poles the strongest magnetic attraction.

211 Straight Through

Results The paper is not attracted to the magnet, but the thumbtack is. Moving the magnet caused the thumbtack to move.

Why? Around every magnet is an invisible magnetic field. Some materials, such as paper, do not stop or disrupt the pattern of the force field. Materials that allow lines of magnetic force to pass through without any disruptions in the magnetic field are said to be nonpermeable. Nonpermeable materials are not attracted to a magnet. The lines of magnetic force pass through the paper with no change in their direction; thus, the paper is nonpermeable and nonmagnetic.

Results The boat moves forward with the first trial and backward when the paddle is turned in the opposite direction.
Why? Newton's Law of Action and Reaction states that when an object is pushed, it pushes back with an equal and opposite force. Winding the paddle caused it to turn and hit against the water. When the paddle pushed against the water, the water pushed back and the boat moved. The boat moved in the opposite direction to the paddle, changing direction when the paddle direction changed.

213 Paddle Boat

Results The straw with the attached balloon jets across the string. The movement stops at the end of the string or when the balloon totally deflates.
Why? Newton's Law of Action and Reaction states that when an object is pushed, it pushes back. When the balloon was opened, the walls of the balloon pushed the air out. When the balloon pushed against the air, the air pushed back and the balloon moved forward, dragging the straw with it. The string and straw keep the balloon rocket on a straight course.

214 Balloon Rocket

Results The rotation speed increases as the weight increases, but a point is reached where additional weight pulls down with such force that the wings move upward and the plane falls like any falling object.
Why? As the paper falls, air rushes out from under the wings in all directions. The air hits against the body of the craft, causing it to rotate. Increasing the weight by adding paper clips causes the helicopter to fall faster, and the amount of air hitting the craft's body increases. This increase in air movement under the wings increases the rotation speed.

215 Helicopter

Results The helicopter spins counterclockwise when the right wing is bent toward you and turns clockwise when the wings are reversed.
Why? Air rushes out from under each wing in all directions as the helicopter falls. The air hits against the body of the craft, pushing it forward. Both halves of the body are being pushed in a forward direction, resulting in a rotation about a central point. The diagrams indicate direction of movement.

216 Right or Left?

Results The sound produced changes from a low pitch to a high pitch as the length of the ruler extending over the edge of the table decreases.
Why? Sound is produced by vibrating materials. The pitch of the sound becomes higher as the number of vibrations increases. The longer the vibrating material, the slower the up-and-down movement and the lower the sound produced. Shortening the ruler causes it to move up and down very quickly, producing a higher-pitched sound.

217 Twang

Results The bottle with the most water has the lowest pitch.
Why? Sounds are made by vibrating objects. The number of times the object vibrates—moves back and forth—is called the frequency of the sound. As the frequency increases, the pitch of the sound gets higher. Tapping on the bottle causes the bottle and its contents to vibrate. As the height of the water column increases, the pitch of the sound gets lower.

218 Bottle Organ

Results A loud chiming sound is heard.
Why? All sound is a form of wave motion that is produced when objects vibrate. Striking the hanger causes it to vibrate. The vibrations travel through the air and up the string to your ears. This is an example of stereophonic sound, which is when different sounds come toward a listener from two different directions. The sounds traveling up the string are slightly different and each sound is directed toward a different ear.

219 Sound Blaster

220
Cup Telephone

Results Your helper's words are loud and clear.
Why? Sound can travel through solid objects like paper cups and string. Sounds are made by vibrating objects. The vibrating vocal cords in your helper's throat cause air molecules to vibrate. These vibrating air molecules make the cup vibrate. The vibrating cup makes the string vibrate, and the string passes the vibrations on to your cup. You hear the vibrations as your helper's words.

221
Streamers

Results The thin paper strips move toward the comb.
Why? Static means stationary. Static electricity is the buildup of negative or positive stationary charges. Matter is made up of atoms, which have electrons spinning around a positive center called the nucleus. Moving the comb through your hair actually rubs electrons off the hair and onto the comb. The side of the comb that touched your hair has a build-up of electrons, making that side negatively charged.

The paper strip is made of atoms. Holding the negatively charged comb close to the paper causes the positive part of the atoms in the paper to be attracted to the comb. This attraction between negative and positive charges is strong enough to lift individual strands of paper.

222
Snap

Results A snapping sound can be heard.
Why? Electrons are rubbed off the wool and onto the plastic. Electrons tend to move from an area where they are concentrated to an area of less concentration. Thus, the electrons move across the span of air between the plastic and the metal clip. The movement of the electrons through the air produces sound waves, resulting in the snapping sound heard.

223
Fly Away

Results The paper strips fly apart.
Why? All materials are made up of atoms that have positively charged protons in their nucleus and negatively charged electrons spinning around the nucleus. When two different substances, such as your hand and the paper, are rubbed together, electrons leave the surface of one material and collect on the surface of the other material. The electrons have a negative charge, so one material develops a negative charge and the other a positive charge. This collection of electric charges that remains stationary in one place is called static electricity. Materials with like charges repel each other. Thus, the paper pieces fly apart because they have similar charges.

224
Attracters

Results The two balloons move toward each other and stick together.
Why? All matter is made up of atoms, which have negatively charged electrons spinning around a positive nucleus. Electrons are rubbed off the hair and collect on balloon A; thus, the balloon becomes negatively charged. Since like charges repel (push away) each other, these negative charges on balloon A repel the electrons of balloon B, causing B's surface to be more positively charged. The balloons now have opposite charges, so they are attracted to each other.

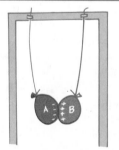

225
Repellers

Results The balloons move away from each other.
Why? Rubbing both balloons on your hair results in a buildup of negatively charged electrons on their surfaces. The balloons move away from each other because they have the same charge and like charges repel.